TransCompetition

TransCompetition

Moving Beyond Competition and Collaboration

Harvey Robbins   Michael Finley

Winners of the 1995 Financial Times/Booz-Allen & Hamilton
Gobal Business Book Award, The Americas

 **BusinessWeek Books**

McGraw-Hill

New York   San Francisco   Washington, D.C.   Auckland   Bogotá
Caracas   Lisbon   London   Madrid   Mexico City   Milan
Montreal   New Delhi   San Juan   Singapore
Sydney   Tokyo   Toronto

Library of Congress Cataloging-in-Publication Data

Robbins, Harvey.
   TransCompetition : moving beyond competition and collaboration /
Harvey Robbins, Michael Finley.
      p.   cm.
   Includes index.
   ISBN 0-07-053082-3 (alk. paper)
   1. Psychology, Industrial. 2. Competition (Psychology).
3. Cooperativeness. 4. Work groups. I. Finley, Michael.
II. Title.
HF5548.8.R574 1998
158.7—dc21   97-48492
                                                              CIP

McGraw-Hill

A Division of The McGraw·Hill Companies

1 2 3 4 5 6 7 8 9 0 DOC/DOC 9 0 3 2 1 0 9 8

ISBN 0-07-053082-3

*The sponsoring editor for this book was Mary Glenn, the editing supervisor was
Fred Dahl, the designer was Inkwell Publishing Services, and the production
supervisor was Pamela Pelton. It was set in Stone Serif by Inkwell Publishing
Services.*

Printed and bound by R.R. Donnelley & Sons Company.

McGraw-Hill books are available at special quantity discounts to use as
premiums and sales promotions, or for use in corporate training
programs. For more information, please write to the Director of Special
Sales, McGraw-Hill, 11 West 19th Street, New York, NY 10011. Or
contact your local bookstore.

Contents

Contents

Preface

Our last book was about change. In it, we tried to catalog all the different kinds of change initiatives companies were undertaking, show how they were failing, and suggest ways to get them back on track. When we came up with the idea, we supposed there were a couple dozen major change themes out there vying for attention: reengineering, TQM, empowerment, benchmarking, and several others. It turned out there were hundreds, many more than we could sort out. They varied from draconian downsizing to New Age hand-holding, from cycle time speedup to the learning organization.

But when the dust of that book settled around us, we realized that all these initiatives had the same metatheme rumbling around inside: They were all about *competition*—they were either fiercely for it or fuzzily against it:

➤ "Fiercely-for" initiatives like reengineering and downsizing see a future driven by intense competition, and seek to adapt to this hostile environment by driving the workforce to supercompete ever harder to increase performance, grab their share of scarce resources, and thereby make the company better able to survive in its markets.

➤ The "fuzzily-against" New Age initiatives take the opposite tack, deliberately softening the competitive impulse within a company to create an environment in which the company can better compete externally, where the money is made. In this paradigm, empowerment and teams are really just two ways to defuse negative competitiveness within organizations.

Two opposite futures, each placing competition at the center of the picture: one seeing it as an indispensable virtue, the other as a regrettable means to an end. Which vision is right?

A World Competing

Time to define competition. The goal of winning, the urge to win, is what competition is about. It is the principle underlying not just basketball, but just about every social endeavor.

In life we compete for the big three: fame, fortune, and love. As kids we compete for good grades, the attention of parents, teachers, and peers. People snore through collaborative endeavors like Sunday services, but they sit up when the local team takes the field. Nonplayers compete for the remote control.

We compete for feelings: for favor, for security, for superiority, for religious primacy, for fun and happiness, for stimulation, for thrills, for sex. We compete for the pure satisfaction of beating others. We compete for money.

We compete for good jobs, choice assignments, prime territories, grade-A clients. We compete for prestige: medals, promotions, recognition, prizes, the trophy spouse, the executive palace.

We compete for inclusion. We want popularity, laughs, the attention of people we find attractive. And we compete for exclusion, to be set apart as "special." We want the patronage of a powerful boss, a corner office, a parking space close to the entrance. We compete to have the best people working for us.

We compete for things we want to have, and for things we don't want the other fellow to have. We compete for titles, status, desk size, elbow room, time off, vacations, special privileges (the executive washroom key!), a better spot in the lunch queue, better food, a place in history, and a fridge full of Evian water.

Managers of product lines or functions compete against one another to meet output quotas, to meet various goals and objectives, and for their own rewards and promotions. One product group competes against the next for allocations. To falter or to finish a close second is to vanish from the race.

Divisions of large companies compete against one another to post the best profit margins. Senior managers compete on matters as important as strategic direction and as unimportant as the direction of the sunlight coming through their windows. Companies like Motorola and Intel compete against one another for market share. Industries, cable companies versus Baby Bells, compete against one another to create the next technological standard. Investors like

Warren Buffett, George Soros, and Donald Trump compete against one another for return on equity and magazine cover appearances.

Competition vs. Collaboration

So the business future promises to be a bloody war between a Push vision of supercompetition and a Pull vision of peaceful collaboration. One side holds that competition is something really good and in need of enhancing; the other side, that it is really bad, and in need of suppressing.

Our task here was to figure out which side was right. As far as we knew, there was no existing handbook on appropriate competition—what kind is good and what kind is bad. There was no guide to when to use the power of competition and when to resort to an alternative power source.

We knew we were perilously close to having an idea, and it wouldn't be our first. In 1988, Harvey wrote a book (Mike helped edit it) called *Turf Wars: Moving from Competition to Collaboration*. It was one of the first books to suggest that competition, which has always enjoyed a place of honor at the American table, isn't all it's made out to be. We made no claim then to a global theory about the nature of competition; we just said too much of it made for an unhealthy work environment.

Another book published at about the same time, however, did make a global claim. Alfie Kohn's *No Contest* was a scathing attack on competition, the celebration of winning over losing, wherever it reared its head—in sports, education, relationships, and business. Here's a sample:

> We have reached a point where doing our jobs, educating our children, and even relaxing on the weekends have to take place in the context of a struggle where some must lose. That there might be other ways to do these things is hard for us to imagine—or rather, it would be hard if we were sufficiently reflective about our competitiveness to think about alternatives in the first place. Mostly we just accept it as "the way life is."[1]

Kohn's was an impassioned portrayal of a society made sick by its own games. The back cover sported blurbs by antiestablishmentarians like Dr. Spock and Noam Chomsky. It was the kind of book that made you want to change everything you did, but gave few practical hints on how to do that. The reason is that an anticompetitive stance goes against the grain of American society. There isn't a lot a single organization, acting on its own, can do to make a difference, unless you believe companies like Ben & Jerry's (ice cream) and Tom's of Maine (natural toothpaste) have altered corporate behavior worldwide.

We're not as anticompetition as Kohn. Although we agree it can be an obstruction to achieving our long-term objectives, we believe competition is an essential aspect of human life, and of business life.

On the other hand, we're not 100% procollaboration, either; teams very often *don't* work, and collaboration has a dark side that is seldom acknowledged, but that we are going to acknowledge.

Both competition and collaboration have their uses in our work and in our lives. The problem is that we resort to them automatically, without thinking; we aren't choosing between the two, or combining them into the third set of adaptive behaviors that we call *transcompetitive*.

We wanted to write a book that would help people and organizations achieve this higher level of versatility. We felt there was a need for a guide:

➤ that would address people living and working in the real world, who sense that all is not right with the way we turn every human activity into a prizefight;

➤ that draws a visible line between competition that works for the common good and competition that bludgeons the group for the good of the individual;

➤ that provides a practical, down-to-earth look at the pluses and minuses of both competition and its counterpart, collaboration.

This is that book. While it is basically business how-to, it doubles as an adventure story of ideas. We will roam through world history, rummage through old books about anthropology and psychology, and not neglect periodic stops at your company's shop floor, where the two great impulses humans feel—the need to survive and the need to get along—bump heads.

What Transcompetition Is

We will be talking a lot about transcompetitive behaviors. Transcompetitive behaviors are not an abandonment of the competitive ethic but a refining of them, a peeling away of the cultural layer of "untrue truisms" competition comes wrapped in, that we cheerfully accept, such as, "Competitiveness is the same as competence." (It isn't, not by a long shot.) We will have a lot to say about these myths, which we call collectively *competitionism*.

Transcompetition seeks to break the deadlock between winning and losing and to provide guidelines for intertwining both the competitive and collaborative impulses, adjusting them to fit your personality, your organization's culture, and your particular vision of the future. It looks for ways of dealing with people with competitive orientations different from your own. It explains how and why different cultures compete differently. It also seeks to demand proof when scarcity of any substance essential to life and growth is posited. "There isn't enough to go around" is sometimes true, but it is always a good way to get people eyeing one another competitively. In our time, scarcity is often one of the Big Lies.

Where competition emphasizes *bottom-line results* ("You lose, therefore I win"), the transcompetitive approach emphasizes the process by which results are obtained.

Where competition focuses solely on *individual performance*, the transcompetitive approach includes group performance. Teams work when the people on them set aside their individual competitiveness and work for a shared goal. They won't do it for no good reason; your job as leader is to communicate a good reason.

Where competition often resorts to *secrecy, trickery*, and *gamesmanship* in order to win, transcompetition strives to be honest and aboveboard in its dealings, with an open-book policy toward workers and customers alike.

Where competition focuses on *bashing one's competitors* on the head, transcompetition knows the value of an occasional pat on the back. By looking for the bigger picture, transcompetition seeks to deliver something valuable to customers that no "competitor" can.

Where people in competitive organizations acquire power by *withholding information* from one another, their counterparts in transcompetitive systems swap knowledge back and forth, with the customer as the eventual beneficiary. Knowledge is truth, and the truth shall set us free.

What Transcompetition Is Not

If you listen carefully, you will hear the sound of knuckles dragging. That is the sound of the champions of competitiveness, supercompeters, drawing near to denounce transcompetition. So, for the record, let us say these things about beefing up one's transcompetitive muscles:

➤ **It does not contradict free market principles.** Cooperative strategies are part of the free market. Organizations, after all, are collaborative by definition.

➤ **It is not communism,** or communitarianism, or a denial of the individual. People are still individuals in a transcompetitive scheme. Transcompetition is a balancing of attention to the group and to the individual.

➤ **It is not a denial of competition.** By moving beyond competition we are not denying its importance and usefulness. We are simply saying there are tools in the toolkit besides the sledge hammer.

➤ **It is not an embrace of all things collaborative.** Competition is good stuff, when used appropriately. And collaboration is often not all it's made out to be.

➤ **It is not an abdication of excellence,** or quality, or people doing their best. It is one of the vanities of competition (and collaboration, too, for that matter) that only *it* can guarantee that people do a good job.

➤ **It is not a flight from "first things."** Transcompetitive work is as focused on survival as the work of the most supercompetitive. But it defines survival over a longer term, requiring greater diplomacy.

➤ **It is not handicapping,** weighting down those who are successful so that those who are less successful will have a greater chance to succeed.

In the transcompetitive environment, the organization has found ways to make the best of each worker's nature, and of its own nature:

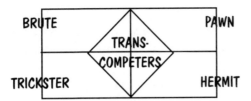

> ➤ The Brute, who has lived solely by personal power, becomes an orchestrator of the power and skills of others.

> ➤ The Trickster, who has lived by manipulation, becomes an entrepreneur.

> ➤ The Pawn, who has had to take what the world dishes out, learns to stand up for him- or herself and become a communicator.

> ➤ The Hermit, who has walked away from the game, returns to it as a player, analyzer, and contributor.

Whatever your competitive style, when you have completed this book, you'll be able to do things you weren't able to do before:

⇒ Define your and your organization's attitudes about competition—whether you are supercompeters, supercollaborators, bullies, or wusses. Lots of people and lots of organizations think they know where they fall along the competitive spectrum, and lots of them are wrong.

⇒ Work with people on your team or under your supervision to coax the best out of them—the best that is competitive and the best that is collaborative—and excise the parts that are counterproductive or toxic.

⇒ Create a climate of mutuality between customer and provider, meeting long-term needs instead of seeking short-term advantage.

⇒ Work with organizations with very different personalities than yours to create a partnering culture that allows both sides to make the most of the relationship.

⇒ Use interactive technology to enforce codes of conduct in your industry to halt the flow of cutthroat competition.

⇒ Connect the things that happen at your workplace under the banner of competition with thousand-year-old stories in legend and Scripture. What once seemed trivial and annoying will soon seem like a page from an ancient picture book.

These are not minor goals. They involve assessing and altering your deepest, most unconscious business and personal habits. Not everyone will have the openness or flexibility to make the change.

But the upside potential of changing is great. By lessening the impact of short-term competition, transcompetitive habits can break the brute cycle of winning (stomping the competitor), then losing (when the competitor stomps you back). Transcompetition builds alliances between individuals and between organizations to make possible a stream of *continuous winning.*

It isn't world peace, but it will make your organization smarter about the competitions it declines and more successful in the competitions that matter.

The Who and the What of It

Harvey is a business psychologist who has consulted with scores of companies around the world on team and change issues. His calling in life is to alert organizations when business fashion or bad management practice leads to wide-scale organizational stupidity.

Mike is an essayist and business writer who specializes in the human side of organizational change.

It has been said of us that Harvey provides the passion in the partnership, and Mike the sarcasm. Together, we operate a patched-together foundation we call the Why Things Don't Work Institute (http://www.skypoint.com/~mfinley).

Our research method requires a word of explanation. During the year we spent reading and writing about competition, we spent perhaps one entire day in a library. We decided that while the existing literature has many valuable things to say about competitive styles, our approach would be less formal. We simply paid attention to the issue of competitiveness, whether we were talking with friends, watching the news, reading the paper, or consulting with client companies. Since competition is all around us, we simply waded into the stream and netted whatever swam by, whether it originated in the South China Sea, the mouth of the ancient Euphrates, or our own Lake Wobegon in Minnesota.

It was the summer of the Mir rescue in space, of the UPS strike, of the anti-tobacco initiative by state attorneys general, of the handover of Hong Kong to China, of Microsoft bailing out Apple Computer—all extraordinary stories of competitive entities doing transcompetitive things.

Don't expect this book to be like most business books. We aren't selling a methodology for welding a transcompetitive face onto your company overnight. Our goal is simply to get you thinking more consciously about your current way of competing, its models, and its costs. We believe too much business thinking is simply habit, not considered choice. Our thinking is presented here to stimulate you in your own thinking and your own choices.

You take it from there.

Endnotes

[1]Alfie Kohn, *No Contest: The Case Against Competition,* revised edition, Houghton Mifflin, 1992.

Acknowledgments

A book like this is never the work of just two people, at least not if we can help it. We selflessly invited everyone we knew to do as much of the work as possible, and many responded with ideas and anecdotes. Meanwhile we shamelessly appropriated everything we came across and liked in our reading. The goal: a nonacademic book about competitive excesses that are really happening in the world around us.

We corresponded, for instance, with dozens of people around the world, to get their perspectives on how competitiveness varies from culture to culture. Many of these observations pop up in these pages. This impromptu blue-ribbon panel of international advisors includes natives of those countries, plus a few Americans and English who have spent time in the countries they talked about: Fabrice Neyret and Jean-Marc Tagliaferri (France), Sandeep Krishnamurthy (India), Roland Wolf (Germany), Busaya Virakul (Thailand), Geoffrey Sherwood and Stephan Haggard (Korea), Margaret Wood (South Africa), Douglas Cymbala (Nigeria), Jorge Send (Argentina), Themin Suwardy (Indonesia), Owen McShane (New Zealand), Luc Bauwens (Belgium), Adriana Bruggeman and J.P. van Bolhuis (The Netherlands), Jun Zhang and Sean Qu (China), Tor Slettnes (Norway), Christina Johansson Robinowitz (Sweden and Denmark), John Cheung (Singapore), and Binh T. Nguyen (Vietnam). Thanks especially to "the hyena women," Susan Marais and Magriet Herman, for their trenchant analysis of affairs in South Africa. We thank them all for their insight and candor.

The biggest intellectual debt we owe any one person is to Edward O. Wilson, author of the seminal *Sociobiology* (Belknap Press/Harvard University Press, 1980). Wilson provided the initial inspiration for our thinking here—the idea that competition is not a human invention, or something immoral, but arises for perfectly natural reasons going back to the most primitive species. His thinking provided us with our book's central metaphor, that people in organizations, just like symbiont species in nature, work together out of self-interest. His contribution cannot be measured in footnotes.

Harvey wishes to thank the clients and colleagues who have chipped in with their travails and triumphs, in particular the executives, managers, and other hardworking stiffs at the Southern Company, Honeywell, the U.S. Treasury, and the member companies of the Institute for Management Studies.

Mike would like to thank his friend, frequent collaborator, and personal management trainer Jerry de Jaager for his many helpful comments, and tips on what previous books on this topic said and didn't say. He thanks friends and neighbors, especially Margaret Ryther and Dr. Frank Mach for their stories and support, and John and Noelle Jacquet-Morrison for their hospitality and encouragement. And he thanks his client, The Masters Forum, a Midwestern executive education group, for the confidence they have shown him over the years, and for the wisdom he's gleaned from the excellent speakers they bring in (Joshua Hammond, Lester Thurow, James Collins, Ron Heifetz, and Rick Ross come especially to mind).

We both want to thank Andrea Pedolsky and Nicholas Smith, our agents and partners in publishing; and Mary Glenn, our editor at McGraw-Hill, whose patience and perspicacity helped us reach new heights of transcompetitive splendor. Thanks to Kurt Nelson for bird-dogging the project during its final stages. Thanks to Diana Witt for helping with the index. And thanks to Fred Dahl of Fishkill, New York, for his copyediting expertise.

Finally, we wish to thank the little people who made this book necessary—our children, Max Robbins and Daniele and Jon Finley. Theirs is the world this book hopes to help build, a world in which people pick and choose rationally between competition and collaboration, to find solutions that advance peace and prosperity for the many without sacrificing the glory of the individual spirit.

Harvey Robbins
Michael Finley

A World of Losers

Cracks in the wall of a powerful theory

What better way to start a conversation about competition than with a stirring story from the world of sports? Not one about big, strapping, testosterone-surging, male pro athletes, but one about high school girls who are finally allowed to play hockey.

It is a drippy February evening in Minnesota in 1997. Girls in our state have been playing hockey for decades, but this is only the third year they have been competing interscholastically. On the TV is the high school girls' hockey tournament. The two teams are the suburban school, Roseville (pop. 34,112) and the Iron Range city of Hibbing (pop. 7,412), home of Bob Dylan and the Hockey Hall of Fame.

The game is supposed to be a laugher. Roseville has never been beaten and they are the odds-on favorite to win the state championship. They even beat Hibbing twice in the regular season, once very recently. But the Bluejackets from Hibbing simply outplay the larger school, 4-3, in a game described as "better, and the competition more nerve-wracking, than any of the 52 previous boys' state tournaments."[1]

After the final buzzer, the Roseville players drift to their locker room, except for one big-shouldered player, a senior with a brown ponytail who sinks into a folding chair at mid-rink and bawls her eyes out.

It is an incredible victory for the Hibbing girls, but you can't shake the image of the sobbing girl in the folding chair. You can tell she is going to go away from this experience—likely the highest athletic event she will ever participate in—thinking of herself as a loser.

If she is a loser, what does that make the girls on the 18 teams that Roseville beat, and the girls on the 18 teams Hibbing beat? And all the players those players beat out to make their teams? At the end of a season there is one winner standing atop a giant pyramid, and below those few are layer upon layer of other girls, hundreds of them in this Minnesota conference alone.

"When all have fallen, one alone remains." This victory pyramid is the metaphor Western societies are built on, the one we use to inspire ourselves. How we love our winners; but in order to have one, we need to create all those losers.

For a generation or more, however, people have wondered, Isn't there a better way? A way to generate the good feeling of winning that a few people feel, without the overwhelmingly worse feeling of losing that everyone else feels? Must the happiness of the few be at the expense of the happiness of the many?

This question does not even get at the hollowness that many winners feel when the battle is over and there are no more worlds to conquer; or when the next season is only a few months away, and winners must start all over again, with all the pressure and sacrifice that repeating will require, at the bottom of the pyramid.

Competition in the Business World

It's true in girls' hockey and it's true in the business world: Intense competition, instead of creating well-being, creates ill will, depression, and pain. Companies and individuals around the world are competing like crazy, but not getting where they want to go. Here are seven true anecdotes from organizations that believed in the power of competition and worked assiduously to increase their competitiveness, but in the end fell victim to their own competitive habits.

▶ The Team-Building Activity That Wrecked the Team

"I was working at a Penney's credit service bureau in Chicago," said Margaret, a neighbor of Mike's. "Our work was to screen people's credit histories and respond to requests for higher borrowing limits, extensions, etc. We were going through a customer satisfaction phase and the group sponsored a contest to solicit ideas on how to put the customer first. The winner of the contest received a few hundred dollars in store credits.

"I submitted several ideas and I won. To my surprise, everyone began to turn against me, whispering, giving me the cold shoulder. It was because I was a part-timer, and they didn't think I should have been allowed to compete, or should have kept my mouth shut. I was disappointed—here was a team contest that was supposed to bring people together, like a pep rally, but it wound up having a very icky, negative feeling."

Penney's imagined that it could take a group of people that it had programmed for years to be afraid of one another, and they would approach the competition with open hearts. It doesn't work that way. People were so burned by a long history of being jealous of and getting beaten by one another that there was no way this contest could improve teamwork. Instead of bonding together, people turned against one another.

▶ The Company Whose Predatory Imagery Backfired

From its earliest days, Lasermaster Corp., a color graphics company in Eden Prairie, Minnesota, was a wholehearted believer in supercompetitive imagery. Looking down on the employees from every wall of the corporate headquarters were paintings, photographs, posters, and velvetized images of animals in hot pursuit of other animals. Mountain lions baring their fangs, bald eagles making off with trout in their talons, giant upright Kodiak bears, poised for action. The pictures were there for employees to identify with. "We are a mean, snarling, carnivorous team," was the message these images conveyed.

The company's CEO is himself a bantamweight entrepreneur fascinated by competitive imagery: He took the name Mel Masters for himself because it sounded masterful.

The carnivore culture developed at Lasermaster. The company held rallies at which employees were encouraged to shout out their determination to dominate their market. Individuals were singled out and challenged to see if they had the right stuff to win. Internal contests were held to model the kind of competitive behaviors Masters expected would carry the company to the top.

But despite the pep rallies, recognition ceremonies, and rah-rah atmosphere, Lasermaster wasn't an especially fun place to work. People reported feeling edgy, paranoid, and disinclined to join group activities. Like predators in nature, they tended to huddle in their cubicles, guarding their catch against interlopers, withholding information from one another like crazy.

After ten years of terrific success and an initial public offering, Lasermaster hit a few bumps in the road. Competitors from entirely new, less expensive technologies moved in. The company's stock price faltered. Invocations to fight back like the predators they were no longer seemed to motivate. Perhaps people were drained by all the bloody imagery. After years of being clubbed over the head about how tough they were, most of the blood they had seen was their own.

Mel Masters learned several lessons the hard way. One was that competitive fire, while necessary and admirable in certain circumstances, must be a rational process, not a habit beaten into people. Unthinking competitiveness actually undermines an organization's true competitiveness, its ability to grow and cope with change.

Another lesson was that predatory animals are not especially competitive. Predators are the number one group of animals on the endangered list.[2]

▶ A Competitive Relationship That Got Out of Hand

One of the worst attributes of supercompetitiveness is that it makes you lose perspective on what's proper. Winning becomes such an obsession that the niceties of doing business get lost.

Our favorite story of competitive obsession revolves around the coffin-selling business in the southern Thai city of Nakhon Si Thammarat.[3] Death is a booming business there. Eight coffin sellers have shops in the city, all directly across the street from the city's largest hospital. Salespeople seem to know no bounds as they vie to outsell one another. Bribes to hospital personnel ("Here's $10, please direct the families of dying patients to us") are common. One salesman studied the admissions list to see which families had already done business with his shop, then sneaked into the hospital rooms of their terminally ill loved ones, and disconnected their oxygen—figuring he would get their business sooner or later anyway, and sooner was preferable.

Think interbusiness competition doesn't get tougher than that? Consider the taxi business in South Africa. In their zeal to carve out market share for themselves, competing taxi companies hire professional Uzi-toting killers. The killers lie in wait and ambush the most productive drivers of competing companies. Between 1993 and 1997, over 100 cab drivers were murdered this way.

▶ A Nonprofit That Pushed the Pedal to the Metal and Got Nothing

A local college decided it wanted to become the "Notre Dame of Minnesota." Frank, the school athletic director, thought that might mean higher scholastic achievement, but it certainly meant winning more games. A lover of competition all his life, Frank was hit for the first time by the power of coercive competition: win or go. Coaches would come to him with problems and he would be unable to provide the kinds of answers that would result in wins. The final result was that Frank, a man of exceeding gregariousness, became clinically depressed, a condition brought on by external competition but which was to rattle his internal chemical cage for many years.

How many organizations, for profit or not, learn that pressing people too hard to win, and punishing them when they lose, eventually lowers their self-esteem and breaks their spirit? How is a team with a tattered sense of itself, and its neurons misfiring left and right, ever going to win anything?

▶ A Company That Was Destroyed by Internal Competition

Jantzen used to be a well-known and highly regarded independent maker of sportswear. In the 1980s it became enamored of the "strategic business unit" concept, and set about to make all its departments into profit centers. The word soon went down from corporate that every department would be expected to show a profit on paper. The logic of this was that competition to match measurable performance targets was a healthy thing. In reality, however, it forced internal units to do things they were never intended to do. Manufacturing units within a company are not supposed to make money off one another. But instead of assisting one another in making an enterprisewide profit, departments raised the prices of their internal services in order to show departmental profits. With all this internal price-hiking, products were soon unaffordable to consumers and unattractive to merchandisers, and Jantzen sales went into a tailspin. In 1986, within two years of the competition brainstorm, Jantzen was acquired by V.F. Corporation, and several of its plants were shut down forever.

▶ A Company Whose Competitiveness Came Back to Bite It

No company is as passionate about competition as Nike, the world's largest seller of shoes. Consider this remark by Phil Knight, onetime track star and founder of Nike:

> Let us never forget what this company is ultimately about: beating the crap out of those sons of bitches. If you have the opportunity to put 15 meters ahead of your opponent you have a moral obligation to do it.[4]

Paul Fireman, Phil Knight's counterpart at Reebok, doesn't hate Knight. But Knight hates Fireman with a burning passion, according to Fireman, because the game is afoot, and Knight has the deranged heart of a marathon runner:

> If I was in a contest with Phil Knight and I won, I'd congratulate him. If he won, he'd dig my grave, throw me in it, throw dirt on top, throw the shovel on top and walk away. Asked about the remark, Knight replied, "Of course I would. What else could you do?"

Now take that attitude and transplant it to a Nike subcontractor (Pouchen Shoe Co.) in Vietnam, where workers' and women's rights are a sometime thing, and where sweatshops are eager to emulate their anchor partner's competitive style.

> On March 8, International Women's Day, 56 women employed at a factory making Nike shoes in Dong Nai, Vietnam, were punished because they hadn't worn regulation shoes to work. Factory officials ordered the women outside and made them run around the factory in the hot sun. The women ran and ran. One fainted, then another. Still they ran. They would be taught a lesson. The ordeal didn't end until 12 workers had collapsed.

A Vietnamese-American businessman, Thuyen Nguyen, had this to say about the event:

> Vietnamese all over the country were outraged that on International Women's Day, when most companies in Vietnam

give women workers flowers and gifts, 12 Vietnamese women were so abused that they had to spend the day in an emergency room.[5]

Picture a group of working women whose offense is not wearing work shoes, as instructed, and instead wearing their own native sandals. Picture a floor manager feeling incensed that the women were not backing company efforts to westernize operations, and feeling supported by the articulated competitive ethos at Nike, and determined to teach the backward women a lesson in the new world order.

➤ An Entire Industry Gutted by Its Own Competitiveness

Want evidence that fighting to win causes you to lose? Look no further than your nearest auto dealership. No business is regarded by its customers as more competitive, and no profession is as disrespected, as car sales. Since the days of Henry Ford, sales managers have been driven by the need to put up sales numbers now, this month, and never mind the problems that come back a month from now. As a result, the auto salesperson is a walking joke in business culture, the commercial embodiment of deception, manipulation, and chicanery.

Tell car dealers they must change their ways and they will laugh at you. Lie, us? Anyway, this is the only way it is done. If you don't buy from Smilin' Sam, go down the road and buy from Dealin' Dale. Even the used car market, dominated by private person-to-person sales, is characterized by the ethic of pawning off problems onto the buyer. It will never change, right?

Wrong. Traditional car dealers are advised by superconsultant Michael Treacy to sit down today and find a buyer for their businesses, because vendors with less competitive practices are coming in now, and they will eat the old-line sales outlets for breakfast. Saturn at General Motors was the first to design a new way of hassle-free, no-tricks car buying. Buying clubs helped customers find the model they want at the price they want, with no arm-wringing. Wayne Huizenga's idea for the automotive equivalent of Wal-Mart, AutoNation, will provide good used cars in a no-baloney buying process. The Internet is even charging in, with outfits like AutoByTel offering choice cars at the lowest price with zero crapola. Bye-bye, Smilin' Sam.[6]

Deming Weighs In

Quality heavyweight W. Edwards Deming was hip to the corrosive power of the wrong kind of competition. Competition is the enemy lurking behind his famous demand that management abandon quotas and "drive out fear." He never spoke about the need to compete, because "winning" is a result, and his abiding interest was processes. "Optimizing the system" was what managers needed to be about, not clobbering employees, other managers, other companies, or customers.

Deming tackled competition head on in his last book, *The New Economics*. The composer of a liturgical Mass for organ, Deming quoted the Bible:

> A body is not one single organ, but many. Suppose that the foot should say, "Because I am not a hand, I do not belong to the body," it does belong to the body nonetheless. Suppose that the ear were to say, "Because I am not an eye, I do not belong to the body," it does still belong to the body. If the body were all eye, how could it hear? If the body were all ear, how could it smell? ... There are many different organs, but one body. The eye cannot say to the hand, "I do not need you."[7]

In the heat of competition, people see themselves as isolated from one another, and justified in cutting corners, bending rules, taking shortcuts, piling it on. What would ordinarily seem excessive is excused by the fact of competition.

"This is what we must do in order to win" is the attitude underlying much of the destructive competitiveness in the business world, and in the world beyond business. It is the logic that leads countries to issue ultimatums of war that they then must back up with action. It is the logic that a general uses to justify sending an army off into certain death—knowing it will mean the death of more of the enemy's army.

It is the logic of mergers and acquisitions, in which companies will even bid against themselves, will bid vastly more than the appraised value of a company, will spend themselves and their existing shareholders into a deep crevasse just to be able to score a win, to make their acquisition offers acceptable to existing owners.

It is the logic of market giants that engage in mutual bloodletting, not to increase market share, but to avoid being handed the "second-best" label. Examples are Coke/Pepsi, GM/Ford, Toyota/Nissan, Fuji/Kodak, News Corp./Time Warner, Disney/Sony, and British Petroleum/Royal Dutch Petroleum.

For really irrational competition, consider the 25-year war between Major League Baseball and the Major League Players Association. In 1995 they had a $3 billion dollar pot to divide, if they could only work collaboratively. But both owners and players are, by disposition, habitual supercompeters. They opted instead to alienate a public that had faithfully bought tickets for generations, by ending the season and calling off the World Series, creating a hole in baseball history with their greed. Customers retaliated by staying home the next season, taking their recreational dollars elsewhere. Baseball is still digging out of that hole. The 1997 World Series, featuring two teams with the highest payrolls, was the least watched in years.

Habits vs. Strategies

What we have learned is that competition and competitiveness are often less *strategies* (things you consciously plan) than *habits* (things you do because that's what you do).

We believe that neither competition nor its opposite, collaboration, are good or bad of themselves. Each has its place, and each has its disadvantages, which need to be considered thoughtfully every time we undertake an initiative.

Companies and individuals most often go wrong in automating the decision to compete or collaborate—doing one or the other not as a rational choice but as a habit, because it suits our organization's culture or our individual personality. By making unconscious a decision that should be fully conscious, we put blinders on ourselves and gallop into action without having a clear idea of the outcome or the consequences. In this unconscious way, we give competition free rein, and it goes bad on us.

We're going to spend the next few pages decrying competitive excess, before turning our sights on the supposed solution to competition, which can have even greater potential for undesired results.

Endnotes

[1] St. Paul Pioneer Press, February 21, 1997.

[2] A rabbit is much more competitive in most ways than the lynx that eats it. There are more rabbits than lynxes in the world—the very definition of competitive success. A lynx may eat one rabbit, not because of competitive fire but because the lynx is bigger and has sharp teeth and claws. And maybe the rabbit was old, or lame.

[3] Originally reported in a February edition of *The Nation* (Bangkok). We caught the story in Chuck Sheperd's "News of the Weird" column, July 31, 1997.

[4] Remarks from James Collins at The Masters Forum, Southfield, Michigan, April 1, 1997.

[5] Bob Herbert, New York Times Syndicate, "Nike factory in Vietnam marks women's day with brutality," *Star Tribune*, March 31, 1997.

[6] Remarks by Michael Treacy, The Masters Forum, Troy Michigan, July 29, 1997.

[7] 1 Corinthians 12:14-21.

The Competitive Sandwich

We're caught in the squeeze between good and bad

The modern world is a world of continuous struggle, in which every moment assigns us to either the winners' or the losers' column. We seem to accept this. We are for it.

Indeed, we spend every day of our lives doing something to make ourselves more competitive. We see that our task in our careers and in our lives is to press the competition throttle even harder, to become better at what we do, to master tricks to triumph over our rivals. We undergo weeks of training every year toward this end; we attend motivational seminars to fan the competitive flame inside us. We work 70-hour weeks to hone our competitive edge. We shell out money for everything from MBA degrees to give us credentials against our opponents, to athletic shoes to make us "more like Mike"—to gain that extra step, that extra jolt of confidence that will allow us to win at will the way Michael Jordan seems to do.

The Dark Side of Competition

But there's a shadow side to competition that can't be dispelled. Say *competition* and one part of you feels excitement and fulfillment. It can be very beautiful and compelling. But there is another part of you that feels sorrow and dread.

For every individual who swears by competition, believing it is the law of nature and the only way any person or any organization has ever amounted to anything, there are scores of others who swear *at* competition, believing it is the cause of a horrible lot of brutality and suffering, in the world and in the workplace.

But people don't attack competition much. The deck is stacked in favor of being procompetition; everyone in power got there by competing. Alfie Kohn's book was unique in taking on the topic. He was often put in a very uncomfortable position, as if he were attacking America or defending communism or belittling masculinity. As Phil Donahue asked Kohn, "Aren't you just against competition because you are a loser?"

Here's a laundry list of the good things we attribute to competition. The list is long, and is interspersed with the side effects accompanying each competitive virtue.

⇧ **It motivates.** Everyone performs better when something is at stake. "The best essay will be pinned on the school bulletin board." "Team Blue came up with the plan we wound up adopting, so they get to park close to the elevator for a month." "In America, any child with gumption can grow up to become president."

⇩ **Sure, it motivates, but it also demotivates.** People do not line up to lose time after time. When it becomes clear that the fastest, strongest, cleverest, and best-connected people will always win top honors, the rest of us start to shut down. Who wants to be a walk-on in someone else's movie? While we all admire champions, no one wants to be the "breakfast of champions."

⇧ **It's fun.** Warriors relish the din of battle and find meaning in it. It is the reason people play sports and reach for the gold ring in business. Doing business without competition is like playing tennis without keeping score, or gambling with matchsticks. The tension of knowing you may lose something of value adds to the enjoyment for many people.

⇩ **It's fun—for some.** To be on the losing end of every competition is no fun at all. What general store operator wants to see Wal-Mart trucks pulling into town? There's an epidemic of clinical depression in America, and one suspected cause is the feeling many people have that they will never make it in a culture that only values winners. Is your company having as much fun as Microsoft? Not many are.

⇧ **It contributes to identity.** Especially nice when the identity is "winner," with all the fanfare that accompanies winning. True competitors know who they are by dint of having competed and found out what qualities are inside them. This is equally true of organizations. Who recruits the top candidates: the company that has been taking a drubbing, or the company that has been dishing one out?

> ⇩ **It contributes to identity—unfortunately.** The worst label you can hang on someone is that of loser. You can beat out hundreds in your scramble for the gold, but if you finish anything but first many people will see you as a loser. Think of the Buffalo Bill's, Woolworth's, American Motors, Montgomery Ward, or WordPerfect.

⇧ **It's social.** What better way to get people together to interact than through a contest between teams. Volleyball, softball, league bowling. Sales quotas, quality competitions, cycle-time contests. Rivalry energizes people, lets them get to know one another better. Competition is like that Pepsi commercial that depicts everyone on the beach diving happily for the ball.

> ⇩ **It's antisocial.** When people compete, there is usually an element of cruelty in the air. Winners identify other people's weaknesses and exploit them; how social is that? Even beach volleyball has a dark side. Clue: It's not a Pepsi commercial if your skull is getting caved in with each spike.

⇧ **It builds character.** To come back from a string of defeats to win the championship or to be a global market leader is the greatest plot in sports, entertainment, or business. Winning too soon is no good—you have to suffer a while, until something changes inside you and you become a true winner.

> ⇩ **Does it really?** For every heroic story of an athlete coming back from untold defeats to win, we know people in our families and careers who lack that Horatio Alger resilience. When they are beaten they stay beaten. There are no body shops for restoring crumpled self-esteem.

⇧ **It stresses individuality.** Being distinct is a virtue, and competition sharpens differences. Sir James Goldsmith's Referendum Party in Britain viewed cooperation with Europe not as "a high tide that lifts all boats," but as a blow to the things that make the states of Europe unique and, because they are unique, prosperous.

⬇ **It quashes individuality.** Being separate means quarreling, which retards progress. Cooperating in the European Union is the best hope those states have of competing with global economic powers. Prosperous confederates will be much more distinct to the world than feudal duchies unable to agree on money and measures.

⬆ **It's emotionally healthy.** Competing is exercise for the soul. It keeps you vital, relevant, someone not to be taken for granted. It sharpens your sense of self. It bestows blessings on everyone involved, winner, loser, and spectator alike. In some cases, it gives you a reason to live.

⬇ **It's emotionally disturbing.** If it is vitalizing to win, it is enervating to lose. Nearly everyone has had the kick-in-the-guts feeling that only the go-to guys get the ball; the rest of us are just fill-ins. Yes, winning is terrific for the winners, but that healthy glow comes at the expense of everyone they climbed over or ignored to seize the loving cup.

⬆ **It trains leaders.** Just as rolling and tussling with siblings helps lion cubs develop adult hunting skills, competing against other managers in an organization allows a natural selection process to occur. The most talented alligator in the swamp eventually asserts itself, and a leader is born.

⬇ **What kinds of leaders does it train?** It also assures that our leaders will be of a single type, ferocious competitors. "When all you have is a hammer, every problem looks like a nail." Why should workers swear allegiance to such leaders? Does it make sense that ordinary people will seek out leaders who have caused them personal pain?

⬆ **It elicits innovation.** Countries that encourage competition between individuals and companies seem to vault to the forefront. America and India have competitive healthcare structures, and lead the world. The U.K., Cuba, France, and Canada have public, collaborative healthcare systems, and are not viewed as breaking fresh ground.

⇩ **The innovation it elicits isn't worth the pain it causes.** Sure, the U.S. and India lead in healthcare treatment and technology. But look at them: The actual healthcare is only available to those societies' winners. Billions are wasted on marketplace duels that destroy the losers and do nothing for the truly afflicted.

⇧ **It consolidates allegiances.** A team that competes against another develops a formidable spirit. The team develops loyalty and camaraderie. Each victory deepens their passion for one another. Picture the football goalie jumping into the forward's arms. Onlookers also form powerful attachments: They become fans.

⇩ **It discourages allegiances.** When you have been beaten often enough, you become resentful. To the rest of the world you are just a punching bag, there to provide the winners with the pleasure of defeating you. Ever wonder how people working in banks, which are losing market share to non-banks on a daily basis, get out of bed in the morning? The "team attitude" your team is most likely to develop will be gallows humor.

⇧ **It allocates scarce resources.** If there is only so much money or so many food rations to go around, what better way to decide who gets it than to make people compete for it? Like the Oklahoma Land Rush, the goods go to whoever is daring, swift, and innovative. By definition, the winner is the most deserving.

⇩ **It allocates resources whether they are scarce or not.** Never mind that people unable to compete for them on an equal footing with the strong in all likelihood have the greatest need of them, like African farmers, urged to grow cash crops for global export instead of food crops necessary for survival.

⇧ **It increases productivity.** If workers must meet individual quotas or are paid according to how they perform compared to one another, they work harder and produce more. This dynamic helped make the U.S. the most productive and most prosperous country in history, and the idea is proving highly exportable to other countries.

⇩ **It may or may not increase productivity.** When workers are pitted against one another to survive, how likely are they to share ideas that will move the entire enterprise forward? And when you die, as beaten companies do, where does your productivity go?

⇧ **It improves quality.** If Teams A, B, and C all want to win the Golden Turkey Award for most quality suggestions offered and implemented, that will be one stuffed suggestion box. If job security depends on quality performance, you will get very high quality performance.

> ⇩ **It compromises quality.** What is there about product quality that requires that teams be made to fight gladiator games against one another? Companies like Nike brag that high style and low cost deliver supreme customer satisfaction, not defining the prison labor they employ through subcontractors as "customers."

⇧ **It tests ideas.** The marketplace is a forum for ideas to duke it out against one another. Marxism, cold fusion, slavery, beta video, and appeasement of aggressive dictators all had their chance to show what they could do. Competition reveals whether one formula for cola tastes better than another, whether one design team's approach is superior to another's, whether one political solution or style is more attractive than another. It makes choices easier for consumers and management alike.

> ⇩ **It kills ideas in the cradle.** Instead of creating an atmosphere in which ideas are allowed to incubate, to show what they can do or how they can be combined, we set them against one another, often before they are ready. How many great ideas have perished because competitive pressures prevented them from getting a decent hearing?

⇧ **It institutes order.** Through the Middle Ages, a philosophy of hierarchy called the Great Chain of Being was popular, in which every creature and every person occupied a rung according to his or her or its worth in the eye of God. God was at the top, followed by Angel, then Man (half angel/half flesh), then Animal, then Plant, then Dust.[1] When a winner is rewarded, people do not begrudge it, because the reward was earned in straight-ahead competition—it made sense according to the Great Chain. Competition legitimizes the pecking order; it establishes a performance-based hierarchy. Who can argue with performance?

↧ **It institutes order, all right—Caesar's peace:** an order built on resentment, bitterness, and a feeling that your defeat is fuel for your competitor's victory. That isn't a game, it's predation.

↥ **It establishes rules of fair play.** No hitting below the belt, no shaving of points, and no intentional grounding.

↧ **It creates loopholes.** There was no cheating until there were games.

↥ **It selects.** In courting, people compete to win the best mate they can. It is survival of the prettiest, the handsomest, the most powerful, the richest. Those who can't win the competition become literally extinct: Their inferior genes are booted out of the pool. Competition shows what sort of people we are, and what group we belong in.

↧ **It selects destructively.** There are schools that screen kids out at age 5, before any child can be expected to take a test. Competition establishes early on who will be given a second chance in life and who will not; whose DNA will be passed on to the future, and whose will not.

↥ **It's fair.** Competition equals competence. Devotees of competition see it as the indisputable arbiter of freedom and justice. What could be more fundamentally liberating or more just than "May the best person win?"

↧ **It's not only unfair, it's unbeatable.** "May the best person win" is circular logic. Competition does not guarantee competence. No one challenges it, because the only tribunals one may challenge it to are themselves victors of competition: the politicians that are elected, the opinion makers of the media, the judiciary, the establishment.

That's a lot of misgivings to have about the glue that supposedly holds the United States together. After all those pluses and minuses, you're probably confused—is winning really winning? Can competition really be all that bad?

If competition is all that bad, should we just stop doing it, as Alfie Kohn suggests? If we did that, is there another skill set we can turn to?

The offsetting skill set to competition is collaboration, or cooperation, or teamwork. It has been all the rage in management literature for the last few years. It is the heart of the team-building, total quality, empowerment, and systems thinking movements. But it too has problems, as we shall see.

First, though, let's look at the range of impulses that stretch between competition and collaboration.

Endnotes

[1]Arthur Lovejoy, *The Great Chain of Being*, Harvard University Press, 1936.

The Realm of Connectedness

Things that go beyond competition

Though competition is important, there are lots of behaviors it can't account for:

➤ It does not explain species identity. Higher animals don't devour their own. Dogs don't really eat dogs, unless they are awfully hungry.

➤ It does not explain "biocivilization"—the grouping habits lots of species (ants, wolves, elephants, geese) besides ourselves have developed to work toward common goals.

➤ It does not explain the interesting mutual relationships between species, like the cleaner fish that passes safely between the killer shark's teeth, picking out the tasty tidbits that lodge there.

➤ It does not explain how some current human societies, ones we are told are "primitive," value group involvement over individual circumstances—while showing more genuine respect for individuals than our ultraindividualized society does.

➤ It does not explain families—individuals who help and support one another, the capable attending to the less capable, often at great cost to themselves.

➤ It doesn't explain the kindness of strangers, why we have hospitals and social agencies, why we lend a thousand helping hands to people who have demonstrated their inability to compete.

➤ It does not explain organizations themselves—people banding together and working not just for individual aggrandizement but for a collective cause.

There are in fact two contradictory impulses in human nature: the urge to wrestle and the urge to embrace, competition and collaboration. Together they encompass a characteristic called *sociality* or *connectedness*. Connectedness is just what it sounds like, the range of ways in which members of a species connect with one another. It describes how social we are, how we deal with one another, how important the self is versus the group.

The scale of connectedness ranges between the two extremes of competition and collaboration. Competition, which says that individual well-being and short-term success are the most important things, occupies the left half of the connectedness scale; collaboration or cooperation, which says communal well-being and long-term survival are more important, occupies the right half.

There is a balance to be maintained between the two extremes of connectedness, one that is right for you and for your organization. What most people have trouble with is telling if their current "balance" is really balanced, or if they are listing perilously to one side.

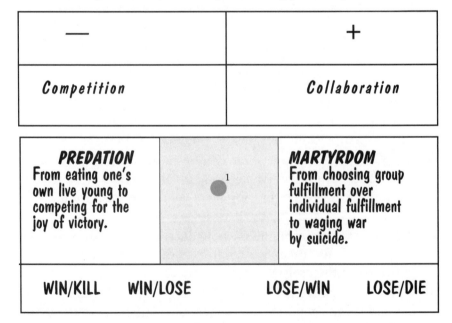

—	+
Competition	*Collaboration*

PREDATION From eating one's own live young to competing for the joy of victory.		**MARTYRDOM** From choosing group fulfillment over individual fulfillment to waging war by suicide.
WIN/KILL WIN/LOSE		LOSE/WIN LOSE/DIE

The extreme ends are occupied by a supercompeter or predator on the left, and a supercollaborator or martyr on the right. The closer to the center of this graph your organization is, the healthier it is. The closer you are to the extreme sides of this graph, the sicker you are.

Both extreme poles are ultimately destructive to their professed objectives: survival and community.

Here are the four varieties of connectedness that typify organizational dysfunction:

➤ **Win/Kill.** The extreme end of supercompetition is sadism: "I shot a man in Laredo, just to see the look on his face." Many blood-and-guts managers measure their success not by profits or per-share price but by the amount of pain they inflict on their way to victory. What surer way to guarantee victory than to exterminate the opposition? This kind of winning goes beyond putting the opponent's king in check, to mashing its chess pieces with a pestle.

Win/kill is blood sport—obsessive, ritualistic competition—and it occurs not infrequently among humans but seldom among other creatures. Genocidal wars such as those fought in Europe in World War II, and more recently in Yugoslavia and Zaire, bear this imprint. Win/kill doesn't occur often in business, although a kind of mock win/kill is evident in the extreme competitive styles of people like Nike's Phil Knight.

➤ **Win/Lose.** This is what most of us mean by competition: "It's not enough that I win; I also have to make certain that you lose." To people caught up in this habit, the brutal trashing of the opposition is the heart and soul of competition. It is more important than whatever is "won"—market share, prestige, an award, etc. Indeed, those are just benchmarks for the real competition, which is for dominance of the other.

While win/lose works pretty reliably in the short term, in the longer term it tends to fail because those on the losing side eventually get even and make the winning side pay for its victory. In politics, win/lose is the main game: In the U.S., Republicans win until they annoy enough people with their negativity, and then it's the Democrats' turn. The pattern looks like this:

Winning

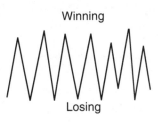

Losing

Win/lose almost always invokes what we call the Brute Cycle, which we describe in a later chapter. (No, it's not an exercise machine.)

➤ **Lose/Win.** This is the martyr's position: "I will lose on purpose, then redefine defeat as victory." This is the perverse strategy of the passive-aggressive.

Many workers and middle managers cast themselves in the role of lose/win, dragging their feet or maliciously complying with the terms of an agreement. "But you said ..." is how they defend actions that undermine organizational goals. Some managers display it by indecision, trying to achieve contradictory goals simultaneously and thereby dooming both.

Former tennis champion and commentator Rosemary Casals said she could tell the moment when every match changed from a contest to see who would win, to a search by the loser for a reason for losing.[2] It is a sad aspect of human nature that, faced with probable defeat, we search not for a solution but for an alibi.

Lose/win can be a victim mentality often displayed in codependent and dysfunctional relationships. We blame it on nature by calling it "mother love," but it is devious in the way only humans can be.

➤ **Lose/Die.** This is anticompetition arising out of hatred, as when Samson brought down the temple, killing both himself and his enemies, the Philistines: "If I can't win, I can at least prevent you from winning." The kamikaze pilots of the Pacific War were knights of lose/die. Bees that give up their lives in order to defend their community are lose/die. Timothy McVeigh in Oklahoma City probably saw himself this way.

In business, we see it in companies with troubled pasts, like Eastern Airlines, that have to ask the same employees they have systematically betrayed to make concessions "for the common good." Eastern's employees took twisted pleasure in voting the company out of existence and themselves out of jobs.

> People who decry lack of participation in elections or avoidance of organized conflicts such as collective bargaining should consider that the disenfranchised see voting and organizing as lose/die propositions. Staying away from the polls, or refusing to stand up

for better conditions, weakens the hand of whatever government or management is put in place, while undermining their own influence over affairs. But at some desperate level it is a statement they feel compelled to make. Their vote for despair is the only "victory" they feel they will experience.

What links these four categories? First, they all lead to behavior counter to the interests of any sensible organization (though they can be found in every sensible organization).

Second, they focus on short-term, not long-term results. As such they are emotional indulgences, not part of a rational plan for sustainable success.

Third, they are all *habits*. They are patterns of behavior that we all characteristically slip into. They require little actual thought. We see the green light, and we step on the gas and go off in our customary direction.

As we progress through the following chapters, our goal will be to surface these unconscious mental models at the outskirts of the scale of connectedness, and to replace them with rational choices closer to the center.

Endnotes

[1]An astute reader has noticed the large gray spot at the center of the scale. Watch that space. It's where all the good stuff is.

[2]Remarks by C. Terry Warner at The Masters Forum, Minneapolis, June 1993.

Not-So-Great Stuff about Collaboration

Why "teamwork" can't solve every problem

Though our work lives are marked by competition, the parts we most cherish are collaborative in nature. It is one of the human pleasures to team up with others. It is a relief to set aside the anxieties and pressures we associate with competition, the scarcity mentality, and the great people-compartmentalizing power of the Chain of Being. If competition is the repository of our most passionate values, collaboration is the repository of our most revered values: peace, love, and understanding. We have a soft spot for collaboration that our rough competitive exteriors belie.

All our utopias are collaborative in character. That is their appeal, and also, ultimately, their undoing.

The Idea of Collaboration

The thesis of collaboration is that there are many things individuals cannot do by themselves or do as well by themselves. Collaboration is a dynamic by which people increase the amount of knowledge at their disposal in order to perform a task at hand.

Think of any complex task two people may face, like building a house or running a business. We'll call them *you* and *I*. Think of the range of choices you and I have as we set about to perform that task. Two fellows named Joe and Harry (not you and I) came up with a concept in the 1960s called a JoHari Window.[1] The trick is to imagine that the four panes can shrink or expand, according to how much is in them.

What We Know Together (The Known)	What Only You Know
What Only I Know	What Neither of Us Knows (The Unknown)

This particular window divides the universe of what the two individuals know and what they don't know. In the upper left is the collaborative pane, where I share what I know with you, and you share what you know with me, adding permanently to what both of us know. This is exceedingly valuable.

The two shaded panels are things you know, and things I know. When we hoard our information from one another, we are triggering the Brute Cycle—information is power, and information withheld is a lethal weapon. The only way to move from the brute boxes to the collaborative box is by trusting one another, and by uniting in some sort of common vision—peace, prosperity, full employment, stable boundaries, etc.

The whole point of "society," according to collaborative theory, is to continually share information with one another so that the remaining panel, The Unknown, remains of manageable size. The Unknown has traditionally encompassed everything that is terrible— disease, famine, the death of the planet, or the failure of an enterprise. When The Unknown shrinks to nothing, the theory goes, we'll know everything and people won't get sick and all the religions of the world will have sleepovers with one another and eat s'mores. It is, after all, a utopian theory.

The problem with collaboration is that the world doesn't work like that. With the Internet, satellite uplinks, and free flow of information worldwide, The Unknown, instead of shrinking, has been expanding. It is as if the more we know, the less we know. Technology and the ability to deliver megatons of information by the second contribute to this expansion. What we are learning about the universe we live in—the peculiarities of matter and energy at the subatomic level—accounts for much of the rest. Shared knowledge is not setting us free; it is drawing us deeper into a world of paradox, doubt, and uncertainty.

The challenge is not to invest in a utopian dream of universal collaboration that will usher in a worry-free era, but to take a different path, one that confronts The Unknown head-on.

"Fire Bad, Smoke Good"

An important point needs to be made. It is wrong, and it is crazy, to equate competition with "bad" and collaboration with "good."

Pure collaboration is as problematic as pure competition. Both have their purposes. But each at its extreme, practiced unconsciously, results in breakdown.

Supercompetition, like a Panzer division rolling over Poland, creates a spirit of over-the-top, scorched-earth absolutism, legitimizing whatever means result in victory: treachery, deceit, corruption, murder.

But supercollaboration has problems, too. It is the sworn enemy of individuality, progress, diversity, and change.

Here are some of its hallmarks:

➤ **Sameness.** Competition is brutal one way, and pure collaboration can be brutal in a less direct way. Collaborative groups adopt rigid standards and impose them on themselves, foreclosing creative deviation. Think of certain churches, fraternal organizations, and professional groups whose codes of conduct have shut down the thought process.

Groupthink leads to inquisitions of perceived outsiders, and stultification of insiders. Think of corporate cultures so symbol-driven that they cause individuality and ultimately their own organizational freshness to wither, and prevent the truth from being spoken. Many ex-EDS'ers complain about that company's white-shirt uniform, as have escapees from the team rigors (morning calisthenics, pep rallies, group apologies) at Nissan.

➤ **Blurriness.** When everyone has input into planning, planning loses focus. Think of the way Congress, the ultimate collaborative body in the U.S., works, and you have a fair critique of extreme collaboration: gridlock, waste, lack of critical judgment, and countless false starts. An organization that doesn't pick winning ideas just keeps adding all ideas—good, bad, or indifferent—to its knowledge and operations base. This inclusiveness results in democracy's downside: bloat.

➤ **Slowness.** Consensus doesn't "snap to" the way intimidated agreement does. It is a slow ooze forming, and organizations lose momentum waiting for the ooze to arrive. In the time it takes your team to put on a play, you could have read it by yourself. Oftentimes, you could even have written it.

➤ **Leaderlessness.** When everyone is encouraged to lead, the usual result is that no one does. Or leadership is replaced by alternating pressures: "You got to do it your way last time, now it's our turn."

➤ **Defenselessness.** When everyone knows everything, because sharing is so important, there is no confidentiality, and no fire-walls. You are at the mercy of whoever sees you are vulnerable and crosses the street to beat you up. "Flattened" organizations, where only two job descriptions may exist ("chief customer satis-faction officer" and "customer satisfaction associate") sacrifice defense to simplicity. Effective organizations often find they need role variety, including the roles of warriors and champions.

➤ **Interiority.** Collaborative groups have a way of becoming cross-eyed over time, focusing on subjects of interest exclusively to the group. Politics often forces collaborative groups to think in severe us/them ways, and to invest all resources in immediate concerns. This tendency is why Lee Iacocca scoffs at worker-owned enter-prises: "Somebody's crazy. It can't work. What do you think will happen when it's a choice between employee benefits and capital investment?" Collaboration, critics say, has no guts.[2]

➤ **Mercilessness.** "The many are stronger than the one," is the motto of supercollaboration. It is also the motto of fascism. The *fasces* of Mussolini was a bundle of Roman sticks bound together. Individually, each stick could be snapped; together, they were unbreakable. A supercollaborative group is ferocious in its intol-erance of outsiders, and oppressive in its domination of minority insiders.

Perhaps the worst thing about supercollaborative environments is that there is no way to fight them. Jeane Kirkpatrick, American ambassador to the United Nations, caught a lot of heat in the 1980s when she said that authoritarian or totalitarian governments were preferable to communist governments. Kirkpatrick was a hard-line anti-Communist, so the remark predictably aroused the ire of people on the left, who replied that a firing squad is a firing squad, regardless of whether the dictator is on the right (Somoza in Nicaragua) or the left (Castro in Cuba).

What we suspect Kirkpatrick meant was that it is easier to overthrow a single bully than it is to undermine an entire system. Heroic stories abound of individuals who bring down a giant, or minotaur, or dragon. There are fewer tales of individuals who had that kind of impact against the consensus of an entire culture. When they do prevail they often pay a high price: Jesus, Gandhi, Martin Luther King, Jr.

We agree with Kirkpatrick that supercollaboration poses a greater danger than supercompetition. Killing the king is an easier assignment than ending the Dark Ages single-handedly.

A lot of this book, for that reason, is about how to handle brutes in the marketplace—the people we work with and for, and the organizations they make up. Handle them we must, because handling the alternative to them is so difficult.

The Play's the Thing

If you think of your business as a stage production, and the people in it as actors in a play, you can imagine three kinds of theatrical performance:

1. **The competitive cast.** In this production the actors are insecure, and they are all mugging like crazy in hopes there is a famous producer in the audience who will discover them and take them away to something grander. Competitive actors have no loyalty to the play or to the author or to the director or to one another. Imagine an all-egomaniac play starring Jack Nicholson, Kathleen Turner, Jack Lemmon, Barbra Streisand, and Pauly Shore. It's every actor for himself and herself, and agony for the audience to watch.

2. **The collaborative cast.** These actors are the exact opposite—well-mannered, trained in the art of working together, sensitive to the slightest nuances of one another's performance, and eager to do justice to the play as a whole. They encourage one another and embrace frequently. Indeed, they are repertory theater in the highest sense, people dedicated to staying together for this play, and for another, and then another, and then another. Picture a cast in which everyone wears a black body stocking and wears a mask—like Mummenschantz or Cirque du Soleil! The theater is their life, but that does not protect them or their audience from the tedium of their authenticity.

3. **The transcompetitive cast.** To these actors, the play is everything. It is valuable in and of itself, but it is also their ticket to better things individually. There are experienced stars and aspiring new actors, but they have found a way to work together without resentment or conflict. The great actors pick the lesser actors up, and the lesser actors provide a foundation for the stars to play off. No one imagines the cast will be together forever. There is no pretending that actors don't have egos and are not trying to outdo one another on stage. But it is all within the context of the play, making it a success in order that everyone can share in the proceeds. Now you've got a cast with life that is not trying to suck the life out of one another.

We think the best choice of play and performance is obvious.

Endnotes

[1]After psychologists Joseph Luft and Harry Ingham, who came up with the idea in 1963.

[2]Adam Bryant, "After 7 Years, Employees Win United Airlines," *The New York Times*, July 13, 1994.

The Big Vague

The catastrophe of supercollaboration

Given its downsides, we should approach pure collaboration just as carefully and consciously as we approach pure competition. Teams don't always work, and not every task is suited to team solutions.

But wait, it gets worse. When pundits worry about where our supercompetitive age is heading, they usually talk about the haves eventually getting everything, and the have-nots losing everything. That is not a vision of an end, but of a brief, unstable condition occurring just before the real end, a snapback from supercompetition to its exact opposite, supercollaboration.

Think of the fall of the Roman Empire. Think of the Dark Ages. Think lengthy. Super collaboration spawns a world full of martyrs, in which progress is nil because no competitive fire is pushing individuals to achieve and "codes of conduct" curtail all experimentation.

To get a bead on what the coming supercollaborative age might be like unless we come to grips with supercompetition, let's examine recent history.

Since the end of World War II, the competitive dynamism of the world's economies was held in check by the Cold War. Because the U.S.S.R. and the U.S. both had nuclear weapons, neither was willing to expand recklessly. Neither side wanted to do anything too provocative or supercompetitive.

Domino theory to the contrary, fewer national borders changed during this period than did after World War I. The threat of mutual destruction forced a kind of "limited modified competitive hangout" upon the postwar period. Two powerful rivals, with opposite philosophies, each did everything in its power to avoid doing something to set the other off.

The limited modified hangout ended when capitalism won the cold war. Competitive restraint has been replaced by an urgent new breed of nearly pure competitiveness. People from the mightiest to the lowliest are aware as never before that they live in a world in which people far away can snatch the meat off their table.

We fret about our personal ability to compete, be employed, and bring in money.

We fret about our organizations and whether they will be lean enough and able to learn fast enough to continue to compete.

We fret about our schools and whether they are equipping our kids to compete against the schoolkids of Japan, Russia, and Singapore.

We fret about our whole society caving in competitively, letting the hordes of more competitive countries march in and help themselves.

Our response to stepped-up competition is reminiscent of the arms race: We step it up even further. If everyone is competing, we shift into overdrive and supercompete—take no prisoners, give no quarter, duel to the death.

The spirit of capitalism, competition, is finally given free rein. Every industrial and developing power on earth is locked in a struggle to establish and maintain footholds in world markets. Manufacturing plants in Malaysia and Bolivia belch smoke around the clock. Supercompetition is a car driving all out, with the pedal to the metal.

Everyone is working harder to do better—to win.

How long can this continue? The Brute Cycle tells us that supercompeters are usually brought down by the very people they thought they had squashed. Speeding cars eventually burn up their engines, run out of gas, or go out of control, and when they go out of control, as Japan's economy has in recent years, the momentum of the catastrophe threatens to take out every other car on the track.

Signs that this kind of collapse may be drawing near abound. In the business of professional sports, runaway player salaries have resulted in higher ticket prices and stadium bail-out plans that take public money and invest it in one of the most speculative businesses.

When 21-year-old basketball center Kevin Garnett announced in August 1997 that he would decline an offer of $103.5 million to play for the Minnesota Timberwolves of the National

Basketball Association, the decision sent shivers all the way over to another professional sport, baseball, where the Minnesota Twins have been lobbying for public support of a stadium.

"There is a greater fear today—the most legitimate fear—that the whole thing is escalating so much that it's not sustainable," said a state representative.[1] How do you sell the public on underwriting a game they can't afford to attend? But how do you get talented, super-competitive players to ask for anything less than the richest teams in the biggest markets are willing to pay?

It's happening in big-bucks book publishing. HarperCollins, one of the most respected publishers, announced in August 1997 that it was canceling over 100 titles from its fall book list, letting 420 people go, and writing off $279 million in losses. The reason: The company had lost too much money publishing celebrity blockbusters, like Johnnie Cochran's *Journey to Justice*, that didn't sell. As with sports, publishers must compete to deliver the highest contract to celebrity writers. When a celebrity book fails, publishers cut costs the only way they can, by eviscerating the budgets of noncelebrity authors. It doesn't help when the publisher is supercompetitor Rupert Murdoch.[2]

In each case the pigs—the top athletes, the publishers, the celebrities, and their agents—get to feast while lesser figures pick up the tab. In each case the loser is the public, which grows wearier of empty books and superstar egos every season. These industries are competing their way to collapse.

Snapback

If competitive expansion were infinitely possible, that would be bad, but people could probably muddle along. The rich would get richer and the poor would get poorer, indefinitely.

But it isn't possible. All trends ultimately reach a tension point such that they reverse themselves. A world stretched to the breaking point by supercompetition is likely to snap back to its diametric opposite, supercollaboration.

We are not likely to like supercollaboration much better. It won't be mild collaboration like teams and empowerment and democracy. It will be more like mob anarchy. The center will no longer hold.

Already we are seeing it in the rise of tinpot fiefs, run by people no longer afraid of the big powers—Saddam Hussein in Iraq, the

Russian Mafia, the Freemen of Montana, the Independent State of Texas, the Aum sarin gas cult of Japan, and Heaven's Gate in San Diego, groups wielding coercive power over their members because there is no balancing power to offset their tyranny.

Pure collaboration is an environment in which progress is forbidden and individual achievement is discouraged. To those who like that sort of thing, it will have the relative serenity of a hermitage. To those for whom hermitages hold no special appeal, it will seem like, well, a hermitage—silent and constraining, like a straightjacket and gag.

When the world is all Martyrs and no Predators, we'll miss the Brutes' verve. There will be no armies vying for one another's territory; on the other hand, we'll all feel like we're in the army.

Imagine a complete rejection of the competitive spirit, blaming it for all the evils of recent times. Conformity and sacrifice for others will be primary civic values. Entrepreneurialism and innovation will sound like fingernails on a chalkboard to people. Anyone with any sort of individual spark will have it preemptively snuffed. Anyone with a better idea will think better before expressing it.

That is the dreaded supercollaborative scenario. A little short on specifics, true; but when it comes, that will be its hallmark. Call it the Big Vague. Anything that seems individual, unique, or nonfuzzy will be shaved, sanded, or guillotined back into shape.

Something like that will happen sometime, and maybe soon—unless people become more conscious of, and more appropriate with, their competitive habits.

Endnotes

[1]Jay Weiner, "Contract rejection may hurt stadium effort," (Minneapolis) *Star Tribune*, August 14, 1997.

[2]Jeff Guinn, "Writing is on the wall: Book publishers scrambling," Fort Worth *Star-Telegram*, August 12, 1997.

The Pyrrhic Fallacy

The unbearable cost of winning

The worst aspect of pure collaboration is that when it occurs, it tends to last a long time, like the Dark Ages. The redeeming aspect of its opposite, pure competition, is that it is often over almost as soon as it begins. Supercompetitive people and organizations, those who revel in the brute delight of winning, can practically count the hours their victories will last.

Pyrrhus, a king of fourth-century BC Albania, was widely acknowledged to be a brilliant military strategist, but he was unable to capitalize on his victories because they always came at too high a cost. His campaigns in Italy and Greece were triumphs in terms of crushing the enemy, but he lost so many men and resources in them that the vanquished enemies simply ignored his demand for terms. He could never maintain what he won. Thus his name comes down to us as a metaphor for the ruinous, or Phyrric, victory.

And so it is with the unthinking competitive drive. Left to itself, it seeks to win at whatever cost. A company like AT&T in the 1960s will knock all other companies aside in its rush to success until it is brought down to earth, in this case by Judge Harold Greene. IBM in the 1980s, the consummate marketing company of the era, was done in by the little people it thought nothing of—the chipmakers and operating system companies that supplied parts for its neglected microcomputer lines.

More often than not, brutal victory comes back and bites you, preventing winners from enjoying their winnings. Tyrants do not endure, because there is no collaborative weight counterbalancing their regimes, and because mere "strongmen" are seldom able to ensure peaceful succession.

Bullies in the marketplace tend to cause their enemies to unite and defeat them. This comeuppance, which we call the Brute Cycle, always seems to take supercompeters by surprise. They expect, reasonably enough, that the challenger they beat will learn to accept an inferior position and not come around except with head bowed. This generally works in the short term, so the order of competition ("I win, you lose, and you like it") is logical and acceptable to all.

But in the longer term, and especially in a democratic culture with free flow of information, bully rules don't play well. The *social* ethic of equal opportunity holds that one can be whatever one sets one's mind to. The *business* ethic of continuous improvement holds that nothing is better forever—thus there is no ordained ruling class. If a Brute kicks sand in your face, why, you bulk up, learn tae kwan do, and go alter the hierarchy in Chuck Norris style.

Because of this cycle, traditional winning is often a prelude to losing. Winning in a way that humiliates and angers your competitor almost guarantees that your turn to lose will come next.

The Brute Cycle explains why the bigger and meaner you are, the harder and earlier you fall; why species at the top of the food chain appear most often on the endangered list. Mussolini[1] wound up hanging upside down in a square in Milan. Hotelier Leona Helmsley[2] wound up tucking sheet corners at a women's penitentiary in upstate New York. In the same way, companies that deliberately throw inside tend to get knocked down when it is their turn at bat.

The compleat Brute organization is a criminal entity, taking every shortcut and walking over everyone, exhibiting zero social conscience and maximum cruelty. The irony is that its very brutish nature and its confidence in its own superiority hasten its demise.

The Brute Cycle is not something that "happens" to bullies. It is what people who have been bullied do back to the bully. It is the only defense people have against aggression and exploitation. It involves three steps that organizations and individuals have followed unconsciously since the days of Pyrrhus:

➤ **Exchange.** This is the information stage, in which victims make contact with one another and with potential allies and exchange information. They decide on a strategy for dealing with the bully. If possible, they extend a peace offering to the bully to cut it out.

➤ **Encircle.** This is the stage in which victims and allies move together to surround the bully. They link arms and focus attention on the predator and keep it focused until the predator's behavior changes.

➤ **Exact.** This is the action stage, in which victims and allies compel the bully to negotiate or concede. The bully who refuses stays encircled forever.

The 3Es worked sporadically in ancient times. Information flow was usually inadequate to really encircle a predator. In modern times, though, information has been more readily available. Boycotts, whereby a group not only stops buying a product but urges others not to buy it either, use the 3Es. Whistle-blowing, the act of exchanging information about the misdeeds occurring on one's own side, never succeeded in other centuries, but works in ours (sometimes).

The 3Es are not a game, and they are seldom pleasant. They are never assured of success. But they are the primary transcompetitive tools for dealing with supercompetitors.

"Chainsaw Al"

The best contemporary example of a supercompetitive manager is "Chainsaw Al" Dunlap, CEO at Scott Paper and author of an aptly titled book (*Mean Business*) promoting his own brutal and deliberately shortsighted view of business. Dunlap is a gleeful celebrator of stratospheric CEO salaries and draconian downsizing, and a harsh dismisser of corporate philanthropy and good neighborism. He's been called everything from "Corporate Killer" (*Newsweek*) to "Rambo in Pinstripes" (*The New York Times*).

When Dunlap moved Scott's corporate campus from Philadelphia to Florida, he was met with severe criticism from the Philadelphia newspapers, which deemed the move self-serving.

Like Mel Masters at Lasermaster, Dunlap is into imagery:

"I like symbolism," he explains, motioning to the paintings of lions in his office. "Predators don't order out for room service. I respect that. I'm a classic Leo: gregarious, outgoing, very self-confident, someone who likes center stage and is probably a little egotistical." There are more lions at his home—and a few sharks in case the theme gets a little too predictable.

The move to Boca Raton cost 11,000 employees their jobs. But Dunlap made no secret that the only constituency he cared about was Scott's shareholders. His pay before the cuts was $618,000; his pay in the year following the cuts rose to $3,575,500.

To his credit, he makes no claim whatsoever to being a patient manager with a Japanese 100-year plan.

> Albert J. Dunlap admits there is "some truth" to the charge that he is no long-term manager. "Once a business becomes business-as-usual, it loses its appeal for me."[3]

Dunlap is still out there, doing that voodoo that he does so well. Will the Brute Cycle come round for him?

It doesn't come around for everyone. Bullies are hard to topple, and fighting them is costly. As we type these words, Cambodian leader Pol Pot has been taken prisoner in the umpteenth insurgency since the 1972 United States intervention in that country. Pol Pot, dubbed "the Hannibal Lecter of Asia,"[4] was the worst of the lot, having stacked 2 million of his countrymen's skulls during his bloody tenure as head of the Khmer Rouge. Pol Pot survived the Brute Cycle for many years in part because information flowed so poorly in his country. The cycle is no guarantee that injustice will be avenged. It is simply the shape retribution takes when it occurs, as victims and allies exchange information, encircle the malefactor, and exact a settlement.

Chainsaw Al Dunlap may escape it if he keeps moving and keeps cashing people in for another short-term fling. Like Billy Martin in baseball, there is always a call out for a manager who can rattle the cage of a company that needs change, and whose previous managers were unable to effect it.

Part of Dunlap's charm is that he knows he is so politically incorrect, and that he can hide for a long time behind the kind of short-term results (176% stock price rise in one quarter alone) his slash-and-burn tactics achieve.

Another part is that he is himself contributing, with his penchant for publicity, to the encircling that is already well underway.

Endnotes

[1]"We must learn to grow less likable and to become hard, implacable, and full of hatred."

[2]"Taxes are for the little people."

[3]"Scott Paper Profit Rises 176 Percent," Palm Beach *Post*, October 19, 1995.

[4]Lucy Komisar, "Counting the Bodies," *American Reporter*, July 19, 1997.

The Brute Cycle in Action

Fighting back against supercompetitors

A recent news story described how surrounding communities rise to take down brutes in their midst. A man named John Harper, Jr. was the scourge of Spring Valley, California. Though he lived with his parents—which suggests something about delayed development in bullies right there—Harper spent much of his time antagonizing people in the San Diego suburb. He deliberately tailgated drivers and tried to run them off the road. He picked fights with people, threw rocks at them, and threatened to burn their homes down. One of his repeat victims, a retired Navy commander named John Palm, begged authorities to do something about Harper. But the justice system was too clogged to cope with the man besides wagging a finger at him. On November 28, 1995, an enraged Palm cornered Harper and emptied two ammunition clips into him.

During the trial, the Brute Cycle kicked into high gear. Neighbor after neighbor spoke up in defense of Palm's action. The jury found Palm guilty of murder and sentenced him to 15 years in prison. But the judge threw out the verdict, claiming that Harper was a "jerk" and brought about his own death, and reduced Palm's conviction to manslaughter.[1]

Bullies like Harper are everywhere. They may share a cubicle with you, or they may run the entire company. The business media tend to glorify managerial sociopathy, handing the most egregious offenders mock-villainous nicknames like "Chainsaw Al." We all admire an executive with will, much as people in other times admired dictators who got the trains to run on time (never mind who had to be pushed onto the tracks). They have what we wish we had, an instinct to kill and to get what we most want.

We overlook two things in our admiration:

1. Most of these people would still be vicious even if there were no defensible objective guiding their actions.
2. The simple, brutal philosophy of terror is useless in achieving any long-term goal.

Richard Nixon and the Pepsi Gambit

There are two psychological side effects of the Brute Cycle. The first is the Brute's diversion into paranoia and obsessive-compulsiveness, and the "defactualization" or reshaping of truth that occurs.

Brutes may appear indifferent to the suffering they cause, but in fact they are always processing the consequences of their own behavior, and they respond by becoming afraid of retaliation, which diverts their attention away from production and toward defense and the formation of a story that legitimizes their behavior.

In 1972, Ken (One-Minute Manager) Blanchard suggested that a peculiar disconnect occurred whenever workers compete against one another. The very things about competition that bring a team together against outside opponents tend to corrode its internal cohesiveness:

> While competition and the responses it generates may be very useful to a group in making it more effective and achievement-motivated, the same factors which improve intragroup effectiveness may have negative consequences for intergroup effectiveness.

When win/lose confrontations occur between two groups or teams, even though there eventually is a winner, Blanchard said, the loser is not convinced of having lost, and intergroup tension increases rather than diminishes:

> If the win is clear-cut, the winner often loses his edge, becomes complacent, and is less interested in goal accomplishment. The loser in this case often develops internal conflict while trying to discover the cause of the loss or someone to blame. If reevaluation takes place, however, the group may reorganize and become more cohesive and effective....

During such competition, Blanchard said, paranoia and obsession kick in. Each group starts seeing the other as the enemy and distorts its own perceptions of reality, seeing themselves as virtuous and the other group as the sum of all badness. Hostility toward the other group increases, while communication decreases. Soon it is no trouble at all maintaining a fever pitch of animosity toward the other group. Forget ever setting the record straight at that point. If the groups are made to talk face-to-face, it is a charade. Neither side really listens to the other—they hear only those cues that support their side's arguments.[2]

The classic example of a bullying business team going bonkers involved the Pentagon Papers revealing the brutal disregard for the truth about Vietnam during the Johnson and Nixon administrations.

The people in the White House and the Pentagon had become so abusive in their withholding of information that they lost all connection with reality. Historian Hannah Arendt comes down hard on the paranoid mystique that developed in high places. Without the relatively free flow of information in the U.S., the truth would still not be known about these men.

> I am not sure that the evils of bureaucracy suffice as an explanation, though they certainly facilitated this defactualization. At any rate, the relation, or, rather, nonrelation, between facts and decision, between the intelligence community and the civilian and military services, is perhaps the most momentous, and certainly the best-guarded, secret that the Pentagon Papers revealed....

In the Pentagon Papers we are confronted with people who did their utmost to win the minds of the people, that is, to manipulate them; but since they labored in a free country, where all kinds of information is available, they never really succeeded. Because of their relatively high position in government, they were better shielded against this public information, which told the more or less factual truth, than were those whom they tried to convince and of whom they were likely to think in terms of mere audiences, "silent majorities," who were supposed to watch the scenarists' productions:

> Probably because of their high station and their astounding self-assurance, they were so convinced of overwhelming success, not on the battlefield, but in the public-relations arena, and so certain of their psychological premises about the unlimited possibilities in

manipulating people, that they anticipated general belief and victory in the battle for people's minds.[3]

And since they lived in a defactualized world anyway, they found it easy to pay as little attention to the fact that their audience refused to be convinced as to other facts.

No ivory tower of the scholars has ever better prepared the mind for ignoring the facts of life than did the various think tanks for the scholars and the reputation of the White House for the President's advisers. In this atmosphere, defeat was less feared than admitting defeat.[4]

The second psychological side effect of Brute behavior is a kind of guilt. Our favorite illustration of the guilt phase involves two friends of ours who happen to be identical twins, Jim and John Thornton. Not all twins are competitive, but these two were super-competitive as kids, ferocious in their determination that neither would achieve the smallest advantage over the other. While growing up in relative affluence, they behaved as if every substance were in critically short supply. That being the case, even the sharing of a bottle of Pepsi became an opportunity to seek advantage.

They would pour and repour until the two glasses were equal to the satisfaction of both boys. They even devised a "fake swallowing" gambit to take advantage of one another. Both boys would appear to drain their cans. But one would save a last mouthful and dribble it back into his glass, to sample and savor for the next hour or so, to get the other's goat. No way could spit-out Pepsi be as good-tasting as the flush of victory over one's DNA-mate.

Their entire boyhood was consumed with the need to beat one another, and out of it they perceived a cycle. When one twin won, two things happened: The twin who lost was enraged and brought fresh rage to the act of retaliation, and the twin who won felt guilty about it and therefore let his guard down just a bit. Result: A continuous cycle of competition, fired by defactualization, then weakened by guilt. Winning could only be a momentary pleasure, because guilt immediately wiped it out and set in motion the victor's replacement by the vanquished, which never lasted long, either.

So what were they fighting for? Was cola precious enough to justify that level of perniciousness? What scarcity could account for the energy of their infighting? Parental approval? (Their parents were by all accounts loving and generous people.) Identity within their own twinhood?

The truth is that they were both natural-born supercompeters, and nature had given them to each other as foils.

Brute Behavior in the Marketplace

The Brute Cycle is as repetitious a story in the marketplace as it is in the jungle. It is repeated over and over again, between grocery stores, between professional groups, within consumer product categories, and between nations.

Commodore and Leading Edge were major computer companies in the 1980s, and they sold millions of computers by hardballing everyone: suppliers, distributors, and customers alike. Everyone was afraid of these companies because of their ruthlessness, their unwillingness to take prisoners.

But eventually both companies came crashing down, due at least in part to the ferocity of their competitiveness. In the case of Leading Edge, stores frustrated with Leading Edge's indifference to customer complaints refused to stock their computers any more. In the case of Commodore, suppliers rose up in revolt against the company's savage style of supplier relations.

Killing the Competition

The sure sign of a Brute company is how it behaves when up against someone smaller than it.

Consider the notorious McLibel case that hypnotized British readers through 11 months of 1996 and 1997.[5] In the longest trial in English history, a pair of unemployed, lawyerless vegetarians held off powerful McDonald's in a battle for the hearts, minds, and arterial passages of the United Kingdom.

Former postman Dave Morris and bar worker Helen Steel circulated brochures outside London restaurants condemning the chain in just about every way—labor relations, environmental practices, cruelty to animals, false advertising, and the nutritional merits of their hamburgers.

McDonald's, seeking to head off attacks by other "publicity seekers," sued the two for libel. The verdict, a partial victory for the restaurant chain, was of the Pyrrhic sort—an award of $94,000. The trial is said to have cost McDonald's $16 million.

The Brute Cycle is on naked display in electoral politics. Politicians are told by their handlers that unless they "go negative" against their competitors, they will certainly lose. So the mud flies and the defactualization accumulates. By the time voters cast their ballots, the reputations of both candidates are in tatters and voters are no longer even interested in the issues or the candidates' stands—they are too disgusted with the process. The ability of the winner to govern effectively is thus severely compromised, a classic Pyrrhic victory.

Win today, lose tomorrow. It is a cycle that can only be broken by redefining interests so that heads no longer crash into one another and organizations master a kinder, gentler, longer-term approach to winning.

Endnotes

[1] Associated Press wire, April 17, 1997; found on CompuServe.

[2] Ken Blanchard and Paul Hersey, *Management of Organizational Behavior,* Prentice-Hall, 1972.

[3] Hannah Arendt, *Crises of the Republic,* Harcourt Brace, 1972.

[4] Arendt, ibid.

[5] Associated Press, June 19, 1997.

Belling the Bullies

The relative magic of exchange, encircle, and exact

There is a force that can contend with outlaw competitiveness on a global scale, but it is not the United Nations and it is not the World Bank. It is the informed power of a watching world that has learned to identify cheaters and bullies early on, and is taking steps to *exchange* information among themselves, *encircle* the offending party, and *expose* the misbehavior.

Three examples that have appeared in the pages of this book are Nike, Coke and Pepsi Colas, and Microsoft. We picked these companies because each, at a formative moment, did something sneaky or unworthy to get started. These are great, revealing little stories, like George Washington chopping down the cherry tree in reverse:

➤ In 1968, Nike paid $35 to Carolyn Davidson, a graduate student at the University of Oregon, for the "swoosh" design that they have plastered the planet with. Over the next 30 years, Nike profited immeasurably from her design. She never made another dime from it.

➤ Coke and Pepsi laced their original secret formulas with actual cocaine and billed the beverages as health products.

➤ Microsoft, needing some kind of operating system to sell to IBM along with their own BASIC language, paid $50,000 for a young product called QDOS, which became MS-DOS, which became the baseline product driving the PC revolution.

47

None of these acts was illegal, but they were all smarmy, and they suggested what these companies would do to compete. And there's more.

First, you have to love Nike; we do. Their brand of supercompetitiveness is so naked they are the Yosemite Sams of business—loud, obnoxious, and obvious. They extol the glory of winning in their mission statement, their ads, their sales practices, their supplier relationships, and their corporate behavior. When Nike goes over the top for supercompetition, they are just being themselves.

But the whole world is watching. The Internet boasts several Nike watchdog groups, monitoring everything from plant conditions in Vietnam to labor disputes in Beaverton, Oregon.

It's unthinkable that Nike, as charged with the fire of battle as its CEO Phil Knight is, will change its ways any time soon. But every move they make is under the watchful eyes of people like Thuyen Nguyen of Nike Watch, an international group of people who plain hate Nike's values and practices. Outspoken East Timorese Nobel prize winner Jose Ramos-Horta led another anti-Nike group, proclaiming the company an enemy of civilization:

> Companies like Nike should be viewed as enemies, in the same manner we view armies and governments that perpetrate human rights violations. What is the difference between the behavior of Nike in Indonesia and elsewhere, and the Japanese imperial army during WWII?[1]

But the amount of damage Nike can do is circumscribed by the attention the company draws. Fifty years ago, you could make a billion people mad and there was nothing they could do to you (think Ma Bell, or Soviet food lines). In the information age, knowledge makes might, and people can resist.

The best evidence that even fierce Nike can be made sensitive can be found in the headlines. In June of 1997 Nike made peace with Muslims who were offended because the logo on a new shoe resembled the word *Allah* in Arabic. The play on words was distressing to Muslims, and having the name of Allah on shoes was seen as particularly disrespectful because, used properly, the shoes get dirty, muddy, and sweaty, which is tantamount to sacrilege.

Read, and ask yourself if this sounds like the Nike we have come to know and love:

Under the written agreement between Nike and the Council on American-Islamic Relations, Nike will apologize to Muslims and recall shoes with the logo. In exchange, the council will urge Muslims worldwide not to boycott Nike products.

"We wanted to reinstate confidence in our community that whenever they see something offensive, there could be something done about it," said Nihad Awad, the Islamic council's executive director.

He said his group would have called for a global boycott of Nike products, especially in affluent Muslim communities in the Middle East and Asia, had the two sides failed to reach a settlement.

"From the outset we have sought to avoid any offense to Muslims," said Nike spokesman Roy Agostino. "We have, through this process, developed a deeper understanding of Islamic concerns and Islamic issues and ... have opened up a broader dialogue with members of the Islamic community."[2]

Lo, how the mighty are fallen. This announcement was issued the day before the floor manager of the Vietnamese factory forced women to run until they collapsed as punishment for not wearing the right shoes. Nike was so encircled by Nguyen's group that it hired former U.N. ambassador Andrew Young to conduct an inquiry into its own practices in Asia.

Finally, in October, 1997, Nike offered a payment in stock to Carolyn Davidson, in part due to the bad publicity that had encircled the company for 30 years.

In Coke and Pepsi we have two companies that pledged, back when there were no global companies, to become global companies. Coke led the way, pledging when the company went public in 1919 not to stop until it was possible to purchase a bottle of Coke in any village in any country anywhere in the world, 195 nations in all. Pepsi was the first American consumer product in the Soviet Union, and it is the leading seller in India and South America. (The people of Guam, incidentally, are the world's biggest Pepsi lovers, quaffing 512 cans per person per year.[3])

To make good on their commitments, these companies invented saturation marketing. Pepsi invented the radio jingle. Coke took the form to its greatest heights with the global anthem, "I'd Like to Teach the World to Sing" in the 1960s.

But beyond the image of people holding hands are the images of two elephants trampling the global grass. Both companies positioned themselves as the answer to countries experiencing problems guaranteeing potable water. Coke and Pepsi both were excoriated on *60 Minutes* for their practice of demanding that stores allot a set percentage of shelf facings for their products. This is why, when you buy soda, 40 percent of the aisle is filled with Coke products, another 40 percent is filled with Pepsi products, and the remaining 20 percent of space is divided among 20 or so smaller companies. Stores must allot this percentage to do business with the two big companies.

These two Brute companies owned the mass marketing age lock, stock, and barrel. Whole advertising campaigns have been based not on the benefits of the products, but on amusing wrinkles in the Coke/Pepsi positioning rivalry. There is the famous Pepsi commercial in which cola deliveries to a frat house and a senior center are switched. The seniors get the Pepsi and party down, while the frat brothers drink Coke and rock gently on their front porches. And Coke has ingeniously positioned itself, via its artsy commercials, as both hip and nostalgic—a tough combination.

But people no longer care about the rivalry of global elephants. The knowledge age is unfriendly to corporate arrogance and indulgence. Formulas are easier to duplicate, and in an information age the masses don't have to be asses. The two giants are seen increasingly as charging premium prices and twisting the arms of retail channels to purvey sugar water.

Copycat companies like Cott of Toronto and retailers like Wal-Mart, with enough clout to say no to the cola companies' shelving demands, have demonstrated that the flavors of Coke and Pepsi can be reproduced and even improved upon and sold profitably for two-thirds the cost of the original brands, and even less. And why not? The new store-brand colas have none of the global advertising budget to make up. Shoppers are buying the once-scorned, now-improved, in-store brands by the vanload. Pepsi has started to fail its own taste tests. Coke loses out to RC Cola in blind taste tests 95 percent of the time.[4]

What has happened is that competing retailers and customers have *exchanged* information on the soft drink malaise, *encircled* the competing giants, and *exacted* from them concessions on their absurdly self-serving market positions. Increasingly, their endless competitive war with one another is seen worldwide as pointless.

Finally, we have Microsoft. Never, not in the cases of John Rockefeller's Standard Oil, AT&T, United Fruit, or Liberian Freighters Unlimited, has the world mistrusted a single company the way our world mistrusts Microsoft. It is a suspicion that is out of proportion to the company's size: It is a $5 billion company in annual sales, compared to AT&T's $75 billion.

But people have memories they didn't use to have. Hardly an American over the age of 7 is unaware of Chairman Bill Gates, the $36 billion man,[5] or of Microsoft's conflictual status as developer of both operating systems (DOS and the many flavors of Windows) and the applications that run on these operating systems. The company's promotion of Windows 95 was the biggest single-product promotion in the history of the world. Microsoft, unlike AT&T, has momentum and ready cash. People see it not as it is today, but as what it is likely to become in ten years—a bigger monopoly than AT&T ever was with tentacles in communicating, entertainment, publishing, and banking.

And so the company is under perpetual siege. At any moment there are hundreds of lawsuits pending against the company. It is the punching bag of every pundit with two pennies and a newsletter column to rub together. Regulators have nothing to lose by maintaining constant antitrust vigilance. When Microsoft sought to acquire Intuit a few years ago, the deal was quashed because it gave Microsoft access to a bank. People flash-forwarded to a future in which all our checks said Microsoft in the lower left-hand corner, and shuddered.

Encircled and exposed, Microsoft feels the heat of the world and pads softly through it, like a cat with a bell around its neck: not neutered by a long shot, but apparent to everyone as a potential danger that must be watched. John D. Rockefeller was never hemmed in as Bill Gates is.

How has Microsoft responded to this encircling? In the summer of 1997, when Apple was in trouble and its CEO Gil Amelio turned out not to be the savior everyone had hoped, Apple looked in every direction for a white knight company to come sweep it up. There were so many companies that made sense as partners: Motorola, Sun, Oracle, and even IBM were discussed in the press.

But the company that actually put up money to keep Apple afloat was Microsoft, in one of the most stunning acts of corporate partnership ever. By all the known rules of competition, Microsoft would have been better off with the disappearance of the #2 maker of operating systems. How easy it would have been for Microsoft to stand by and let Apple choke on its own problems.

Many are cynical of the partnership, and it is true that the $150 million that passed hands is chicken feed in the larger scale of things. One joke that made the rounds went like this:

Q.   What will the new Microsoft/Apple alliance be called?

A.   Microsoft.

But even if Microsoft is playing a clever game of killing with kindness, it is a sign that the company is aware that people are watching and that, as big as it is, it can no longer be insensitive to the eyes of the world.

Endnotes

[1]Gary Gach, "Nobelist Horta: 'Nike Should Be Viewed as an Enemy," *American Reporter*, week of June 30, 1977.

[2]Associated Press, June 24, 1997.

[3]Marginal note, "Obvious," *New York Times Magazine*, June 8, 1997.

[4]Remarks by Michael Treacy, The Masters Forum, Troy, Michigan, July 29, 1997.

[5]"Biggest Billionaire Is Bill Gates - Forbes," Reuters, July 13, 1997.

New Ways of Winning

Naming the transcompetitive habits

In the graph on page 20 we showed four dysfunctional ways of winning. The gray center square, what we call the Transcompetitive Zone, hid four ways that have greater long-term chances of success.

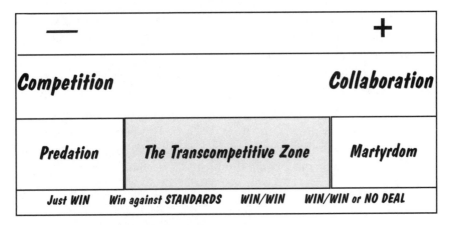

These are the four new ways of winning:

➤ **Just Win.** This will be tough for sensitive people to hear, but there is nothing wrong with winning. Innocent compared to its brutal cousins, the Just Win position simply wants to come out on top in the competitions it enters; it has no interest in the outcome of others in the competition. It is the standard motive in professional sports, where wins translate to bonuses and championships, and it is the minimum expectation of most business owners and workers: "I just want to come out ahead."

➤ **Win against Standards.** Winning against standards means competing against oneself, or against the standards others set—but not against individuals themselves. The Olympics are the best example of this: When Janet Evans won the gold medal in the 400-meter freestyle swim in Atlanta, she was beating her own time and the times of other swimmers, both in person and in the record books. Winning against standards is a very beautiful form of competing. It is about singleness of purpose, about achieving human perfection, not about clubbing the other player on the cranium. It is saying *This is what I can do* to the whole world. This beauty is one reason we make sports competition a kind of unofficial religion.

➤ **Win/Win.** For years, a town in Oregon sponsored an annual Short Fat Man's Race,[1] in which the entrants help each other out along the way and stop at the "stop short" line, wait for everyone to catch up, then cross the finish line together, hand in hand. The point behind the race was that anyone could win and that one party's winning did not preclude anyone else's winning. This insight became the core concept in *Getting to Yes*, the classic guide to negotiating based on mutual interests.[2]

Managed intelligently, win/win results in a pattern any individual and company would kill for—but of course shouldn't. This is a pattern for *continuous winning*, whereby one's victories last longer even in uncertain times, because the people who used to be strictly competitors are no longer ganging up on you. Continuous winning beats the Brute Cycle hands down.

Winning

Losing

CONTINUOUS WINNING

There are probably more books about win/win on business bookshelves today than there are books on golf. That is a problem. Win/win has been overinflated as a collaborative panacea. Find advantages for both sides, the theory goes, and all conflict will be eliminated, and we'll all be living and working in a paradise of teamwork and nonaggression. Easy!

But it is a pipe dream. Collaboration cannot make competition obsolete, not while real shortages of resources exist and multiple businesses engage in head-to-head rivalry. This is the case in a hundred businesses for every one that finds a noncompetitive monopoly niche for itself.

➤ **Win/Win or No Deal.** This is win/win with a commitment, or militant transcompetition. It is a way of certifying that a win/win really is a win/win. Both sides have to agree that the decision is a win for them. Until they find a way both sides can win, nothing goes forward. This compact helps police the looseness of win/win. It's most useful when trust between two parties is incomplete. "You know your intentions are okay, but until you see with your own eyes that working together is to your advantage as well as ours, we are not going to pressure you to agree."

These new ways of winning are what the supercompetitive (and the occasional supercollaborative) individual and organization should move toward. This may sound clear, but it isn't easy because you will be calling into question habits accumulated and rewarded by years of striving. These habits have become entrenched, unconscious, and irrational. Changing them requires understanding a few things about nature, psychology, and change theory.

Endnotes

[1]We thought enough of this contest to use it in the epilogue of our first book, *Turf Wars*, Scott Foresman, 1989.

[2]Roger Fisher and William Uhry, *Getting to Yes*, Penguin, 1981.

The Joy
of Cannibalism

And other rites of natural connection

An interesting statistic: Zoologists say the percentage of species of animals in the world that have achieved the bare minimum of socialization is no more than 20 percent. What is the bare minimum benchmark? Whether or not the species has quibbles about eating its own young. Everywhere you look, if you can stomach the sight, nature reveals its dirty secret:

➤ Tropical fish are known to regulate their own population levels by eating their excess young.

➤ Hyenas eat other hyenas.

➤ Lions, those noble creatures, have been known to attack competing herds and kill the young.

➤ For termites, cannibalism is a way of life. Every termite colony ever observed shows that they eat their own dead and injured.

➤ Then there is the wasp larva, embedded in a host insect, that at some strange timed moment in its development awakens, attacks, and kills other larvae.[1]

Ah, to be a caterpillar and devour one's siblings—it would be tough to define a more competitive act than that. It has got to be a liberating feeling, knowing that if times get tough, or even if they don't, there are always members of your own kind you can snarf up. "My innards request the pleasure of your company...."

If you are not literally gobbling others up, you can absorb and excrete them in analogous ways: downsizing, exploitation, violating their rights to property and privacy, terrorizing them on the job, lying, cheating, walking over them as if they were shag rug, not people.

Cannibals in nature have their reasons: the thinning of the herd, the strengthening of the strong at the expense of the weak. Among so-called primitive human tribes, cannibalism is ritually undertaken only for religious reasons: to ward off evil or to invoke a taboo. It is exceedingly rare and works like homeopathy—a little sin to exorcise a bigger sin.

But then there is cannibalism for the hell of it. That is what we see the most of. Your children, your neighbors, your competitors, your employees, your customers—delicious! Cannibalism and sadism are such accepted ways of doing business, in nature and in business, that we cannot ignore them as a starting point.

But they are only the starting point. The behavior range on the scale of connectedness runs from wild to woolly, from lion to lamb. Here are the faces of competition in nature that also turn up in our places of work. As you read the descriptions, consider the character of your competitive relationships—with colleagues, competitors, family, friends—and how they differ.

➤ **Simple competition.** Simple competition, which corresponds roughly to win/lose thinking, is what happens when resources are limited and two or more creatures both want them. A misunderstood facet of simple competition is that the two creatures don't have to devour one another to compete. They don't even have to fight. They just need to be after the same scarce thing, like breathing the same air or enjoying the same berry. If I eat your peanut, I don't need to fight you. We competed and you lost. I got the food and you didn't. This is more than biology; it's economics in a nutshell.

Giraffes and elephants on the Serengeti Plain, hardly aggressive by disposition, are nevertheless highly competitive. In business all competition is of this sort: Lufthansa and British Airways wage war over market share, not the flesh of one another's boards of directors.

Naturalist Edward O. Wilson, who brought the idea of connectedness in animals and humans to full flower in his book, *Sociobiology*, links simple competition to the idea of scarcity:

> The techniques of competition are extremely diverse.... An animal
> that aggressively challenges another over a piece of food is obvi-
> ously competing. So is another animal that marks its territory with
> a scent [aggressive competition versus competitive prevention]
> even when other animals avoid the territory solely because of the
> odor and without ever seeing the territory owner. Competition also
> includes the using up of resources to the detriment of other organ-
> isms, whether or not any aggressive behavioral interaction also
> occurs. A plant, to take an extreme case, may absorb phosphates
> through its root system at the expense of its neighbors, or cut off
> its neighbors from sunlight by shading them with its leaves.

Competition can occur between members of the same species
(dogs and dogs) or between different species (dogs and cats) and
phyla (cats and catnip). It can and does occur between individuals, families, teams, groups, species, family businesses, corporations, nonprofit organizations, and whole societies.

➤ **Predation.** Many viewers have sat and watched the popular
death-and-mayhem videos being hawked on the tube: "Nature's
Bloody Behavior," "Beasts Biting Each Other," and "Carnivores
with Long Sharp Fingernails."

What they saw was scene after scene illustrating the glories of the
food chain: alligators scarfing down flamingoes, praying mantis-
es munching their mates' chitin heads, wild jackals competing for
first rights to some fetid corpse strewn along the desert floor.

The lesson is simple: Predatory competition, corresponding
roughly to win/kill thinking, makes the natural world go
around.[2] What the predator image overlooks is that these seemingly supercompetitive creatures are also supercollaborative in
their home lives. Wolves live and travel in packs, lions in prides.
Relationships are terribly important to them. Wolves and eagles
mate for life (not with one another, silly).

This is the behavior the business magazines extol in supercompeters like CEOs who stop at nothing to trump their competitors,
or the corporate pirates of the 1980s like Carl Icahn or Kohlman
Kravis Roberts who swooped down on befuddled companies and
made off with corporate assets for distribution to investors before
the victims knew what hit them.

It occurs at the team level as well, in the unit that doesn't think
it can win unless a parallel unit is made to lose.

Special Relationships

Scattered among the usual competitive relationships are several that are unusually intense or occur only between certain individuals.

➤ **Nemesis.** This word from Greek mythology has come to mean "fateful enemy." Your nemesis is your sworn natural enemy, as you are the same to it. These creatures are locked in an obsessive relationship only one can survive. The tarantula and the wasp are a perfect example: The wasp needs a hairy dead body to lay its eggs in, and the giant spider would prefer that didn't happen. Or the mongoose and cobra: The mongoose protects its long-term future (its eggs) from the cobra, who seeks short-term nourishment. One of the most feared creatures in all nature, the cobra cowers at the mere sight of a mongoose. In business we have instances of this peculiar strand of supercompetition: Sumitomo and Intel, Pepsi and Coke, MCI and British Telecom. One suspects, however, that the sworn enmity bit among these players is sometimes a ruse, that their nemesis relationship is a matter of convenience, like the winking agreement among George Orwell's global regions to take turns allying and making war against one another.[3]

➤ **Sibling rivalry.** We looked on with horror in an earlier chapter as identical twins John and Jim tried to pour exactly equal glasses of Pepsi. Sibling rivalry is an intense form of competition occurring within not just a species but a family. In sibling rivalry, children vie against one another despite parental disapproval, apparently out of mutually reinforced habit: You put me down, I put you down. In organizations, the analog is divisional competition, whereby business units within a larger business vie for resources and prestige, often in the face of much more dangerous external competition.

Imagine what it must have been like growing up in the Brennan household in Chicago in the 1940s, within sight of the Sears and Montgomery Ward mail centers. Edward and Bernie, four years apart, always vied to do the same things. During the 1970s, they worked together for Sears, with Bernie splitting when the rivalry grew too intense. Edward rose to the CEO position at Sears. Not to be outdone, Bernie commandeered Sears' lookalike rival, Montgomery Ward. Both were harsh taskmasters, fighting some internal battle colleagues could only guess at. Edward was a bureaucrat by disposition, so Bernie was a ferocious antibureaucrat. But despite their opposite approaches they were alike in their energy levels and fervor to succeed. Though his company wound up declaring bankruptcy, Bernie was in many ways more successful with Wards than Edward was with Sears; point to Bernie. But neither Brennan was able to bring either of these old-line retailers back to glorious form.

➤ **Parasitism.** This is a sad form of competition in which one individual derives nourishment at the expense of another, usually by laying waste to its living tissues, and usually with the result that the "weaker" winds up destroying the "stronger." Unlike predators, parasites do not kill their hosts outright. Rather, they weaken them till they die by other causes.

There is also a limited, nonfatal parasitism. An example is one bird putting its eggs in another bird's nest. The cowbird and European cuckoo have somehow lost their instinct for nest building, so they borrow other birds' nests. Another example is the eagle that robs the osprey of its catch, then catches the fish before it hits the water.

Parasitism occurs less between competing entities in business than it does between supposed stakeholders: "entitled" employees and suppliers with sweetheart deals who drain a company of its resources while contributing little; customers who demand that mature products be supported ad infinitum, guaranteeing that a competitor with a fresh idea will overtake them; shareholders and raiders who extract wealth and sell off core assets; communities that soak businesses for the maximum amount of tax, killing to the most vulnerable ones.

Collaborative Behaviors

Nature also boasts four patterns we may describe as nearly collaborative or fully collaborative:

➤ **Familiarity.** Directly between competition and collaboration on the connectedness scale is familiarity or family instinct.

Familiarity is recognizing that something is the same as you, and according it special (nondevouring) treatment. The opposite of cannibalizing one's young, it means cultivating them as family or clan. Parents of millions of animal species feed, care for, and teach their young. This is the bare minimum you might expect of socialization and thus does not qualify as fully collaborative, just as merely paying your employees will not win you employer of the year honors.

Among humans, family marks the onset of civilization, the moment when the Brute stops fending only for himself or herself and thinks about fending for others, when the hunter becomes a gatherer. Even extremely competitive people live with and work with their own families. It is the most collaborative they allow themselves to be, because the family is seen as inside the same circle as the self. Everything outside the circle is still the enemy. But for supercompetitive people, that is the limit of their connectedness. They never allow others into their sense of community.

One step beyond family feeling is community feeling. Animals live together and feel joint cause with one another. Lions in a pride hunt and feed together. Ants build robotic civilizations. People join together to form organizations.

Family is where competitive and collaborative habits are learned. A healthy marriage is a collaboration, as is the assignment of chores and responsibilities to children. A family is a team in every sense, with a mission, goals, roles, policies, and rewards.

But it is also the seedbed for competitive practices. A father who divides his estate into two parts, as in the story of Cain and Abel, or who divides his attention and love into two parts, creates a condition of scarcity that will haunt the children all their lives. Being expected to live as well as the parents on half the resources is a prescription for intense rivalry.

Taken to the next level, familiarity is an entry-level requirement for healthy organizations. People may not hold hands and sing around a fire, but they recognize one another as belonging to the same group, and they do not eat each other. *Us* and *not-us* is still the defining difference between competition and collaboration: Competers keep the portal as small and tight as possible, while collaborators yearn to widen the aperture for others.

➤ **Association.** In this arrangement, one side benefits and the other neither gains nor is harmed. The barnacles that live on a whale's flanks qualify, until they are so numerous they slow the whale down. When a large business comes to town and every existing business perks up, that is the power of association. When Walt Disney World opened and a thousand other businesses sprang up at its front door, that was association in action. Disassociation also occurs. Ultimately, Disney decided it didn't want those barnacles feasting off its business, and bought them all out.[4]

➤ **Symbiosis.** Literally "living together," or mutualism, symbiosis is what symbionts do. You may recognize the word from Patti Hearst's involvement with the Symbionese Liberation Army, an obscure group of radicals that kidnapped, murdered, and stole in the early 1970s, all in the name of living together.

True symbiosis is a fully collaborative relationship in which close, permanent, and obligatory contact exists. The white egret you see standing on the backs of cattle throughout the southern United States is an example. The bird gets the advantage of insects that are attracted to cattle, and the cattle get the benefit of a professional exterminator service. The flashlight fish lures luminescent bacteria into its body, and then uses the fluorescent microcreatures to light its way through the deep ocean and signal others of its kind about sex and danger.[5]

The relationship between bees and flowers is exquisitely symbiotic: The bees feed on nectar while the flowers are cross-pollinated. It is a perfect win/win situation. We argue that symbiosis is at least as powerful as competition in building a successful organization.

An obvious example of symbiotic businesses is Intel and Microsoft. One makes microchips, the other makes operating systems and applications that run on those chips. Consumers have called this dynamic the "Andy and Bill Show," after Intel CEO Andy Grove and Microsoft's Bill Gates. Each company profits immeasurably when the other succeeds in raising the bar of consumer expectations. In an industry in which everyone sues everyone else, these two have never been anything but symbiotic, sharing and growing together—and devouring one another's enemies.

Many businesses have symbiotic relationships with other businesses without ever acknowledging those relationships. "We provide the legwork, they provide the brainpower." "We provide the muscle, they provide the money." Part of the transcompetitive art is identifying and honoring these vital relationships to keep them healthy and long-lived.

When people talk about teams, they are talking about a direct human analog to symbiosis. Teams are composed of people with different skill sets living side by side, profiting from one another's knowledge.

➤ **Communalism.** On the right end of the connectedness scale are animals that are truly collaborative. In communalism the group is everything and the individual is nothing. There is only one role here, because pure collaboration has a great sameness about it: the negation of the individual and the exaltation of the group.

Examples are bees in a hive, communism in its utopian form, monks in a monastery, and the police force of a major city. A rich and ironic example is the body of followers any original thinker leaves behind: Their derivative style provides stark contrast to their departed leader's genius.

Listen to biology-watcher Lewis Thomas rhapsodize about the power of termite connectedness:

> There is nothing at all wonderful about a single, solitary termite, indeed there really is no such creature, functionally speaking, as a lone termite, any more than we can imagine a genuinely solitary human being; no such thing. Two or three termites gathered together on a dish are not much better; they move about and touch each other nervously, but nothing happens. But keep adding more termites until they reach a critical mass, and then the miracle begins. As though they had suddenly received a piece of extraordinary news, they organize in platoons and begin stacking up pellets to precisely the right height, then turning the arches to connect the columns, constructing the cathedral and the chambers in which the colony will live out its life for the decades ahead... They are not the dense mass of individual insects they appear to be; they are an organism, a thoughtful, meditative brain on a million legs.[6]

And that's just the beginning of termite connectedness. You may think that termites eat wood, but in truth they are unable to digest cellulose. To do that they require the help of as many as 40 different kinds of bacteria, spirochetes, and protozoa living in their guts. "Without their helpers, termites could chomp wood ad nauseam, but they'd starve to death."[7]

But wait, we're not done yet. One of the symbionts of the termites, a protozoan called a polymastigote, itself has symbionts—thousands of spirochetes attached to it like hair on a dog. "Propelled by these spirochetes, the polymastigote swims about the gut, scooping up and digesting wood fragment."[8] Now, that's community spirit.

But lest we wax too rhapsodic about the communal life of termites, keep in mind that they are lusty cannibals of their own. You see, cannibalism occurs at *both* extremes of the connectedness scale.

Biologists and social scientists have isolated several factors that affect how connected a community feels and behaves. Each has its analog in the working world:

➤ **Group size.** Even when animals gather in great numbers, they usually belong most tightly to subgroups—bigger than the family, but smaller than the herd or flock. This size correlates to human teams—flexible enough to change greatly without ceasing to "belong." Organizations can use slogans like "Team GM" or "The Marines can use a few good men" if they like, but actual teams know this is nonsense. Big organizations are inevitably flotillas of many teams, groups, subgroups, and subteams, like organisms made of many cells. Identification with the whole is useful and important, but identification with what is small, local, and intimate is almost always stronger. The way to control and shape group behavior may begin with the vision of an individual at the top, but must be implemented at more local levels.

➤ **Demographic distribution.** "All young males" is a formula for a short life in any enterprise, whether you are a street gang or Menudo. One could argue that a group of identical units—clones, say—is no group at all. Diversity is essential to group success, diversity of knowledge, in particular. Diversity along racial, gender, age, and cultural lines is useful and valuable primarily in the way in which these differences contribute to knowledge diversity. Some forms of diversity are toxic, however: Diversity of core values, wherein members of a community have diametrically different views of the group's goal, is poison to any community or organization.

➤ **Cohesiveness.** Cohesiveness is the will to be together, what we have called "desperately seeking teaming."[9] It is one of the more mysterious group attributes that no consultant has found a way to package and no leader has found a way to mandate. It is a critical requirement the group must provide by itself. Cohesiveness is the result of balanced chemistry and shared values. Noncohering groups come apart because crises drive a wedge between conflicting values. Cohesive groups weather these crises because they have the will to stick together.

Does your group hold together of itself or does the environment of crisis it finds itself in want to pull it apart at the seams? Do not underestimate the importance of this attribute. People will not commit to being long-term shipmates if they believe the ship may sink at any second.

➤ **Permeability.** Can outsiders immigrate into the group, or is there police tape keeping them from drawing close? Many birds will reject their own eggs if they feel they have been contaminated by outside elements. Bull wildebeests drive off straggler males who threaten their hegemony. Management is notorious for creating elite environments that rank-and-filers never see. Full-time workers are notorious for keeping part-timers on the outside, looking in.

When Republic Airlines merged with Northwest in 1986, an unresolved issue was how to blend the two tiers of employees together. Northwest was unwilling to raise Republic workers' salaries to equal its own, and the merger still has problems more than a decade later. A transcompetitive organization is a hospitable one, finding ways to treat newcomers fairly and with dignity—and avoid the competitive quagmires of first- and second-class forms of citizenship.

➤ **Differentiation of roles.** A healthy herd is one in which animals know their roles for defense and nurturance. A herd in crisis forgets its roles; they stagger thirstily across the plain. An organization in its death throes does likewise, order dissolving into an every-member-for-itself retreat.

Different people in organizations do different things, and that is the source of their value to the group. People enamored with the flattened or dehierarchized organizations like the simplicity of their structure. But simplicity of structure (bosses and masses) is no guarantor of cohesiveness. It is very similar to the model in place at sweatshop factories, where everyone is doing the same low-value thing for an indifferent organization.

➤ **Integration of behavior.**[10] Does what all members do fit together into an effective unit? This factor complements the previous one.

➤ **Information flow.** Being social is less about emotion than about information. Information is what dogs get when they sniff each other and what makes a bee's antennae tingle. A connected organization is like sparkling water: Its energy forces information to rise through every level. A disconnected organization fosters gray-market information in the form of gossip. Gossip is the trunk line of the disconnected organization: who is saying what about who did what to whom. When people obtain information they need to survive entirely through gray channels, that is a sign the organization is not long for this world.

➤ **Time devoted to being social.** Lemurs, a lonely species, spend only 20 percent of their time attending to one another. By contrast, pigtailed macaques may spend 80 percent of their time mixing, grooming, playing, and checking one another out.

Companies whose people do not see one another as people, but as opponents to be beaten, will not be able to tap into their human potential. Disconnected organizations spawn workaholism, a grim breed of estranged loners, running out the clock and avoiding one another.

Connected organizations spawn picnics.

Endnotes

[1]Edward O. Wilson, *Sociobiology*, abridged edition, Belknap/Harvard, 1980.

[2]A convenient corollary: Therefore it must make our business, Amazon Deforestation Unlimited, go around, too—we wouldn't want to go against nature!

[3]George Orwell, *1984*, Secker & Warburg, 1949.

[4]Remarks by Adrian Slywotsky at The Masters Forum, Minneapolis, May 6, 1997.

[5]Anne Fausto-Sterling, "Is Nature Really Red in Tooth and Claw?" *Discover*, April 1993.

[6]Lewis Thomas, *Late Night Thoughts on Listening to Mahler's Ninth Symphony*, Viking Press, 1983.

[7]Anne Fausto-Sterling, "Is Nature Really Red in Tooth and Claw?" *Discover*, April 1993.

[8]Fausto-Sterling, ibid.

[9]Harvey Robbins and Michael Finley, *Why Teams Don't Work*, Peterson's, 1995.

[10]These first six characteristics are extrapolated from Wilson's work on the social life of animals.

Fugues and Variations

Other factors in competitive style

When we talk about competition in the workplace, it is useful to remember what competition means biologically: winning (securing survival) by depriving others of scarce resources. In nature these resources are food, status, territory, and reproductive abilities. In business they are still food, status, territory, and reproductive abilities, with the added factor of economic leverage—competing for wealth.

Of these four, food is the simplest to understand and the most easily explained. Subsistence farmers "compete" against the weather and insects. They compete against other farmers for prime real estate. They compete against the clock to bring in their crops at the most advantageous moment. And they compete against a finite economy—none of the things they need to survive are in infinite supply. Scarcity is thus the primary driver for competition. When there is plenty for all, no one needs to compete.

A Bad Penny

Scarcity is a word that keeps coming up, like a bad penny, in nature studies and in human competition. What's scarce in the natural world could be eucalyptus leaves or wallowing water or grazing space or meat on the hoof. In the human world, it can be money, time, attention, or opportunity. Consumers are always being reminded that nothing is limitless:

➤ call today, or lose out on this once-in-a-lifetime chance...

➤ while supplies last...

➤ the first 100 customers will receive absolutely free...

➤ last chance for gas next 110 miles...

Warnings of scarcity make us anxious, which is their intent. We know the feeling of going to the cupboard to get the dog a bone and finding none. From quite another sector, our new environmental awareness is contributing to this sense of limited resources.

Many things are truly scarce. There is not enough money in the world to make everyone a billionaire. There is not enough land to give everyone 100 acres. Companies cannot hire every applicant that comes in the door.

On the other hand, we all have a tendency to create mental scarcities where none really exist.

One of the transcompetitive habits is to know what you are competing for and to establish whether its scarcity is real or imaginary. Too often, what is scarce is not money or physical resources, but information and the goodwill to share it.

Competing for Bandwidth

Most wild creatures overcome scarcity problems by creating niches: customizing their habits so that they aren't competing against the whole wild world for food, territory, and reproductive ability. Ecological niches are not simply places; they are jobs, or more precisely, lifestyles that get you what you need.[1]

The story of the transcompetitive age is one of businesses avoiding the old head-to-head confrontations in which competition is bruising and profits are accordingly narrow. Instead, they are finding niches for themselves, places where they can be unique and charge the kinds of prices that unique providers customarily obtain.

It is surprising how many businesses, and people in business, ignore this fact known to every other creature. The inclination to be plain vanilla may arise from management theory, which holds that the skills of management are universally applicable to any industry. This may help explain why big companies line up to recruit Harvard and Stanford MBAs. It also explains why big companies have a harder time changing than their smaller counterparts: They define themselves as diversity-adverse, in the face of the clear dangers of being a me-too organization.

Our sense is that plain-vanilla companies feel safer that way, disguised as one among many, like wildebeests on the veldt. But hiding in plain sight provides a false sense of comfort and camouflage. It merely stakes out a position of mediocrity.

On the other hand, diversity is setting us free. Thanks to post-assembly-line manufacturing and advances in global information technology, a vast array of groups are establishing viable niches for themselves. The Usenet on the Internet boasts over 20,000 special-interest newsgroups. Many hundreds of thousands of businesses are creating websites for themselves. Many never win an audience and die in a fortnight. Others will attract markets and customers unthinkable to them a few short years ago, extending their organizational life by many years.

Many of us pass through this drumming of differentiation unaware of the activity. Alvin Toffler, author of *Future Shock*, has noticed:

> On the radio it is possible to turn the dial and find stations dedicated to certain types of music, from classical and contemporary to bluegrass, zydeco, salsa, tejana, tropical, bomba, and bangra. To a thousand different strains, the tastes of individuals are emerging as a market force to be dealt with.[2]

➤ Mega-brute Wal-Mart is so huge it can even put Fortune 500 companies like Black & Decker on the defensive. Wal-Mart's usual approach with suppliers is to try to force them as low as possible on the value chain, until they are supplying commodity products—in Black & Decker's case, electrical appliances—at commodity prices. But Black & Decker fought back with a bit of dazzling nichecraft, creating a website offering consumers help with home remodeling projects. Customers worldwide are flocking to Black & Decker (the French are said to describe anything nifty yet practical as "trés Black & Decker"). Turning the exchange-encircle-exact model to its advantage, the company is proving that unique service can overcome the plain-vanillifying effects of Wal-Mart.[3]

➤ What could be more plain-vanilla than office cleaning? Yet a Danish company, International Service Systems, has turned this once-lowly calling into a $3 billion business, simply by staking out a higher level of quality. Founded in 1901, the small company once known as the Danish Cleaning Company discovered it could create solid relationships with its corporate customers by cleaning up its own vision of the industry. Instead of hiring low-paid, uneducated immigrant workers, it trained intelligent, entrepreneurial people, rewarded and recognized their efforts, and promoted from within. ISS has a different feeling than any cleaning company in the world.[4]

Make your niche specific enough, companies like these are saying, and you may be able to forestall head-to-head competitive striving altogether.

Niche-making is not the only alternative to head-to-head competition. Other outcomes include:

➤ **Suing for peace.** If you don't fight back, it is possible they won't hurt you. You may achieve peaceful coexistence simply by acknowledging that the bigger player on the block is your lord and master. The 113-year-old Italian in Joseph Heller's novel, *Catch-22*, ascribes the survival of Italy through so many world and local wars to raising the white flag. "You conquer us," he said, "and we outlive you."[5] But are those the terms we envisioned for continuous winning—lowering our standard of winning?

➤ **Losing slowly.** This is the condition many businesses are in during the long period in which they restructure like mad, downsize, implement one change initiative after another, reengineer their processes, and do everything but grapple with the enemy. It may take decades, but whole cultures can be slowly erased this way: American Indian tribes, the Irish language, the Amazon rainforest, Western Union, the buggy whip industry. Picadilly Circus in London was created by the inventor of a fashionable collar pin. Today the grandeur of the architecture may live on, but the stickpins have ceased to be. Organizations hide this protracted beating behind a wall of words and exhortations and letters from the chairman. We call it attrition; there are better ways to go out.

➤ **Mergers & acquisitions.** You can be acquired and call that survival. If partnering (two organizations with different cultures deciding to work together as autonomous equals) is like marriage, with all the potential conflict marriage affords, hostile takeovers are comparable to ethnic cleansing—one organizational culture wiping out another by forcibly inseminating it.

While we are on the subject of mergers, we have a favorite question we ask of organizations experiencing change. It is a discussion-starter unlike any other, and can make people laugh or ball their fists. The question can apply to teams, partnerships, alliances—even to marriages and families. The question is:

Do you consider your relationship to be a merger or an acquisition?

➤ **Bistability.** When head-to-head competitors are evenly matched, victory goes to the home team. If you invade their turf, they win; if they attack your homes, you win. You may not think this insight has much applicability at first, until you picture Napoleon on his horse retreating across Russia.

Bistability is the reason the United States dropped the A-bomb to end World War II. It forces you to make an appraisal: Who is strong and who is weak? If you are weak but committed to competition, and you are Nissan, you ship four cars to the United States in 1961 and hope for the best. If you are strong but not up to the competition, and you are Detroit in the 1970s, you will try everything but head-to-head competition on Japanese soil.

Competing for Fun

We confuse so many concepts relating to competition.

Competitiveness is not the same as *bigness*. Though many of us are leery of sheer physical power, a person or organization is not "competitive" merely because it is big. In fact, bigness may connote power, but seldom long-term survival. Bigness implies certain competitive advantages—financial and political resources. But it just as surely implies inflexibility and slowness, which are clearly noncompetitive traits.

Competitiveness isn't the same as *badness*, any more than collaboration is the same as virtue. We get carried away with our noble expressions of group endeavor: "We came in peace for all mankind."

That's what the Apollo message left on the moon says. But the United States had many reasons for going into space.

There is a famous anecdote about three stonecutters. Asked what they were doing, the first replied, "Finishing up my shift." The second answered, "Carrying this hod of bricks to the fourth level." The third, with the right, virtuous, visionary, collaborative answer, said, "I'm building a cathedral to the glory of God." Nice story, but all three workers were right.

The truth is that you can be competitive and good or collaborative and bad. Hitler's SS were wonderfully collaborative in the sense of working well together, rounding up people who were outside their collaborative circle and killing them. Working together by itself has no moral weight. Competitive and collaborative traits are found equally in both saints and sinners.

Competitive is not the same as *intelligent*. We all think that people who win at whatever they do have a special spark, and that that spark is intelligence: survival of the intellectually fittest. But there is very little correlation between high intelligence and high achievement, versus average intelligence and high achievement. To the contrary, the world is full of great minds that never blossom, never fulfill their promise, as well as overachievers who perform stratospherically beyond expectations: Nineteenth-round draft picks who become star athletes and C students who go on to stellar careers. Call the spark that drives them to achieve intelligence, if you must, but it isn't the kind of intelligence that IQ tests attempt to measure.

Finally, and most important, competitiveness is not the same as *aggressiveness*. The tendency to equate competitiveness with aggressiveness is great, because supercompetitive people are usually aggressive as well. But there's a difference between wanting to win and wanting to maim.

Aggression is a tool of competition, but not an indispensable one. It is really just one of the two ways people and other creatures act when confronted with the fight-or-flight message their brains send out when there is trouble. In nature, it is exhibited mainly between males demonstrating how macho they are: the horn fighting of sheep, deer, and antelope; the spectacular displays and fighting among grouse and other birds; the heavyweight battles of elephant seals for the possession of harems.

In business, aggression is less violent but geared toward the same objectives: chasing rivals off and staking claim to the best turf, the highest roosting place, the juiciest territory.

Most aggressiveness is just noise—activity that accompanies another behavior. It is the other behavior—stealing a carcass, impressing a peer, doubling market share—that is really important. The aggressiveness is window dressing, to underscore a point. Consider the machismo of males during rutting season, and especially the sartorial splendor of certain male birds parading on their communal display grounds. It's for show.

But then you have actual aggression, which is something else: the urge to win/kill. Aggression occurs when you are no longer putting on a show. Now you mean it, and someone is going to get hurt. Knowing the difference in your organization is vital: It allows you to distinguish between people beating their own chests, which is merely annoying, and people beating other people's chests, which is alarming.

Aggression is a response to a threat, as identified by the amygdala. The less stimulus you need, or the more violently you react to it, the more aggressive you are. And the more aggressive you are by nature, the harder it will be to graft transcompetitive behaviors onto your everyday set.

Here is the nub of it all. People with higher aggression thresholds will be able to adapt to transcompetitive behavior sets without much difficulty. People with low thresholds, who become aggressive at the drop of a hat, must work at it the way alcoholics fight off temptation.

It is said that bullies are their own biggest victims, because bullying is one of the hardest behaviors to subdue. Why is it so difficult? Because of the fear it instills in others. Bullies who have not raised a hand to anyone in years must still climb a wall of distrust created the last time they swung in anger. The burden of those years usually prevents them from sharing in the collaborative goodies of civilization.

Competing for Status

Status in people is the same thing as dominance in animals. We all have ambivalent feelings about the word *status*. We dislike *dominance* even more.

Here are some of the ways various forms of dominance pop up in the workplace:

➤ the team member who has to have his or her way;

➤ the blabbermouth who constantly oppresses people with his or her ideas, and shuts off input from less assertive types;

➤ the brute who has to win every collegial altercation;

➤ the boss who is not happy unless he or she is treated at all times and in all ways like The Boss.

In nature and in human society, dominance results in behaviors that, while not always pleasant, serve a clear survival purpose:

➤ **Xenophobia.** The boss unites the herd against strangers. Canada geese attack any alien bird flying in their midst. So do some people from a single function, a single alma mater, a single skin color.

➤ **Elitism.** The old must not dominate the young, or vice versa. Males dominating females serves a purpose in the lion pride, but not in the workplace.

➤ **The will to power.** Dominance creates nested cliques of in-groups and out-groups. Gangs are examples of groups seeking dominance. The fact that they are usually made up of young bachelor males, eager to survive by showing nerve, is classic, on the veldt or in the beltway. Divisional cliques, central administration cliques, functional cliques: Dominance is the object of most turf wars.

But dominance is not always obnoxious. The "go-to" player whom we know we can trouble with an idea, even when he or she is busy, has achieved a level of functional dominance within the group. The quiet leader who we know will stick to issues and not personalize them is exercising a powerful kind of dominance. The boss who knows that decisions must be made and makes them even when they are politically difficult to make, because ignoring them will keep the group from achieving its goal, is exercising dominance.

Dominance is not a one-way street. Individuals who accept the dominance of others also receive their protection, which beats being driven out into the desert to die, hands down. People who butt heads with the dominant and lose are not killed; they are often encouraged to rest up, heal their wounds, and try again when the mood hits them. This is social liquidity: Challenges are welcome, up to a point. Sometimes the passage of time by itself will improve the status of a challenger: Dominants do die, eventually, or they get hired away by organizations turned on by their competitive fire.

Edward Wilson notes that, in nature, the more cohesive and durable the social group, the more complex and liberal the dominance order.[6] Dominant order in antelopes and sheep is all based on size and age; with Old World monkeys, it stems from the mother's rank, to membership in coalitions, and to dumb luck: Being in an established family beats being a still-damp immigrant. A young steer lucky enough to catch an old bull off guard has refreshed many a corporate hierarchy.

The best part of dominance is that people suck up to you. In the goose flock the lesser geese groom the leader. In the corporate flock the dominant are complimented, patted on the back, and accorded special privileges. True leaders will run like hell from this peel-me-a-grape treatment, as it is divisive and decadent. The merely dominant will luxuriate in it.

We don't like the brutal kind of dominance, but we easily make room for the interactive kind, because it serves an important role in nature of resolving disputes: Whoever dominates gets to decide who stays and who goes. Sophisticated dominance systems are valuable for establishing long-term security, succession, and peace.

Our objective, then, is not to make dominance illegal but to mold it into ways that extend group life and make the team transcompetitive.

Because it is premised on a single strong leader, dominance guarantees peace in the near term, and the near term is important. But when a single person dominates this way, the group must be rational enough to remember that the long term is also important. When the dominant leader starts chasing away people and ideas that may be crucial to long-term survival, it's time for the dominated to rise up and overthrow the brute.

Competing for Love

Gender and competition are like liquor and drugs: Dangerous by themselves, lethal in combination with one another.

As you examine your organization's competitive culture, do not overlook the fact that a lot of competitive behavior is males showing off for females and vice versa. Men ask to be on certain teams to be close to attractive women; women do likewise to be near attractive men. Executives set out to save their companies and get confused along the way when they discover that power is an aphrodisiac. Women executives become cold and hard because they know if they show their sexuality for even a second they become vulnerable and lose power.

Consider this analogy:

> men : goal-driven :: women : bitches

Isn't that about how we think?

Many books have been written just about the way males and females compete. How do you ignore the apparent male advantages? They are bigger and stronger, they are natural hunters, focused on a single outcome to the exclusion of all others, they know how to fight, and they seem to relish the opportunity. They are socially free to roam and improve their competitive skills, while females are strongly encouraged to stay home, away from the competitive realm, have babies, are natural multitaskers and thus less focused, and exist in a collaborative toyhouse realm designed just for females. Pushed to extremes, men become predators, competing to the point of death; women become martyrs, collaborating with no thought of themselves.

So opposite are males and females encouraged to behave that it is tempting to characterize the competitive end of the connectedness scale as male, and the collaborative end as female. Tribes send boys on walkabouts to learn the skills of contending with the world; Victorian society sent girls to finishing school to polish their "female" skills of nurturance, hospitality, and accommodation.

One of the sickest aspects of male competitiveness is that it undermines the ability of men to be friends to one another. Not "sitting around on Sundays watching football and chasing down some brews" friends, but friends who can open up with one another and admit to weakness.

Rabbi Harold Kushner, author of *When Bad Things Happen to Good People*, says that our society trains men to be skilled at competition and inept at relationships, and trains women to be the opposite, collaborators skilled at knitting relationships together. In such a pairing, women are the ultimate winners, because as theologian and philosopher Martin Buber said in *I-Thou*, relationships are where God is to be found. Buber never mentioned football.[7]

Despite stereotyping, women are as likely to have competitive personalities as men and vice versa. It is only in the supercompetitive and supercollaborative dimensions that gender starts to make a difference. Men who vary from the party line may suffer as much from the war of gender expectations as women. We may not call men bitches but we have names just as bad: wimp, whiner, doormat.

Remember the Barbie Doll math controversy of a few years ago? Mattel was selling Barbie Dolls that "talked," one of whose messages was: "Oh, math is so hard!"

The spit hit the fan when feminists got wind of the message. Bad enough to be insipid, but to embed an already hopelessly sexist toy with the suggestion that girls should take a back seat to boys in the study of arithmetic—it was really too much. A protest ensued, Mattel yanked the product and reconfigured it, and the human race limped on, a scintilla safer from the killer instinct of its own males.

Are males better at math than girls? Let's think about that. It might be true. It is one of the most male-dominated disciplines in academia. On the other hand, it is also one of the most underpaid. People good at math generally do not rise to positions of leadership. They wind up as accountants, actuaries, financial officers, and researchers.

Math is not the problem. Competitiveness is. Are males more competitive than females? No, but they are often more supercompetitive, more aggressive. Boys get called on more in school because they insist on being called on. This male insistence puts girls at a disadvantage, especially in male-dominated spheres.

Recent research seems to indicate that if girls and boys in school are separated at their most vulnerable social age (10–13), girls accelerate at the same pace as boys. They learn from one another and collaborate among themselves to achieve the same interest and competency as boys in all subjects, including math.

Curiously enough, the boys benefit too. Since they are not competing for the attention of the opposite sex, they are free to concentrate on their schoolwork.

In the workplace, this me-first demand of males may look enthusiastic and vital at first, but it exerts a long-term tension that forces many females to despair of getting a word in edgewise, much less a promotion or equal consideration.

> The general rule is that American males are simply trained to win. The object, a boy soon gathers, is not to be liked but to be envied, not to reflect but to act, not to be part of a group but to distinguish himself from the others in that group. Being number one is an imperative for boys, so a good deal is invested in whether one makes it.[8]

Take a second and rephrase that paragraph, saying the exact opposite about females. These are the female's supposed objectives: being liked, reflectiveness, blending in with the group, caring for others, not beating them. Our entire system expects females to be good collaborative people and males to be competitive SOBs. It doesn't matter if males and females are naturally this way; many are not, and no one has the right to force these identities on everyone. The only police officer is nature, and nature is enjoying a doughnut.

Eliminating bias against women in your organization is beyond the scope of this book. All we will do is point to the benefits of eliminating this kind of competition and replacing it with true competitive free-for-all, in which people collide, but gender is neither a handicap nor an advantage. Call this utopian state, oh, free enterprise.

And here's a refreshing note. Recall the infamous case of the Vietnamese shoe company that made shoes for Nike, and whose floor manager forced the women who refused to wear the right shoes to run until they collapsed. It was not a story of mean male bosses tyrannizing poor female employees. The manager in question was a woman.[9]

Until conditions are fair to both genders everywhere, that factoid constitutes progress.

Competing for Space

Competition is related to population. When crowded, cats go cuckoo. Play grinds to a halt. Hierarchy breaks down, and eventually a despot emerges. The despot cat is every group's worst nightmare, a leader with a license to torment everyone in the group. The crowded cats grow increasingly neurotic, obsessing about maintaining what is theirs at all costs. Pariahs are designated, and the community turns into a spiteful mob, attacking the pariahs, apparently in the hope that the sacrifice will improve their condition. In the end the cats achieve a kind of sick stasis, constantly hissing, growling, and even fighting.

Crowded rats don't do well, either. In one famous experiment, crowded Norway rats became hypersexual, trying to have sex with everything and everyone they came in contact with. Some animals became exclusively homosexual. Some managed to keep up appearances, building nests as if everything was still okay—but the nests were distorted and nonfunctional. Infant mortality ran as high as 96 percent.[10] Some rats reached the end of the connectedness scale and indulged in cannibalism.

Edward Wilson again:

> The lesson for man is that personal happiness has very little to do with this. It is possible to be unhappy and very adaptive. If we wish to reduce our own aggressive behavior, and lower our catecholamine and corticosteroid titers to levels that make us all happier, we should design our population density and social systems in such a way as to make aggression inappropriate in most conceivable circumstances and, hence, less adaptive.[11]

When Harvey was a bright-eyed lad in graduate school, he conducted his own crowding experiment with gerbils. He created a virtual apartment building of the animals, and then played with the population level. He provided the same proportionate amount of food and water as the population increased, so behavior changes wouldn't be about scarcity, just closeness. His expectation was that the animals would become more aggressive as their numbers increased.

That was true, up to a point. As comfort space between the animals diminished, they became visibly more snappish with one another. At a certain point, the connectedness scale disintegrated, and it became every animal fighting for itself. Males, females, young, old—all were competing for the sanity of elbow room. Harvey had created a supercompetitive world.

But when he kept adding gerbils, he observed the snapback. When they were all literally sitting in one another's laps, they reverted to docile, nonaggressive behavior. Males stopped their characteristic fighting. Motion subsided. Conditions had become so intolerable, they reverted to supercollaboration, grooming one another incessantly. Compare that scenario with our description in "The Big Vague" (page 31) of a world driven beyond supercompetition.

We have all worked in different environments, and we are aware of our own responses. An empty room in which one can hear a pin drop is a hard place for brutes and tricksters and pawns—for most people—to work. But fill the room up, with different kinds of people, and the dynamics change radically.

Unlike the termite colony in which every individual contributed to a seamless whole, people jostle and bump into one another, both physically and emotionally. A team of five or six or seven people who have had time to get to know one another and have worked out most of the issues that set one against another have a chance to reach a very high level of functionality. The presence of one another nearby is compelling and exciting.

But flood the office with strangers—people making tours, solicitors passing from desk to desk, too many documents dropped in too few in-boxes, too many lights blinking on the phone banks, too many meetings with too many people—and the sweet spot of transcompetitive give-and-take implodes. People burrow into their cubicles and hope the noise dies down and the extra people go away. The original team, surrounded by the extraneous players, look at one another with sorrow and longing. Functionality has fled. The team is like a frightened family, huddling in a shelter waiting for a storm to blow over.

Competing for Time

Though we all follow our preferred competitive styles (brute, trickster, etc.), our styles are not set in concrete. In life, there is a typical curve, a competitive life cycle, that we all follow.

We are born struggling to survive, wailing, bleating, and thrashing for the nipple. As we grow, we discover the pleasure of performance. Performance is the sweetest form of competition, because we are not competing against others, just ourselves and our previous performance. It is what drives a toddler to take the second step after the first step—competing against one's best previous work.

Competition at its most poignant is when we do our best to show what is in us. We see it in a proud child's schoolwork, in the earnest efforts of a worker outpacing others in hopes of being discovered. Competition is like an exultant shout to the world: *See me, know me!* It is 100 percent functional, and often it is the glory of our species.

Much dysfunctional competition occurs when the desire to be known and valued is in some way frustrated: The death of or abandonment by a parent are common experiences of supercompeters. Unable to achieve the normal level of validation, they push themselves to extraordinary lengths to achieve approval mere spectators are unable to bestow.

In the healthy individual, competitiveness decreases with age. As we grow, our interests tend to expand beyond our own survival and success to the happiness and sustainability of those we care about.

Employment in the second decade provides a first taste of collaboration. Marriage, an intensely collaborative contract, happens most often in the third decade of human life.

The fourth decade of our lives, our 30s, finds us intensely collaborative as we raise our families, work with teams, join church and other groups, mingle with our neighbors, become bosses, and assume responsibility for other people, other lives.

By the midpoint of our lives, our prime, we are teachers, and our purpose is to share what we have learned. In all it is a transcompetitive arc, from the struggle to survive at one end to survival beyond struggle at the other.

Endnotes

[1]Karl Sigmund, *Games of Life*, Penguin Books, 1995.

[2]From remarks by Alvin Toffler, Tomorrowday, The Masters Forum, Minneapolis, September, 1995.

[3]From remarks by Don Tapscott, The Masters Forum, 1997.

[4]Remarks by Christopher Bartlett, The Masters Forum, Minneapolis, January, 1996.

[5]Joseph Heller, *Catch-22*, Simon and Schuster, 1961.

[6]Wilson, *Sociobiology*.

[7]Remarks by Rabbi Harold Kushner at The Masters Forum, Minneapolis, December 10, 1996.

[8]Alfie Kohn, *No Contest,* Houghton Mifflin, 1992.

[9]Associated Press, June 28, 1997.

[10]Wilson, *Sociobiology*.

[11]Ibid.

Competition and Culture

How it varies from people to people

Both of the authors are Americans, and Midwesterners at that—the most provincial of our kind. So we have to work to avoid the American chauvinism that applies to competition.

To us, competition *looks* American. No country has erected as many shrines to competition as the U.S. Competition, free enterprise, and equal opportunity are the cornerstones of our constitution and laws. Professional sports, railroad barons, and corporate raiders follow as direct corollaries.

"May the best person win" is a sacred mantra to Americans. It transmutes our highest civic value, personal liberty, into the opportunity to do the best thing people can do, in our minds—win.

Americans talk about rooting for the underdog and we pay homage at the base of the Statue of Liberty to the value of the lowly masses we have taken in. But our strong preference is for underdogs who triumph in the end, like Rocky and the Karate Kid. If the huddled masses don't get their act together within a generation or two, Americans say to hell with them.

Deep down, Americans treasure the lessons of competition: that there is an inherent pecking order in all things, and that spirited contests between individuals and groups are nature's way of settling differences.

Other Styles of Competing

But while American culture has a strong flavor of competition, it has no lock on competition. Other peoples have gone other ways with it, and each has developed its own flavor. Japan may not have heard of Vince Lombardi[1], but Japanese sports and business contests are every bit as brutal as a rout of a Green Bay Packers' game.

Things get interesting when competition overflows national borders and the flavors are forced to mix. IBM, Fujitsu, and Siemens are locked in a global contest to sell information systems and services. But each defines the contest in ways peculiar to the culture around it. Likewise, the world is a village market for the bankers of Berlin, Tokyo, and New York to lend money to. But loan talks with representatives of Sumitomo or Daiwa will be very different from talks with Citicorp, Chemical Bank, or the Deutsche Bank.

A good example of cultural competitive differences appears in Thomas Berger's novel, *Little Big Man*, about the 120-year-old Jack Crabbe who lived two lives in the Wild West, one as a white man and one as an adopted Pawnee brave. The settler culture was supercompetitive. "First come, first served" was the essence of homesteading. "Shoot to kill" was their method of resolving disputes. The Pawnees, being tribal, were supercollaborative by nature, and they resolved many disputes ritually. A mock battle using coup-sticks, in which the enemy is embarrassed rather than hurt, was one of those rituals.

Both methods worked well enough within cultural bounds, but were toxic when cultures mixed. A Pawnee seeing a man with a rifle thought it was a gesture of ritual intimidation, while a white settler seeing a brave brandishing a coup-stick saw it as a clear physical danger. By the time one culture understood what the other meant, the other was nearly extinct.

Let's look at competitive business cultures today that are clashing because of globalization.

On the one hand, we have the competitive culture that we are all familiar with, America's. Americans believe in liberty for individuals above all else. So we are a nation of scrambling individualists, inventing, wild, often violent, and often a bit confused—but extraordinarily vital, because self-interest compels us to differentiate like mad. We affiliate, but ever so loosely. We long ago invented drive-through church services, and have moved on to even looser vehicles of connectedness—cell phones, e-mail, and car-fax.

But compare the way Americans connect in business versus the collaborative style of doing business in Japan. When the Japanese industrial breakthrough occurred in the 1970s, books were written about Japan being a "samurai nation." Americans, who had done battle with the Japanese fairly recently and were aware of how ferocious they could be, took *samurai* to mean warrior, as in all the samurai swords brought home by GIs. Conclusion: The Japanese were warriors who were going to hack us to bits, Toshiro Mifune-style.

What we neglected to do was look up the word *samurai* in the dictionary. Its meaning is simply to serve. In Japan's collaborative culture, there is no aspiration as lofty or as ennobling as the humble process of serving others. This collaborative notion is what underlies the terrific success Japan has with its work teams, and its networks of interlocking industries (called *keiretsus*):

> The word keiretsu does not translate neatly into English, and that is the beginning of the problem. The most common Japanese meaning is something close to the English verbs "link," "affiliate with," or "connect to."[2]

A keiretsu can be anything from a network of thousands of companies all working for a single large firm to something even more stupendous, a consortium of dozens of enormous firms joined together—plus all the thousands of companies that link to them. That's what is meant by the phrase, "Japan, Inc."

It's all hard for Americans to conceive of. We like our big things to be discrete and object-like: Babe Ruth, dinosaurs, redwood trees, $7 trillion debt loads. (We are disappointed to discover our largest living thing is a collaborative effort: a huge fungus growing on the forest floor in Northern Michigan. Altogether it is 37 acres across, weighs 10,000 tons, and is estimated to be 1,500 years old. But, like a keiretsu, it is unphotographable—no frame can contain it.)

In short, it is very hard for Americans and Japanese to understand the competition they find themselves in, because our values are so different.

Differences in competitive styles may have nothing to do with the United States, of course; countries can get plenty confused without our help. Asian managers, for instance, have had a dickens of a time meshing with Mexican workers:

> What happens when Asia's workaholics, accustomed to employment for life, meet a Mexican labor pool where 20 percent turnover per month is not unusual? Alan Wong, the Hong Kong

Trade Development Council's director of the Americas, baldly replies: "It makes it difficult."

Asian firms cope with this culture gap in several ways. Some executives have applied a global manufacturing mindset anchored in the home country, such as Samsung Chemicals, which produces television sets in 20 countries.

Sanyo's Carlos de Orduña makes the necessary allowances. He gives a 6- to 12-month adjustment period for entry-level people. After that, workers who cannot meet Japanese quality standards either weed themselves out or are dismissed. "We hire workers who are willing to learn," he says. "We want workers who are proud to say that a television made in Mexico is good enough to be exported to Japan."[3]

What we learn as we traverse the globe is that different people have stumbled upon different ways of doing things. While Europe is doggedly competitive, Africa is just as determined to be supercollaborative in its approach, possibly even as a response to European imperialism. The Shona tribe of Zimbabwe and Mozambique, for instance, are a Bantu-speaking people numbering nearly 9 million. As the Belgian and English and French and Dutch invaded Africa in the nineteenth century, groups like the Shona had to hunker down with their own values to prevent assimilation and destruction.

Out of this defensive attitude arose a social philosophy called *Ubuntu*, which permeates the village cultures of southern Africa and, according to South African consultant and author Lovemore Mbigi, extends to protect African people everywhere in the world, from Brixton to Harlem:

> The cardinal belief of Ubuntu is that a man can only be a man through others. [It emphasizes] the need to harness the solidarity tendency of the African people in developing management practices and approaches. They have to stick together on selective survival issues and unquestioning conformity is expected from everyone on these issues.[4]

So while Peace Corps volunteers and other well-intentioned Westerners have been coaxing third-worlders to step away from their village cultures, the Ubuntu movement has been urging them to deepen their village identities. Ubuntu is a passionate, charismatic philosophy of survival that is more ambitious than the West can know. Its dream is to become a missionary of collaborative tribal virtues to a world it deems pagan in its individualistic impulses.

As we spin the globe and put our fingers down randomly in other cultures, we see that local definitions of how people connect with one another dictate how they compete as well.

Caution: The random skip around the world that follows is not a statement of conditions ruling the behavior for all persons from these cultures. All cultures are diverse and contain countless internal contradictions and crosscurrents.

In the United States, for instance, the notion exists that reservation Indians are unsuited to manufacturing work. This derives from the politically correct notion ("Everyone knows") that Indians are inescapably collaborative in nature and have no knack for competitive industry. "Factories are not the answer," insists Nancy Jemmison, a Bureau of Indian Affairs planner.[5]

But the Mississippi band of Choctaw Indians, perhaps not knowing better, are successfully making money and reducing reservation unemployment to zero by making car speakers, greeting cards, electronic harnesses, and plastic injection items.[6]

Nevertheless, there is still some truth to these generalizations about competitive cultures, provided to us by people who have lived in these cultures and observed them firsthand:

➤ **Belgium.** Home of the European Union, bureaucratic Belgium may be the world's greatest believer in systems as community. As in Magritte's faceless paintings, Belgians eschew flashy individualism in favor of a centered, orderly system in which all people get their due. As nations go, Belgium gets less respect than most, as in this caustic description:

> Belgian politics enjoy none of the rowdy intellectual contention of the United Kingdom, none of the nuance-loving literary polemics of France, not even a strong national identity. The primary issue in public debate is who gets what benefits, and while commerce and money are gods, neither is served particularly well. The national infrastructure is fraying, with little renewal: Belgians have a high per-capita income and spend it generously on cars and dining, but what Rousseau called the esprit social seems lacking. Crumbling, generic, enervated, debt-ridden, materialistic—is this Europe's future?[7]

➤ **Brazil.** Spain and Portugal did not want to compete against one another for the New World they each laid claim to. As Christian nations, they simply divided the hemisphere into two halves along a longitudinal line 370 leagues west of the Cape Verde Islands. The Portuguese navigator Pedro A. Cabral landed in Brazil in 1500. In a strange gesture of civilization, the Portuguese did not feel they could enslave the unorganized Indian tribes of the region—they saw their task as converting them, instead—so they brought slaves from Africa. Brazil was the last country in the Americas to forswear slavery, a legacy that haunts them to this day. Instability, illegitimacy, and plunder of the country's natural resources undermined the country for decades. On the bright side, the country has preserved a rich diversity (170 languages) and a willingness to form joint ventures with countries such as the U.S., Chile, Germany, and Japan. The country has a transcompetitive insight that may help halt the destruction of the Amazonian forests. Observers of the rainforest agriculture projects over the past 30 years saw that the primary cause of the forest's destruction was not greed but failure. It has been the unsuccessful farmers who keep moving deeper into the forest as their ranches go bust who have caused so much damage. Successful farmers also increase deforestation, but only where they already are. The exchange-encircle-exact formula may be put to work in saving the rainforest, if word can be spread in time that the "sure thing" of forest colonization is not sure at all.[7]

➤ **France.** France and the U.S. have an antipodal relationship with one another; they each work hard to be the opposite of the other. While Americans are adolescent and impulsive, the French are reflective and careful. While Americans throw themselves into the fight and start swinging, confident of eventual victory, the French remove themselves to a zone of mind and temperament that defines victory on its own terms. The phrase *savoir vivre* sums up the French attitude toward competing: Those who live best are the only real victors. Early retirement to the country, which is suspect in the U.S., is an accepted goal in France. Their contempt for a civilization that calls gulping a sandwich from a bag while driving a car "dining" is total.

Unlike the U.S., France seems able to endure high unemployment and endless strikes provided a clear and worthwhile long-term goal is in sight. France is averse to much of American-style competition. In its own view, it does not like an unfair fight, which is how it regards the onslaught of American music and films in French markets. But while it disdains the American orientation to efficiency and mass production in matters of food and entertainment, it has adopted that approach in the education of its people. French public school education, which stipulates that every class teach the same curriculum and that students be categorized early and permanently for eventual specialization, is an instance of one country doing with its children what the country it despises does with its french fries.

➤ **Germany.** Germany, not Japan, is the true home of cross-functional collaboration. Supervisors in German factories in the 1920s mastered the jobs of those working under them, so that they could fill in at a moment's notice. In many ways the German workplace is regulated by a sense of flexibility and trust. Blue-collar workers can vault to the white-collar ranks by taking company-paid instructions in engineering, something that could never happen in neighboring France or Italy. Francis Fukuyama calls this element of trust *social capital*, and it is part of the orderly genius of the German people:

> Social capital is a capability that arises from the prevalence of trust in a society or in certain parts of it.... The most effective organizations are based on communities of shared ethical values. These communities do not require extensive contract and legal regulation of their relations because prior moral consensus gives members of the group a basis for mutual trust. The social capital required to create this kind of moral community cannot be acquired ... through a rational investment decision. It requires [instead] habituation to the moral norms of a community and, in its context, the acquisition of virtues like loyalty, honesty, and dependability. The group, moreover, has to adopt common norms as a whole before trust can become generalized among its members.... Social capital cannot be acquired simply by individuals acting on their own.[8]

But Germany is a nation of many tribes. Historically, it has always felt tensions between its western half and its eastern half. Its democratic and industrial traditions have always looked west, but its darker political moments have looked to the east. It is interesting that the largest institution in the nation over the past century has been Germany's own version of keiretsu, the Deutsche Bank, unique among central banks in the degree to which it has interwoven itself into the operational existence of the country's industrial base. But the enormous ($500 billion in assets) institution has proved itself extraordinarily deft in its 125 years of existence. It could be unpopular with the left (Bertolt Brecht: "What's breaking into a bank compared with founding a bank?"[9]) and with the right (Hitler used the finance policies of the Deutsche Bank to vilify the Jews as responsible for the Depression).[10] Throughout, it has remained a symbol of German unity in work and international competition.

➤ **India.** Americans regard India as noncompetitive, citing the restrictions of the caste system and the historic disinclination of Indians to take the advice of the U.S. on matters such as agriculture and birth control. But this view overlooks India's ability to adapt to changing, often challenging circumstances. When India achieved nationhood in 1947, it moved to reestablish Indian tradition uprooted during its colonial period. This meant a hostility to foreign business (at one point they threw out almost every multinational corporation) and a reliance on the ancient discipline of central management. Government figures decided who would be in business and set quotas for production for these companies. In such an environment, large-scale entrepreneurialism withered, and parties pursued deliberately obtuse industrial policies like "computer chips, not potato chips"—never mind that people liked potato chips. Only in recent years has it dawned on people that the government is not good at running very much, and a more modern (though still not Western) spirit of competitiveness is growing in the country. Large companies are again investing in India, and people are once again unhappy with their foreignness. Throughout all these upheavals, however, one thing has remained constant: the strong Indian preference for family-run businesses that take care of their own. When Indians compete successfully, it is usually within this familial configuration.

➤ **Indonesia.** It is interesting, in light of the anticompetitive prejudices of modern-day Holland, to see how competition has fared in a former Dutch colony. The Dutch record in the East Indies is one of astonishing incompetence. The Dutch East India Company held onto posts that operated at a loss for as long as 30 years in a row. They only really turned a profit during a few seriously exploitative eras like the 1860s. It was a 200-year con game that didn't fold up until Napoleon moved in, in 1800.[11] Since becoming independent in 1945, Indonesia has mostly carried on the tradition of bungling, squandering its many powerful competitive advantages: an educated populace, a great work ethic, and an unparalleled location for global trade. The country's strong central government has helped a business establishment grow, but it has severely hamstrung entrepreneurialism and innovation with a raft of protectionist and bureaucratic regulations.[12] So long as businesses are enjoined from competing with one another, they will be unable to compete at all, and Indonesia, for all its resources, will lag behind Singapore, Malaysia, and Thailand.

➤ **Japan.** Japan is a paradox. On the one hand it has a fiercely competitive culture, whose people work with intense commitment to achieve huge goals together. On the other it has the most collaborative of all the industrial cultures, with a sense of *us versus them* that makes Japanese businesses cohesive internally and spurs them to great achievements globally. They have a great gift for trust. They believe that if you are like them, Japanese, you are almost automatically a person they can work with. Since they are able to do business with large numbers of people, they create large companies of strangers, then proceed to make a huge family of the strangers. The trust network then spills over to other companies and industries and banks, to enormous keiretsu. Because they do not high-five or spike the ball when they win, the Japanese do not get the credit they deserve for their competitive craft from Americans, and this rankles. Many Americans have bargained with Japanese counterparts and left a meeting thinking they got the better of them, to learn otherwise upon careful review of the terms. A favorite trick of the Japanese is silence. They are culturally accepting of periods of quiet. By contrast, silence drives Americans crazy. Many times an American, in a negotiating session with the Japanese business people, has blurted out a concession just to get the comforting flow of words going again. Another Japanese ploy is "by-the-bye negotiation": just as negotiations are concluding and you are glancing at your watch and thinking of your airline departure time, they propose add-on, "by-the-bye" riders to the agreement. In your anxiety, you agree to everything. Only when you are in the air again do you realize you were played like a Stradivarius or a koto.

➤ **Korea.** Everyone seems to agree that Koreans are different from the other peoples of East Asia: more individualistic and more inclined to American-style competition. The English have called Koreans the Irish of Asia, suggesting an extroverted and boisterous nature, but one must consider Great Britain's understanding of the Irish.[13] Koreans see themselves as eclectic survivors, which is close to what we call transcompetitive—imitating the West when that works, and holding fast to traditional norms of family and country at other times. Relationships and patriotism are critical to Koreans. Family and hierarchy are not called into question lightly. Koreans are eager to maintain their appropriate rank in the community, based on their age and social position. Their eclecticism extends to admiring Japanese ways of doing business. The Korean corporate *chaebols* of Samsung and Hyundai imitate the Japanese keiretsu, though Korea retains a deep abhorrence of Japanese culture. Even at their most corporate, Koreans retain powerful traits of agrarian life, stemming from a village culture in which people depended on each other in good times and bad. They don't form lines to board buses because they know how to move together without the device of standing in single file. So it is with business. Linked by work and intermarriage, Koreans look out for one another as no other people in the world do.

➤ **Mexico.** Mexico has always enjoyed competition, as evidenced by its passion for football at every level, including the company team. But competitiveness in Mexican business is a fairly new skill, and it is developing as you read this in a random and sometimes self-destructive manner. Under autocratic rule from the Aztecs to Cortez, to single-party rule under the PRI, the country has practiced severe protectionism, which tended to make Mexican companies lazy and indifferent to quality and to customers. NAFTA changed all that. When Wal-Mart came riding into town they took Mexican stores by surprise, not so much because of Wal-Mart's size and resources but because of their concepts of the customer, continuous improvement, quality, and empowering employees. Immediately after NAFTA, Mexico slumped badly—some say because of crooked politics, others because so many little factories went down the drain, leaving tons of unemployed and thus a grand reduction in purchasing power. But Mexico is bouncing back and with its still unfulfilled potential as an energy-producing nation promises to be a world-class competitor in the near future. The election in July 1997 of a non-PRI mayor of Mexico City suggests a break with the brute political realities of the past and a determination to be a new Mexico in the new millennium.

➤ **The Netherlands.** Of all the cultures of western Europe, Holland may be the one least attracted to American-style competition. One Dutch correspondent told us point-blank that "unadulterated competition goes well beyond good into evil." An American who lived several years in the Netherlands described the difference between the two cultures. In America when a boy comes home from school with a mediocre grade on a paper, his mother asks, "Why did you score so low?" And the boy responds, "Well, it was one of the highest grades in the class." The mother says, "Oh, then it's a good grade." In the Netherlands, the mother answers, "I don't care, I know you can do better than this. Next time, you start researching your work earlier." In the American case, being better than your peers is the important thing; in the Dutch case, it's doing things as well as you are able. Despite this anticompetitive flavor, it should be noted that Royal Dutch Petroleum is still ranked by *Forbes* as the single most powerful corporation on earth.

➤ **Nigeria.** Africans generally have a powerful sense of community. In most African societies it is unacceptable to enrich oneself at the expense of others. In order of importance are the family, one's elders, the community at large, and then and only then one's personal success. In the eyes of most Africans, the American competitive system is profoundly flawed. Nigerians are proud people who see themselves as the marvels of Africa, entrepreneurial and adaptive. But they also see themselves as handicapped by anti-third-world stereotypes of corruption. Fraud and corruption are frowned on in Nigeria. The sense of community is so strong it will not stand for unfair competition. When billionaire Chief Mashood

Abiola appeared to win election to the presidency in 1993, Nigerians saw through the machinations and threw him in jail. Of course, to the outside world, it looked like a coup d'etat by a group of unelected thugs. Amnesty International has condemned the new government's repressive tactics. But from appearances, the coup is more popular in Nigeria today than the election ever was. In any event, how many billionaires are in jail in the U.S.?

➤ **Russia.** There is no nation as troubled about its own competitive culture as Russia; and when a nation straddles 11 time zones, its troubles are important. For 70 years the people of the Soviet Union had drummed into them the collaborative imperative that group success outweighed individual success. Even when they knew that utopian "truth" to be illusory, they had no ethic to replace it with. Since the fall of the U.S.S.R., Russians are being told the opposite ethic is the true one, that societies are built by individual success and that their fate hinges on the deployment of a market economy. Meanwhile, the West, especially America, is impatient for Russians to develop their own version of the American dream. But what Russians dream of is understanding what is happening to them:

> An analysis of the emergence of the market economy in Russia is that it is not a "goal" to the Russian people as we perceive goals. The change to a market economy cannot be a goal for 150 million people. [It] ... rather, is a strategy that is supposed to lead or bring the Russian people to a conclusion, whereby it will be possible to realize the dream. The Russian people want to know where they are going—they are less concerned about the method of getting to their destination.[14]

The identity crisis engulfing Russia is analogous to the radioactive release at Chernobyl, invisible but deadly nonetheless. In part because of this crisis, Russia is passing through a period of unparalleled grief in a long and grief-filled history. The uncertainty is sapping people's ability to live. Mortality due to illness is five times the world average. Violent crime is 100 times higher than during the days of the Soviet Union. In this slippery climate, businesses and other organizations are struggling to get a grip. It is a country of many problems, few of which can be solved until the people achieve a consensus on who and what they are.

➤ **Scandinavia.** Norway and Sweden have a long and mostly genteel history of collaboration. Their politics, even when retreating
from socialism, retain a pronounced flavor of connectedness.
Leading the way worldwide in teaming, AM Volvo of Sweden is
the world's sole worker-owned automobile corporation. But no
one expects Volvo ever to become a world-beater, giving Toyota
or Ford a run for their money. In the company of car makers,
however, Volvo's attention to safety and utility make it a mini-
monopoly. Josh Hammond, author of *The Stuff Americans Are
Made Of*, argues that Norwegians are less collaborative than
Swedes because the more rugged topography keeps people from
coming together. But there is also a tradition called "the Jante
Law" that proclaims that one should not believe one is better
than anyone else. Showing off or flaunting one's success, staples
of American behavior, are considered poor taste in Scandinavia.
Horatio Alger's plucky heroes who rise from poverty to head successful companies, so admirable to Americans, would strike many
Norwegians as morally repulsive. In Sweden, kids aren't graded in
school until the eighth or ninth grades. The reason: Comparing
kids is seen as overly competitive and destructive to the children's
prospects.

➤ **South Africa.** South Africa these days combines a potent mix of
competitive and collaborative impulses. The first settlers of
Dutch, French, and British descent competed with each other and
their emphasis was on group winning. Group competition
reached its apex with British imperialism, and it was brutal group
competition. The Anglo-Boer War, with its "scourged earth" policy, was by many measures the most destructive war the world has
ever seen, leaving the country in total ruin. It was the occasion of
the first use ever of concentration camps. This was followed by
the rise of Afrikaner nationalism, resulting in apartheid, which
excluded the black population from political and economic life
until 1992, when Nelson Mandela was freed. In 1996 the Truth
and Reconciliation Board was set up to conduct hearings on
apartheid atrocities. Hearings revealed many horror stories of the
habits of South Africa's "winners."

The new constitution of South Africa is sensitive to the impact of
group competition; therefore individual rights and community

needs, empowerment and sustainability are entrenched. White and black "peace vigilantes" have joined together to prevent the sickness from taking root again. They have outed a ruthless soccer coach, Andre Markgraaff, by taping and replaying racist remarks he made, and are planning to dethrone an even more ruthless sports figure, Louis Luyt. Likewise, the public is overruling the government by cracking down on street crime. A brave vigilante is more likely to catch the headlines than the gold magnate whose quarterly results put the glitter back in gold. In the new South Africa, say our friends there, the real winners are the people who protect the community rather than filling their own pockets.[15]

➤ **Switzerland.** Neutrality in time of war may *seem* transcompetitive. It's rational, it's opportunistic, and it's safe. Sweden's Volvo, for instance, thrived during World War II, making tractor engines instead of taking sides. Coca-Cola, too global to be political, served up sparkling beverages to the Nazis even during the darkest days of the war. But seemingly neutral deeds can come back to haunt one. Switzerland has long been noted for its orderliness, confidentiality, and stiff community-mindedness, including universal military service and gun ownership. But the collaborative spirit seems to come to an abrupt halt at the borders. The country did well during the war,[16] lending money to both sides and accepting funds transfers from Nazis and then denying for 50 years that the money ($41 million) belonged to 1,800 murdered Jews. "I am somewhat ashamed," said Swiss Bankers' Association chairman Georg Krayer. "I have not found a figleaf big enough to cover up the negligence of my banking colleagues in the period after the Second World War."

Switzerland has taken many hits in recent years for collaborating with Nazi Germany, Ferdinand Marcos, and other worthies. For years Nestlé SA fought world opinion on the topic of marketing infant formula supplement in third world countries—poor mothers were watering down the formula to cut costs. The Jewish accounts scandal might have dealt the country's banking industry's image a crippling blow, had it not been revealed the same week that Israeli banks, too, diverted the money of Jews to their own investments.

➤ **Taiwan.** Competition in Taiwan is circumscribed by the Confucian value of reverence for the past. Competition is not worth any action that will bring dishonor onto a family. Do what you want, be as successful as you please—but do not darken the door to your ancestors' house. A rat race clearly exists in the country, where work brings material reward which requires more work, but people are alert to the emptiness of this cycle. In their view, Americans have so little regard for the past that they are inevitably an insubstantial people.

➤ **United Kingdom.** The U.K. is a muddle of conflicted feelings about competition and collaboration. Despite its professed egalitarian values, classism and the bitter relationships that class entails remain embedded in the civil consciousness. The 1997 Mark Herman film *Brassed Off* painted a vivid picture of the entrenched irrationality of worker-management relationships in an embattled Yorkshire coal town. So bitter and so deep was the feeling of to-the-death competition between Labor and Tory that each was perfectly happy to die to cause the other side grief. On the other hand, the movie was about a colliery brass band that pulled together despite severe hardships to win the national band competition at the Albert Hall. Both strains— rigid class-bound competition and dutiful "Englishman" collaboration—run deep through the British personality. Margaret Thatcher despaired because British businesspeople were happy to retire after making their first million and live a non-business life. She wished more Britishers had the competitive spunk and stamina of their American counterparts. But there is no denying the British ability to form successful teams despite these sharp divisions. Our team consulting in England suggests to us that workers there are not as naturally sullen about teaming as Americans are. We attribute this to a greater acceptance of rules and roles in the U.K., acquiescing to the way things are. While the American cries out, "Don't fence me in" to teams, the British worker sighs and gets on with it. In a world of fractiousness and divisions, there is still something to be said for keeping a stiff upper lip.

➤ **United States.** While it sets the modern standard for individual competitiveness and lacks many common features of a collaborative culture, the United States remains a leader in collaborative business strategies. The learning organization, empowerment, participative management, and Theory Y are all American ideas, and they are implemented more in America than in any other country. Total quality management (TQM) is a curious amalgam of American (William Edwards Deming) and Japanese (Kaoru Ishikawa) strains. Despite this country's often impetuous footprint abroad, it is still communitarian enough to have invented the world's first and most stable republic and built a common infrastructure that is the envy of the collaborative world. While the record on racial tolerance is far from perfect, the U.S. has expanded the circle to bring outside groups in more than has any other nation in history.

The Hong Kong Story

The great world example of transcompetitive dynamism isn't happening in Europe, or America, or Japan. It's happening along the east coast of China, which is undergoing fantastic change in the aftermath of China's reabsorption of Hong Kong in the summer of 1997.

The West characteristically did not know how to understand the handover of the British colony to China. Americans focused on issues of individual liberty. The British focused on the continuing diminution of empire and influence. Japan focused on the alarming potential of a China led by a community that knows how to compete in a way that not even Japan can match.

While Japan enjoys a naturally collaborative culture, China, with its many ethic and language divisions, occupies the neutral zone on the scale of connectedness, in the space between competition and collaboration reserved for family feeling. Though the Chinese are cheerfully international in their outlook, brilliant traders and savvy managers, they are not as given to trusting one another, except within families. As a result, the companies of Hong Kong have generally not been very big and they tend to be very closely held, because they are based on the extended family of the owners. People inside the family can be trusted, and the obligation to hire and help cousins one may not ever have met is very strongly felt; people outside the family (contractors, customers, and unknown stockholders) are not to be trusted. This is why Hong Kong, successful as it is, can't boast big native keiretsus and zaibatsus like the Japanese. The biggest companies in the city are foreign-owned.

The question everyone is asking is: What will happen now that capitalist Hong Kong is fully Chinese again?

Our sense is that the city's return was natural and inevitable. Hong Kong has always been Chinese, and for its part, China has been striving in its own way for many years to become more like Hong Kong. The province of Guangzhou surrounding Hong Kong—and until recently separated by barbed wire—is an example of civic mimicry, the walled creature trying desperately to ape the behavior of the free creature on the other side of the wall. The city of Shenzhen, directly across from the older city, has obvious aspirations to one day blend into Hong Kong and become its twin city.

Though China was a Communist country for 50 years, Communism took root less well there than in the Soviet Union. Since family is still the dominant power in Han China, China is happy its brilliant prodigal child is back.

The 1989 massacre at Tienanmen Square was a nightmare in part because it ran counter to Chinese family values, which tolerate dissent within the family. It was perhaps the low point of the last 1,000 years of Chinese history. But the Chinese are telling us it was also a learning experience.

> There was a tantalizing report, not yet officially confirmed, that Deng showed deep remorse about the Tienanmen crackdown on his deathbed, calling it the regret of a lifetime. If that view wins wide support, China is in for some changes. Any reevaluation of Tienanmen that acknowledges the patriotism and generally good behavior of the students will shake up China's view of herself and how she is seen by the outside world. Even so, human rights concerns won't just disappear by themselves, and democracy won't sprout up overnight. Just as important as the truth about Tienanmen is the right to disagree with the party line. As long as the Communist Party has monopoly on political ideology and leadership, it can revise history every week and it won't bring freedom.[17]

China has felt the power of exchange-encircle-exact, and will think three times before raising its hand against its own again. But trust, of the kind so common in Japan, will take root slowly:

In the eyes of many Chinese, the communists lost the moral right to govern after the Tienanmen Massacre, and are tolerated only as long as the economy continues to perform so well. However, the Chinese leaders likewise do not trust their citizens to wield political power: the memory of the Cultural Revolution is particularly fresh in the minds of those who, like Deng Xiaoping, suffered horribly at the hands of the young Red Brigade.

While massacres may have worked so far in quelling political dissent, there is serious doubt of their future efficacy. For one, the whole world has China under a media microscope, particularly with regard to Hong Kong. In this decade, satellite TV and the Internet have opened information floodgates. If the families of the troops and politicians are able to see their youngsters being killed live on BBC and CNN, such violence may be impossible to conduct for any length of time.[18]

Despite all the troubles, the outlook for China is bright. Mao's sick supercollaborative regime is gone, and Jiang Zemin, China's leader after the death of Deng Xiaoping, has it in his power to be China's Gorbachev, to preside over the dismantling of the Brute state that remains in place and the creation of a transcompetitive nation that will write a surprising new page about human progress, combining the best of the two worlds it knows. What China brings to the table, no other country can: the knowledge, gained over many centuries of frustration and denial, that long-term survival is the sweetest success of all.

Endnotes

[1]"Winning isn't everything. It's the only thing" is the quote everyone remembers. "I wish to hell I'd never said the damned thing," Lombardi said later. "I meant the effort. I meant having a goal. I sure as hell didn't mean for people to crush human values and morality."

[2]Kenichi Miyashita and David Russell, *Keiretsu: Inside the Hidden Japanese Conglomerates*, McGraw-Hill, 1996.

[3]Marlene Piturro, "Turning Japanese: Asian managers find conditions in Mexico more than they bargained for," July/August 1995; Nafta Web Page, http://www.nafta.net.

[4]Lovemore Mbigi, *Ubuntu: The Spirit of African Transformation Management*, Knowledge Resources, Ltd., Pretoria, 1995.

[5]Damon Darlin, "Rebellions on the Reservations," *Forbes*, May 19, 1997.

[6]Competitive styles can vary in something as unimportant as driving habits. We have noticed that, late at night in Boston, many drivers do not even stop for red lights.

If the intersection looks clear, they drive right through. This seems to us very much in keeping with the competitive social style of the east coast. In broad daylight in Minneapolis, where old Scandinavian cooperative customs still linger, drivers wait a moment before entering an intersection, out of consideration for whoever may be coming from the other direction, passing through a changing red light. Both acts are illegal, but one arises out of competitive fieriness, the other out of a kind of misguided neighborliness.

[7]Anna Luíza Ozório de Almeida and Joáo S. Campari, *Sustainable Settlement in the Brazilian Amazon*, The World Bank/Oxford University Press, 1996.

[8]Francis Fukuyama, *Trust*, The Free Press, 1995.

[9]Bertolt Brecht, *The Threepenny Opera (Der Dreigroschenroman)*, K. Desch, 1949.

[10]Lothar Gall et al., *The Deutsche Bank 1870–1995*, Weidenfeld & Nicholson, 1995.

[11]From a conversation with Charles Gimon, a friend and student of Indonesian lore.

[12]Andreas Harsono, "Indonesia Notes Thailand's Mistakes to Avoid Speculative Crash," *The American Reporter*, July 14, 1997.

[13]"Tips, Tricks and Pitfalls to Avoid When Doing Business in the Tough but Lucrative Korean Market," *Business America*, June 1997.

[14]Tankred Golenpolsky et al., *Doing Business in Russia*, Oasis Press, 1996.

[15]From correspondence with Susan Marais and Magriet Herman of Pretoria.

[16]Marcus Kabel, "Banks Admit Shame Over Holocaust Accounts," Reuters, July 23, 1997.

[17]Phillip Cunningham, JKC Communications, "Springtime in Beijing: China after Deng," May 30, 1997, http://www.pelago.com/0202/story4.html.

[18]Arun Mehta, "China needs a Gorbachev," *American Reporter*, June 30, 1997.

The Mirage of the Beagle

Supercompetition is never "Nature's way"

The beagle is a dog we are all familiar with. He is a rabbit hound who, let loose in the woods, will run until he has caught a rabbit. He will do this even when there is no rabbit.

The *Beagle* was also the name of the ship biology-watcher Charles Darwin sailed on in his famous 1831 voyage to the Galapagos Islands. In 1851 he published *On the Origin of Species*. Recap: Darwin saw evolution as a natural mechanism by which species became more competitive or survival-worthy over the course of many generations. Survival-negative characteristics get weeded out of the gene pool, while survival-positive characteristics move the species to new heights.

Darwin's views were vigorously opposed by the legitimate academics of the Victorian world, then befell an even worse fate—they were adopted by post-Victorian pseudoacademics. "Survival of the fittest" became the slogan under which all sorts of uncivil excesses were excused: the imperial violence of the British Empire, the capitalist excesses of the robber baron era, the permanent primacy of the rich over the poor.[1]

Tons of bad sociological commentary can be traced to this distortion of Darwin's teachings. In the right hands, it can turn everything that is bad and immoral, from slavery to fraud, into something "natural" and thus defensible. In the Dark Ages, according to *The Great Chain of Being*,[2] the status quo was excused because it was God's will that the king rule over the people. In Social Darwinism, God's will is replaced by science, or nature.

But Social Darwinism was a crock, as anyone with multiple brain cells and not occupying a seat of privilege understood. Why was it that society only mirrored the competitive realities of nature (dog-eat-dog brutality) and ignored the equally powerful collaborative realities nature displayed (community action, familial love, teamwork, symbiotic relationships that worked for everyone's mutual benefit)? As Lewis Thomas said, "The survival of the fittest does not mean those fit to kill; it means those fitting in best with the rest of life."[3] Not competition, but transcompetition.

Most dysfunctional competition excuses itself using the logic of Social Darwinism. We see it in sports, in education, in careers, in politics, and in the way organizations are run:

➤ "We're doing these people a favor even hiring them. We don't want to spoil them."

➤ "It's fine to target low-income groups with our advertising, but you wouldn't want to hire them."

➤ "The fact that I sold more policies than you has nothing to do with the fact that I get the good leads and prime territories. I'm just a better salesperson."

➤ "This company is out of gas. Sell off the assets and make a fresh start. The people here will be better off."

➤ "If customers can't figure out our products are unhealthy, that's their problem."

➤ "This company is for winners only. If you haven't made a mark after two years here, you belong somewhere else."

These attitudes are destructive in the extreme to the spirit of community that organizations need to build in the century ahead.

A wonderful moment in the discrediting of Social Darwinism occurred in Ethiopia during the war Mussolini initiated in order to impress Hitler. Mussolini wanted to show his fellow Fascists on the Axis side that Italians, like Germans, constituted a superrace, and that they could easily sweep over the primitive non-Aryan nation of Haille Selassie. The African war was to be the feather in Mussolini's competitive cap.

One morning in 1935, a busload of trained, well-armed Italian soldiers ran out of gas in the territory of a fierce tribe of geladas—baboon-like monkeys. For over an hour the animals pelted the bus with sticks and stones, shattering glass and banging on metal, terrifying the soldiers with their hostile screeching. Finally, the soldiers made a mad dash for the bus doors and ran across the plain to escape the enraged primates, abandoning their food supplies and shedding their carbines and gunbelts as they ran.[4]

Monkeys are not supposed to overpower their betters or put them to rout. But working together against a group less cohesive than their own, they handily prevailed.

Endnotes

[1]Not everyone believes in Darwinian evolution. Many reject it on the grounds that it shows people coming from a rung pretty low on the biological ladder—pond scum, if you take it all the way back.

This conflicts with the revelations of their religion, which show that humankind has developed, not evolved, from a rung near the top of the ladder. Pictures of paradise often show humans, lions, lambs, and mosquitoes all living amicably alongside one another. It is a stunningly noncompetitive view of the world.

[2]Arthur Lovejoy, *The Great Chain of Being*, Harvard University Press, 1936.

[3]Lewis Thomas, *Notes of a Biology Watcher*, Knopf, 1974.

[4]Gerald Durrell, *My Zoo*, Liveright, 1958.

The
Burgeoning Brain

Why "rationality" doesn't work

The myth most people subscribe to is that early man was an unspeakable brute, an Alley Oopish warrior who killed for pleasure, ate the hearts of his enemies, clubbed women and dragged them back to his snuggery. If you want to call someone you work with mean and uncouth, you use the epithet, *Neanderthal*.[1]

But the first people were nothing like that. Buried under mountains of dust in an outcropping on the Serengeti Plains of northern Tanzania is a place called Olduvai Gorge. It's famous because this is where anthropologists Louis, Mary, and Richard Leakey discovered fossils and later, tools, belonging to human or hominid beings who lived here across a span of almost three million years.

The hominid creatures that had such little brains traveled in a band, and as such rated high on the connectedness scale of that day. Still, the creature's social life was meager. The day was consumed with moving, searching for food, and being on the lookout for boars, lions, other predators, plus other animals and situations that could do it harm. It had no tools, it ran with its knuckles on the ground, and the only sounds it could make were yips and grunts, like the geladas. It could learn, but it had no way of passing knowledge on to its offspring. When it died, what little knowledge it had amassed died with it.

The animal-human was probably a skilled collaborator, grooming its mate and offspring, sharing food, and helping defend the group against enemies. Prehistoric people were competitive only in the sense of having to scratch to survive.

But the little animal had star quality, because every hundred thousand years or so, its descendants changed a bit and broadened their scope. Eventually the little animal would chair General Motors, but for now it settled for a more erect posture and slightly larger brain pan.

The Little Fellow

Picturing what people acted like then is a challenge. At the far end we (or they, if you don't feel like claiming them as relatives) were simply animals, perhaps a little brighter than dogs. Hominid brains were like other animal brains: a fist-sized lump useful for running the body, feeling things, and a minuscule amount of learning.

Embedded in this little brain was an organ called the amygdala. Every brain has one. It is the body's danger detection system, and it is unsubtle in the extreme: All it can do is signal to the body how it should react. When an animal encounters something it does not understand, an unknown, its amygdala sounds an alarm that galvanizes the entire nervous system and forces the animal to make a choice between fighting and fleeing.

In the course of an ordinary day in the wild, the amygdala may have gone off a hundred times—many times more than ours go off. The animal's choice, when the alarm sounds, is unrigorous: fight or flight. Very little actual choosing or thinking is involved. For a million years or more, the amygdala and the binary habits it engendered ruled.

But inside the skull, something was happening to the little brain. After a while, it was not just getting bigger, but it was changing in its very nature. By the dawn of recorded history, a few short thousands of years ago, it was creating clever new parts for itself that were actually inventing themselves. Brains making brains.

Growing around the old primitive brain was a curly mantle called the neocortex. This new human brain had the cognitive powers that humans most prize—reason, detachment, and language.

According to anthropologist Julian Jaynes, this new brain first attained what we consider modern consciousness about 5,000 years ago.[2] Where prehistoric humans (as well as some scattered aboriginal cultures today) were tribal and collaborative in orientation, the renaissance human had the tools to become self-conscious, individualistic, and personally competitive. From gentle beginnings, we evolved into creatures with the capacity to be mean.

Because the human being had language, it could communicate in wonderful and subtle ways, efficiently passing on information to others in real time. Eventually people would acquire the skill of literacy, and knowledge could be passed on to succeeding generations via written documents.

The 5,000 years that followed the development of consciousness and competition are like an eyeblink in the whole of human history. Yet in this short time we have evolved almost as an act of will. The neocortex allows people dominion over time. Animals can have ideas, and ideas can live long after the individual animal has perished, through stored knowledge.

To the amygdala and the neocortex the current age added data technology that allows us to amass and share immense amounts of information instantaneously, planetwide if we wish. This technological explosion (tech) has been accompanied by a global political revolution, in which everyday people expect to be included in decision making and to be personally fulfilled (touch) by the world available to them.

People in this new age treasure our rights and exult in our power as consumers. We have examined and partially broken with the competitive *isms*—individualism, nationalism, imperialism, racism, sexism, Social Darwinism—that had limited us during the age drawing to a close. In their place we expect to see philosophies adopted and practices implemented that are less brutal, less destructive, and less habitual in character.

Endnotes

[1] Recent studies appear to prove once and for all that current-day humans are not descended genetically from Neanderthals. Associated Press, July 11, 1997.

[2] Julian Jaynes, *Origin of Consciousness in the Breakdown of the Bicameral Mind*, Viking Press, 1972.

Mythic Faces

The Brute, the Trickster, the Hermit, and the Pawn

More than anything else, more than a study in money or numbers, your organization is a story. It is a story of people and the ideas they were able to come up with; a story of growth and peril; of original people learning to take on additional people, and having to teach them, and trust them, to keep the story going. It doesn't matter if you sell doughnuts or consult to the United Nations—your story is profound, because it's yours.

Our premise in this chapter is that an ancient struggle lies at the heart of your organization's successes and failures. The battle rages inside us with seemingly contradictory goals: survival as individuals and connection to one another as a group. We all view the battle a bit differently. Some stress personal history, others place emphasis on group success.

Let us look at a few mythic stories to see what they have to say about competition and what they imply about our ability to rise above it. These stories will reveal four faces of connectedness: the Brute, the Trickster, the Hermit, and the Pawn. We will start with the Brute, and work our way clockwise through the connectedness model to the Trickster.

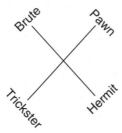

Unless you comajored in business and the classics, not all these stories will be familiar. Unlike Harvard case studies, they get better with age. Homer's *Odyssey* was compiled around 700 BC. The book of Genesis was first drafted around 1200 BC.

But let's start further back, with the book of Gilgamesh, the story of a Sumerian warrior-god who may or may not have lived nearly 5,000 years ago in the fertile valley formed between two rivers in what is present-day Iraq.

The Brute

The mere mention of Sumerian literature is enough to send sensible managers heading for the hills. But hold on. The story is about a giant leap forward for humankind, from the realm of Brute action to a new level of connectedness.

There are many stories about Gilgamesh. The earliest were basically shoot-'em-ups, stories of how Gilgamesh overcame one monster after another, John Wayne-style. Gilgamesh, like so many legendary heroes, from Samson to Hercules to Thor, was simply stronger than everyone else and made everyone else pay. In a land known for brutality from Nebuchadnezzar to Saddam Hussein, Gilgamesh was the good brute who always beat the bad brute.

The Brute is a member in good standing of most any organization today. The Brute is like a dog that will not stop until it has achieved its objective. At their best Brutes embody the will to achievement. The law of the Brute is the law of the self: Do what I want or suffer the consequences. It is nearly as prevalent in organizations today as it was in Gilgamesh's day.

At its worst, of course, the Brute is just a bully, like the boss who rules by terror, like the team member who enjoys making the rest of the team look bad, like the first incarnation of Gilgamesh.[1]

But something stunning happened in the later versions, composed about 2700 BC. Traditional supercompeter Gilgamesh and a Brute monster from the distant hills became collaborators.

The monster was a creature named Enkidu. While early versions of the story described Enkidu as a fierce Brute, in later tellings he mutated into a vegetarian hermit-hero, a combination Samson and Dale Carnegie, friend of nature and seeker of peace. A hunter witnessing Enkidu in action ran to tell his father:

> I saw a hairy bodied man today
> at the watering place, powerful as Ninurta
>
> the god of war; he feeds upon the grasslands
> with gazelles ... he has unset my traps and filled
> my hunting pits; the creatures of the grasslands
>
> get away free. The wild man sets them free.
> Because of him I am no longer a hunter.

When Enkidu and Gilgamesh first meet, at a wedding feast, they are astonished and threatened by one another's strength, and they engage in a colossal crowd-pleasing battle.

> Stormy heart struggled with stormy heart
> as Gilgamesh met Enkidu in his rage.[2]

As they vie, their respect for one another grows into a ferocious affection. Gilgamesh appears to have the upper hand, but they break off fighting to embrace and pledge lifelong loyalty to one another. They go off together on many adventures, with the understanding that the two of them together are stronger than any power. Enkidu taught Gilgamesh, and the two continually remind one another, that "Two people, companions ... they can prevail against the terror...."

The story of Gilgamesh is the story of the elevation of consciousness of the value and power of cooperation. It is not enough to save Enkidu or Gilgamesh from death, but it is enough to signal a new spirit in the evolution of humankind.

The Pawn

The story of Adam and Eve plops people down in Paradise, fully cerebrated and ready to go. They eat the apple, the ax falls, and the two are ushered out into the cold hard world where dog eats dog and bread is made with brow sweat.

One can think of the story of the Fall in two ways. Look at it one way and you have an ontology (a legend that explains why things are the way they are) about competition. In this version, God expects us to *win* our way back into Paradise. To prove our worth we must engage in an endless series of contests or competitive events. In this scenario, all of history—conquering other countries and enslaving their people, selling people things they don't need, brutalizing our employees, and cheating our own communities—is a series of feats we must perform in order to deserve readmission to the garden.

This scenario presents God as a kind of cosmological venture capitalist, setting us up to prove our mettle by hacking and bashing one another. In this stance, we are barely conscious pawns in a game we don't understand.

This would sound dreamlike and fantastical, except that it is how hundreds of millions of people spend each day, performing rote tasks to which they have no logical or emotional connections, and accepting them as the price of daily life.

Adam and Eve were thus Pawns in the free will scheme of a capricious creator. The Pawn is very important in our study because he or she is the basic player in the game of competition. Pawns are all of us who take the situation handed to us and do our best with it, never quite understanding the degree to which we are being manipulated. Pawns never have the information they need to become more powerful. They are not considered to be rational—they are just out there, like serfs or cows.

Nature is full of Pawns, and most Pawn species are very successful. They survive by having large litters; those not taken by predators will live to swell the herds. Their sheer numbers guarantee their continuance.

You may wonder why is it that we never hear of a competitive individual within a noncompetitive species. Why are there no "fighting deer" or "battling geese"? The reason is that nature has designed Pawn species to be food, not fighters. There is a level of aggressiveness beyond which fitness is lowered, not increased. It may be that, within these species, aggressiveness in males does not turn the females on. Animals who are skittish by nature will not appreciate a lion in their midst, not even a lion in lamb's wool.

Most people's workplaces are comprised mostly of Pawns. Most employees are Pawns. Some entire companies—those content to be plain-vanilla providers, supplying midlist products and acting as fodder in the corporate bidding process—are Pawn companies.

Of the four characters of the connectedness model, Pawns seem the most necessary. They are there, it sometimes seems, for

Brutes to brutalize and Tricksters to trick. They are like grass underfoot: Their apparent purpose is to be trampled or browsed.

But despite what Brutes and Tricksters want them to think, Pawns don't need to remain Pawns, because there is a second possible interpretation of Adam and Eve's banishment from the garden. This story is not an ontology of competition but an ontology of collaboration.

Before biting into the apple, there was no sense of teamwork between man and woman, for in Paradise there was no need for teamwork. Problems did not require free flow of information, because there was no information. It was a world innocent of all knowledge. There was not even family. Things being perfect, and conflict and ignorance not posing any survival problems, there was no need for community action.

From this view, banishment from Paradise may have had a very different meaning. God may have been challenging people to see how close we could come to recreating Paradise on our own. Our tools for simulating Paradise would be the things that got us thrown out—collusion and knowledge.

To remain a Pawn in the face of such a challenge is unacceptable. Thinking ourselves Pawns is, from a biblical perspective, the work of the devil, a lie we tell ourselves to accept our helplessness and to deny responsibility for the condition we find ourselves in. You can practically hear the serpent hissing these cop-outs into our ears: "You can't fight city hall." "What's the use in trying?" "Education is for losers." "You're damned if you do, damned if you don't."

Managers like having Pawns to manage, because they are manageable. But Pawns pose problems too. On the one hand, Pawns are the units of all competitive action, the footsoldiers of competitive wars. If Bill Gates wants to create a networking animation product to go head to head against Corel, he needs his Pawns—his development team—to move with brilliant dispatch. But being Pawns, they need a lot of motivating to do their best. The challenge, for kings of long ago and managers today, is how to motivate Pawns to do what they are told without going too far and motivating them to think for themselves. Most motivational schemes—exhortation, brass bands, pep rallies, awards and recognition—deliberately stop at this patronizing level. Henry Ford is credited with this gem: "All I want is a good pair of hands. Unfortunately, they come attached to a person."[3]

So it is odd to hear managers complain when change initiatives stall. Why didn't people respond more favorably to a proposal that might save jobs and extend careers? Might it not be because we trained them to shy away from conscious change? How can we expect Pawns to take our initiatives and become different creatures overnight—bold, entrepreneurial, and brutal? If they became those new creatures, they would be harder to control.

And yet, with the right inducements, Pawnhood is easily outgrown. True adults do it by assuming responsibility for their circumstances. We also move beyond the condition of haplessness by combining the skills of transcompetition: making the rational decision to succeed through a combination of competitive and collaborative measures. Thus we shed the cloak of the unthinking peasant and become true participants in the organizations we are part of and the lives we live.

The Hermit

Enkidu, the hairy half-beast wanderer, was the first Hermit in literature. Another Hermit story, written later than Gilgamesh but taking place earlier, occurs at the beginning of human history. It is the story of Cain.

Adam and Eve had two sons, Cain and Abel. They invented business. Cain, the elder, went into agribusiness, tilling the soil to grow crops. Abel went into livestock.

They also invented religion. Adam and Eve never prayed or sacrificed, that we are aware of. But Cain and Abel, with their industries hanging in the balance, felt it would be wise to offer up their best production samples to God.

And together, they invented crime. When Cain in his competitive jealousy struck Abel and killed him, he became the first murderer.

After killing Abel, Cain fled from all society, becoming a Hermit, the second mythic point on the compass of connectedness. The Hermit forsakes all hope of connecting with people. Betrayed too many times by self and others, the Hermit lives an outlaw existence outside the boundaries of discourse.

The tragedy of Cain is that he had much to offer. He was industrious, entrepreneurial, and inventive. But he pitched his tent way to the left side of the scale of connectedness. He could not bear that Abel's offering found greater favor with God than his own. As in the competitive ontology many people impose on the story of the Fall, he saw life as a series of contests, and victories as pleasing to God. His competitive instincts aroused, he took violent action. Any further to the left on the scale and he might have eaten Abel.

What lesson should we take from the story of Cain? That unrestrained competition, far from being a spark to human creativity, leads to the deepest kind of social infraction, in which the part cuts itself off forever from the whole?

Every organization has a few Hermits. They are the people who never join in and never get over their suspicion of the enterprise. "Just leave me alone and let me do my job" is their motto. They operate on the sidelines of teams, providing the minimum requirements and exerting even at the best of times a negative pull on group endeavors. It is not that they are opposed to the goals and objectives of the group, but that they have given up on them. They are afraid of being made fools, of exhibiting an optimism contradicting their years of perceived betrayal or disappointment. Hired Hermits are organizational ghosts, never leaving, never expressing a wish or desire of their own, but haunting the best efforts of all who are near.

The story of the Hermit is not usually one of redemption—by taking themselves out of the game, they make themselves nearly irredeemable. It is harder for a Hermit to change to a more transcompetitive style of connecting to people than it is for a Brute to stop beating on people. The Hermit role must be set aside completely, and a new one adopted.

None of us is ever far from this state. Organizations are inherently disappointing places. Promises cannot all be kept. Many are waffled on, many more are simply forgotten amid the crunch. When the "partnership" employees believe exists between them and the organization is ignored, the Hermit in each of us chuckles softly and says, I told you so.

The Trickster

The myth of a fallen universe can be found in almost every culture.[4] In ancient Greece it was the Age of Gold, when flawed heroes like Odysseus walked the earth. In Judaism it was the age of Patriarchs, when people like Abraham, Isaac, and Jacob lived.

Odysseus, the hero of Homer's epic about soldiers returning from the Trojan War, supplies our next mythic character, the Trickster. Not a hunk like Hercules or a deity like Zeus, Odysseus was a modernist who lived by his wits, manipulating other people's knowledge to achieve his own ends. Time after time, adventure after adventure, Odysseus thinks his way out of impossible traps. He was the Captain Kirk of mythology—always thinking, always pushing the envelope, willing to try just about anything. In today's business world he would be a dazzling supersalesperson, a Michael Ovitz or Tom Peters.

Jacob was likewise a modernist, a person born too late to be a traditional hero, a person whose character flaws were papered over with tricks, deals, and the savviness of a riverboat gambler.

In the book of Genesis, Jacob was the son of Isaac and the brother of the firstborn Esau. Esau is described as powerful, hairy, and relatively straightforward—a Brute. One day Esau returns from the hunt and begs for a treat. In the story he appears to be hypoglycemic, and willing in his depleted state to give away his primogeniture (rights as firstborn son) for a "mess of pottage."

A hero would have fed his brother and refused the deluded offer. Jacob not only takes advantage of Esau this way, but later poses as Esau (wearing lambswool on his arms to get the desired hairy feel) to obtain his blind and dying father's blessing.

At every step in his early career, Jacob wheels and deals to get his own way. Jacob, like Odysseus, eventually becomes a better person, but before he puts his trickery behind him, he is a perfect rascal. God saw something in Jacob though, because it is Jacob, not the more heroic Abraham or Isaac, who is given the new name of "Israel," and becomes the namesake for a nation.

Needless to say, modern organizations don't get very far without their share of Tricksters. They are the ultimate heroes of business, creating markets, luring customers, reassuring investors, and shaping the perceptions the world has of the organization.

Organizations themselves are Tricksters. Corporations have been described as "legal fictions" whose managers pull a screen over their true intentions while they delicately manipulate different constituencies—workers, investors, customers, government, the industry they are part of—to secure their ends.

The Machiavellian approach to controlling large numbers of people requires the ability to limit the information each person has. Management itself (just think about the implications of "managing" people) is a Trickster's game. Shading, shaving, spinning, hyping—we live in an age of trickery. When Tricksters control the information, they win in a much bigger way than the most brutal Brute.

Superficially, the Trickster is the easiest of the four types to change, to advance to the more transcompetitive role of Negotiator. The reason is that Tricksters are mentally very capable of considering change: They can make it in their minds, and then unmake it in a moment. They are naturally flexible characters.

The difficulty for them is finding firm enough soil so that the change will take root and grow. Conviction is everything in the transcompetitive sphere. Tricksters must believe that community goals matter, and that to be a leader one must have values and be consistent and believable over the long haul. It is not an impossibility; indeed, for this wily archetype, becoming credible to others and making it stick is the ultimate trick.

Playing the Survival Game

Brute, Pawn, Hermit, or Trickster, all are alike in one regard. Each uses his or her mode of connecting to *survive*. Deep down, that is all any of us does; what distinguishes us is how we define survival.

Think of life as a tug of war between our animal and angel sides. On the one end of the rope is our need to survive, both individually and as a species. On the other end of the rope is our crying need to be with other people, to play, work, love, to know and to be known: to be social.

Nature doesn't give us many clues for resolving this tug of war. When animals court and couple, is that survival or sociality? When they go to war, is it to survive or to have a good time with their buddies? When we bash our colleagues within our companies and double-bash competitors outside our companies, are we exhibiting a will to live or are we just being jerks?

The four mythic faces see the rope-ends of surviving and being social as irreconcilable. Transcompetitive personalities, by contrast, have learned to make a lasso of the rope, to see how each connects to the other.

For animals lower on the food chain, what may look like social behavior is still survival: the need to procreate, to cluster to gather food more efficiently and for shelter and comfort (reduced stress and fear). When a bee gives up its life defending the hive, it is not sacrificing itself, it is defending the only life that matters to it, the life of the group. We personify animals' social behavior by comparing it to our own; but theirs is driven by genetic instincts to continue on.

While humans are also programmed to fight for survival, we have an additional intellectual capability that allows us to see beyond today or tomorrow; we can choose to procreate to fulfill whatever political, religious, or social covenant we feel needs fulfilling. We think about our environment and make choices—some reactive, some proactive. We socialize, in part, to fill a higher need for intellectual stimulation, mental challenge, and self-esteem as well as a good cup of coffee.

This tug of war between our animal past (old brain: instinct for survival) and our human potential (new brain: need for stimulation) creates a push–pull or yin–yang force within each of us. We all have the capability to shift between being viciously competitive and compassionately collaborative, depending on changes to our external and internal environments. This ability to switch from one brain to the other is what makes us transcompetitive.

Our internal circumstances color our view of our external situation and determine how we react. How much sleep you had (or didn't have: sleep deprivation), what you had to eat and when you ate it (blood sugar levels), good news vs. bad news, hormones (testosterone, seratonin, acetylcholine, etc.), physical injury or pain (endorphin levels): All these factors help decide how you view your surroundings.

Our inner variations affect our outer variation of behaviors, within a definable range of both competitive and collaborative styles. The extremes of this sociality scale (between competitive and collaborative) can be defined as antisocial. The social rules of civility are designed, therefore, to help people make choices within the normal or functional range.

When the rules of civility are broken, whether supercompetitively or supercollaboratively, people endure the consequence of antisocial behavior—social shunning. They are sent to jail, they are ignored, or they are driven forcibly out of the community.

Within each of the four mythic faces, then, is moment-to-moment variability. One moment you may be a Hermit, the next a Brute. You can occupy a zone with one foot in each of two personalities. Or you can be a little of all four, which is what we are after in this book: greater versatility in making competitive decisions. The more thoroughly a person can achieve this variability (via stress-threat reduction, eating well, exercising, etc.), the more trust that person will engender and deserve.

A Gallery of Competitive Types			
BRUTE	*TRICKSTER*	*HERMIT*	*PAWN*
George Steinbrenner, the biggest brute in sports, and living proof that living to win makes winning unachievable.	Wily promoter **Don King**, destroying boxing with his showmanship and big-bucks baloney.	**Howard Hughes**, one of the world's most powerful men, reduced to using his thumbnail as a flat-head screwdriver.	**Mother Teresa**, whose late-life celebrity did not diminish her compassion for the downtrodden of Calcutta.
Chainsaw Al Dunlap, Scott Paper. The amputator of other people's limbs, he jokes that he is the kind of guy who cries during a horror story.	The Artist Formerly Known as **Prince**. Another day, another disguise. All that attention and nothing much to say.	**Robert MacNamara**, numbers-driven whiz kid at Ford Motor, then defense chief during the Vietnam War, now publicly atoning for his sins.	Farm worker organizer **Cesar Chavez**, the ultimate little guy who made a difference for his people.
Hotelier **Leona Helmsley**, doing time upstate because she needed to win uptown. "Taxes are for little people."	**Mary Kay Ash**, $800 million cosmetics queen. Her sales rallies are like religious revivals. She has made entrepreneurs of thousands.	**Ralph Nader**, a recluse by nature, has put more ideas into play than a dozen corporations. His feud with Bill Gates is like a fight between brothers.	**Charles Harper**, ex-CEO, ConAgra: "No charisma, fat, bald, and he stutters," said John Kotter. "But he is a brilliant leader."
The eyes of the world are on Hong Kong governor **Tung Cheehwa**, as he makes good on his pledge to combine the best of the collaborative East and the competitive West.	**Percy Barnevik**, charismatic head of the world's most decentralized organization, ABB. He has grown from a world-class speaker to the world's top listener.	**Nelson Mandela**, whose character and sense of justice to all, white as well as black, were tempered by 30 years in prison.	**Kazuo Inamori** of Kyocera, a philosopher-king whose genius is to "value the heart of people." The amoeba is small, he says, but indestructible.
ORCHESTRATOR	*COMMUNICATOR*	*ANALYZER*	*ENTREPRENEUR*

A Gallery of Competitive Types

Transcending one's natural competitive or collaborative role means modifying different behaviors for each type. It means beefing up the Pawn, beefing down the Brute, straightening out the Trickster, and luring the Hermit back to the feast.

Put all four of these mythic characters together—Brute, Pawn, Hermit, Trickster—and you have a basic typology of the ways people are inclined to connect with one another. In each myth—Gilgamesh, Adam, Odysseus, and Cain—long-term success was severely limited by the individual's personality type. In every one but the tragic myth of Cain, the characters learned new behaviors to grow beyond the limits of type, to transcend their competitive natures. We know what Cain had no way of knowing: that even terrible crimes can be atoned for and learned from.

Valent Particles

Valence is a term that you may remember from high school chemistry class. It refers to the capacity that different substances have at the molecular level to combine. Some atoms are all too happy to fuse with other atoms. They have open doors, begging other atoms to come courting. Other atoms are stony and inert; they would no sooner take up housekeeping with another substance than they would paint themselves blue.

So it is with human beings. Every team and every organization employ a wide variety of people. Some have a high degree of sociality or valence; they are not happy unless they are mixing it up with others, sharing what they know, and moving the enterprise forward. Others are unable to do this; they insist on their solitariness no matter how the enterprise tries to gather them in.

In his 1974 book, *Competition*, Harvey Rubin (not Harvey Robbins) broke connectedness into two dimensions, aggressiveness and directness.[5] According to his scale, the connectedness each of us exhibits can be pinpointed on a graph showing where our typical social behavior falls. He called them *Dag* (direct and aggressive), *Indag* (indirect and aggressive), *Dinag* (direct and nonaggressive), and *Indinag* (indirect, nonaggressive).

We liked the scale, but thought the terminology was pretty confusing, so we expanded it into the typology of the four contrapuntal characters we have been discussing: Brute, Trickster, Pawn, and Hermit. The images and the scale match up well. The Brute really is a Dag. The Hermit really is an Indinag.

There is more to competition and personality than these four caricatures. The names typify the extremes of each box, the far left or far right. Rather than fence you into predictable behaviors, they indicate what your inclinations are, your default behaviors. Very few of us fall cleanly into any of these four, and a test that simply hung one of these labels on you would be of little practical value. People are complicated, and we tend to be moderate—for every individual stalking the outer perimeter of Trickster or Brute behavior, there are a thousand of us huddled closer to the middle.

And that's good, because the middle is where transcompetitive behaviors occur, where we cut deals with one another to achieve win/win solutions. The middle is where we do business and live.

Endnotes

[1]"It is better to live one day as a lion than a hundred years as a sheep!" Benito Mussolini.

[2]David Ferry, tr. *Gilgamesh: A New Rendering in English Verse*, Farrar, Straus, and Giroux, 1992.

[3]Remarks by Christopher Bartlett, The Masters Forum, Minneapolis, January 1995.

[4]The theologian C.S. Lewis has an interesting take on devolution. He says that not just human nature but all nature is fallen. Humans are not the only species who became competitive and violent after the fall. Insects and other animals all entered a frightful cycle of devouring one another and reproducing in huge numbers in order not to be devoured. People who don't like people often turn to nature for quiet; people who don't like nature find the mindless violence of the food chain even worse. C.S. Lewis, *The Problem of Pain*, Macmillan, 1943.

[5]Harvey L. Rubin, *Competition*, Pinnacle Books, 1981. We drew the X and Y axes of our chart, aggressiveness and directness, from characteristics cited in this interesting analysis of interpersonal competitiveness.

Assessment Tools

Finding out what you and your organization are

Before you can change your competitive behaviors you have to know what they are. This is true whether you are a 100,000-employee, multinational organization or a sole proprietor with a pretzel and mustard cart. This chapter provides you with a typology of competition, and tests to see where you and your organization fit in that typology.

Personalities and Organizations

Organizations don't have personalities or souls. They have something worse, called cultures. Cultures are like personalities, only less changeable. Most organizations get their cultures from their top leaders. Organizations that have competing leaders have multiple cultures—one style one moment, another the next. Young businesses have many traits of Brutes and Tricksters. Established businesses often take on a hermetic cast, as the not-invented-here ethic takes hold ("If we didn't do it, it isn't worth knowing about."). Nonprofits are often Pawns. A Brute nonprofit is like a hostile takeover by a charity—rare, but not unthinkable. In government it is quite common.

To describe organizational competitive style, we suggest the taxonomy that we developed for *Why Change Doesn't Work: Pummel, Push, Pull, and Pamper.*[1] These types run the gamut between maintaining control (Old Age management) and distributing control (New Age management):

➤ **The supercompetitive organization.** This is the Pummel kind of company that rules by terror: "Achieve these objectives or do not bother coming to work." The organization seeks to win at any cost, and can be used to force either change or non-change. The worker or supplier is a slave. Nike on a bad day qualifies as this kind of company.

➤ **The competitive organization.** This is the Push competitive company that seeks advantage, but only for the furtherance of its stated mission. It percolates on its own stress, using the desire to do well and stay ahead of the competition to wring the best from its people. The worker is a rat in a Skinner box. Over the past 15 years no big company has better typified this approach than General Electric.

➤ **The collaborative organization.** This is the Pull organization, whose mission is the fulfillment of all the constituents gathered under its roof. It motivates through the companywide vision. The manager is a human being with no power to coerce; the worker is a human being with free will. United Airlines, bought out by its own workers in 1996, is a great example of a company whose culture is driven by people at the bottom.

➤ **The supercollaborative organization.** This is the Pamper organization which exists for its own immediate comfort, long-term survival to the contrary notwithstanding. This description fits many civil service organizations, old-line unions, and cash-cow companies that have lost their hunger to succeed and are feasting on inherited markets until they die.

The best hope for most organizations lies smack dab in the middle, combining the best traits of competition and collaboration.

The Organizational Questionnaire

We all have both a competitive and a collaborative side to our nature, although one side is usually our instinctual or preferred style. Some organizations, based upon their cultures or the personalities of their leaders, only call on one side. If that side isn't your natural style, you are going to be one frustrated individual—drafted to make war when your heart cries out to make love.

The closer to the center your social score is, the easier it is to override these instincts with logic or open-mindedness. The closer you score to the far left or the far right of the scale, the more power-ful these instincts become and the harder it is for you to override them. Supercompeters and supercollaborators are like addicts in the grip of something more powerful than a transient instrument such as a questionnaire can get at.

Directions: *Take a look at how you and others scored each of these questions. Total the scores to see how your organization rates as a whole. Note that some of the scores go from 1 to 7 while others go from 7 to 1.*

STRONGLY DISAGREE	DISAGREE	MILDLY DISAGREE	NEUTRAL	MILDLY AGREE	AGREE	STRONGLY AGREE

1) It is very important that our company gain the upper hand in every situation.

1	2	3	4	5	6	7

2) It is important to our organization to assure that it hear, understand, and meet workers' needs while getting work accomplished.

1	2	3	4	5	6	7

3) Our company has a practice of following the boss's decisions without question up and down the hierarchy.

1	2	3	4	5	6	7

4) Our organization believes it is crucial to exploit its competitors' weaknesses.

1	2	3	4	5	6	7

5) Our company does not consider it a "win" if it can't help its competitor win/save face as well.

1	2	3	4	5	6	7

6) The best organization usually wins.

1	2	3	4	5	6	7

7) Our company believes it is more important to help the customer win than to win itself.

1	2	3	4	5	6	7

8) Our organization does not consider it a win unless we crush our opponent in the process.

1	2	3	4	5	6	7

STRONGLY DISAGREE	DISAGREE	MILDLY DISAGREE	NEUTRAL	MILDLY AGREE	AGREE	STRONGLY AGREE

9) Not winning is the same as losing.

1	2	3	4	5	6	7

10) Our company believes that you win together or not at all.

1	2	3	4	5	6	7

11) In our organization, we believe that you never get a second chance to take first place.

1	2	3	4	5	6	7

12) Our culture believes it is important to involve others in the accomplishment of outcomes.

1	2	3	4	5	6	7

13) A glory shared is not as sweet.

1	2	3	4	5	6	7

14) When we win, we have been known to rub our competition's nose in it.

1	2	3	4	5	6	7

15) Our organization believes that there are enough resources out there for everyone to get what they need.

1	2	3	4	5	6	7

16) Since there aren't enough resources available, only the strong will get what they need.

1	2	3	4	5	6	7

17) Our organization believes in survival of the fittest.

1	2	3	4	5	6	7

18) Our organization survives by helping one another.

1	2	3	4	5	6	7

19) We believe everyone has something to contribute to a successful outcome.

1	2	3	4	5	6	7

STRONGLY DISAGREE	DISAGREE	MILDLY DISAGREE	NEUTRAL	MILDLY AGREE	AGREE	STRONGLY AGREE

20) At our company, there is a moral obligation to help others when you can.

1	2	3	4	5	6	7

21) We don't believe in burning bridges at our organization—we remain civil even in the thick of competition.

1	2	3	4	5	6	7

22) Our culture is such that we believe it is important to show others who is in charge.

1	2	3	4	5	6	7

What It Means

Count up the numbers you have circled. The higher your score, the more competitive your organization is by nature; the lower your score, the greater the tendency to seek collaborative solutions to problems.

➤ **22-44—Communal or supercollaborative.** Your organizational mission is predicated upon inner harmony and social satisfaction. It is urgent that you decide, at your earliest opportunity, if you are a business or not. Seriously. Supercollaborative organizations thrive when they occupy exclusive zones where conventional competition cannot get at them—government, religion, education.

➤ **45-66—The conventional collaborative zone.** Your organization shows a natural disposition toward collaborative effort. Be sure that this tendency does not conflict with the organization's mission and operations. Next step: Look for ways to broaden the behavioral palette through individual incentives and recognition.

➤ **67-110—The vast, in-between, wishy-washy, plain-vanilla wasteland.** Being in the middle is **not** the same as being transcompetitive. More likely it is just an organization with no distinct style. The question here is less "Which are you?" than "How conscious is your behavior, and conversely, how often are you on automatic pilot?"

➤ **111-132—The conventional competitive zone.** Your organization shows a strong degree of competitive bias. You like to win and you aren't apologetic about it. Next step: Building in collaborative strategies that strengthen your long-term prospects.

➤ **133-154—Blood and guts or supercompetition.** The organization is competitive to the point of cannibalism. You can survive and even thrive in the short term, but the odds are you will piss so many people off they will encircle you and take you down. Option: Learn to count to ten before annihilating everything in your path. Your best bet may be to die young and leave a beautiful corpse.

Your numerical score, however, is less important than the discussion the inventory prompts. In discussing it with your team, keep in mind these questions:

➤ Do other team members agree with your assessment of the organization? If not, why not?

➤ Do you see an across-the-board pattern (high, low, or midrange scores) to all your answers?

➤ What is the relative weight of the opinions of managers and workers?

➤ How habitual would you describe your organization's behavior? Is it competitive or collaborative by rote, or by careful decision?

Individual Personality Profile

Now comes the test for individuals. This test looks for evidence of your natural or preferred role for connecting with other people—the competitive archetypes. Once you know what your habitual role is, you can take steps to combine it with other roles, restoring or creating your own "missing transcompetitive links."

COMPETITIVE ARCHETYPES	TRANSCOMPETITIVE LINKS
Hermit	Analyzer
Pawn	Communicator
Brute	Orchestrator
Trickster	Negotiator

Directions: *Choose the one answer from each of the following pairs with which you agree most. You may circle it on the page, or jot it on a separate piece of paper. Many questions will seem redundant. Don't worry about that.*

1

A I feel the need to make certain all the information has been presented in a logical and thorough manner.

B I like being in charge of projects to make certain they run according to plan.

2

A I like to make certain that people's efforts are coordinated.

B It is important to let others know what you're working on so there are fewer surprises.

3

A I am usually thinking about who needs to know what we're doing and how I can get their input.

B I like being in charge of projects to make certain they run according to plan.

4

A It is important to let others know what you're working on so there are fewer surprises.

B The correct answer usually lies between two individuals' differing perceptions. The hard part is finding the acceptable middle ground.

5

A I try to get people to value others' points of view, especially when they're different.

B I am usually thinking about who needs to know what we're doing and how I can get their input.

6

A I feel the need to make certain all the information has been presented in a logical and thorough manner.

B I am usually thinking about who needs to know what we're doing and how I can get their input.

7

A I am best when working alone.

B I expect people to do what they are told.

8
A   I believe in the credo "Lead, follow, or get out of the way."
B   Having to deal interpersonally with others while I'm working hampers my ability to be my most productive.

9
A   Being precise is important to me.
B   I like to make certain that people's efforts are coordinated.

10
A   I believe in the credo "Lead, follow, or get out of the way."
B   I often feel like others are using my talents to advance their own agendas.

11
A   I feel an obligation to do some unimportant tasks to support the rest of the team.
B   I expect people to do what they are told.

12
A   I feel the need to make certain all the information has been presented in a logical and thorough manner.
B   I try to get people to value others' points of view, especially when they're different.

13
A   I am best when working alone.
B   I feel an obligation to do some unimportant tasks to support the rest of the team.

14
A   I often feel like others are using my talents to advance their own agendas.
B   Having to deal interpersonally with others while I'm working hampers my ability to be my most productive.

15
A   Being precise is important to me.
B   It is important to let others know what you're working on so there are fewer surprises.

16
A   I believe in the credo "Lead, follow, or get out of the way."
B   I don't mind presenting differing points of view in order to get others to agree with me or join my cause.

17
A   I try to get people to value others' points of view, especially when they're different.
B   I like being in charge of projects to make certain they run according to plan.

18

A I feel an obligation to do some unimportant tasks to support the rest of the team.

B If possible, most people would manipulate the system to get the results they want.

19

A Having to deal interpersonally with others while I'm working hampers my ability to be my most productive.

B I don't mind presenting differing points of view in order to get others to agree with me or join my cause.

20

A The correct answer usually lies between two individuals' differing perceptions. The hard part is finding the acceptable middle ground.

B Being precise is important to me.

21

A I am best when working alone.

B If possible, most people would manipulate the system to get the results they want.

22

A I like to make certain that people's efforts are coordinated.

B The correct answer usually lies between two individuals' differing perceptions. The hard part is finding the acceptable middle ground.

23

A I often feel like others are using my talents to advance their own agendas.

B I don't mind presenting differing points of view in order to get others to agree with me or join my cause.

24

A If possible, most people would manipulate the system to get the results they want.

B I expect people to do what they are told.

How to score: In the chart on the next page, circle the letters that correspond to your answers for each question. Total the number of circles in each column to get your score for each style.

What it means: If one style stands out by having two or more circles than the next highest style, that is your dominant or preferred competitive style. If your scores are clustered around the middle, that means you are already versatile in the ways you connect with people; either that or you are wishy-washy. Note that having a well-distributed score does not necessarily mean you are transcom-

	Analyzer/ Hermit	Orchestrator/ Brute	Communicator/ Pawn	Negotiator/ Trickster
1	A	B		
2		A	B	
3		B	A	
4			A	B
5			B	A
6	A		B	
7	A	B		
8	B	A		
9	A	B		
10		A	B	
11		B	A	
12	A			B
13	A		B	
14	B		A	
15	A		B	
16		A		B
17		B		A
18			A	B
19	A			B
20	B			A
21	A			B
22		A		B
23			A	B
24		B		A

petitive, nor does an unbalanced score mean you are not transcompetitive. It just means this is your current preference. You can be a Brute and transcompetitive if that way of connecting is your conscious choice. The key to transcompetitive behavior is *that* you choose, not *what* you choose.

Endnotes

[1]Harvey Robbins and Michael Finley, *Why Change Doesn't Work*, Peterson's, 1996.

Transcompetition in Action

Applying the assessment information you just obtained

You've taken the tests and totaled your organizational and personal scores. You've discussed your organizational scores with your team to see if there is strong agreement or difference among you about the company's competitive nature.

Why does the test matter? It matters because you are what you eat, and organizations are a sum of what their people and leaders think, say, and do. If your organization is loaded with supercompetitors in decision-making positions, that's what the world will see you as. That is what you will be.

Here are some hints to break out of dysfunctional habits (either supercompetitors or supercollaborators). Keep in mind that it is more difficult to break your behavioral habits the further away from the middle you are.

General Rules

To become more collaborative:

➤ Try to discover the priorities of your competitors. You can't meet them halfway unless you know what they are after.

➤ As long as it doesn't interfere with your priorities, help competitors network to resources that may help them achieve their objectives.

➤ Remember that it may be difficult trying to collaborate with or help an organization that either is unwilling to accept help or views itself as your sworn enemy—the nemesis relationship. It is awkward to be in a Reebok–Nike relationship, in which one side seeks profitable coexistence and the other seeks scorched earth.

➤ There is still hope if you can find common ground with a nemesis (shared resources) where both sides can win more by collaborating than by competing. But the advantage of changing must be clear to both sides, or you will never break the habit.

To become more competitive:

➤ Improve on your unique knowledge and skills. The competitive downfall of most people remains lack of specific, distinguishing expertise.

➤ Make sure your own and your organization's needs are met before quixotically setting off to help others. For supercollaborative organizations, this can be a tall order. Groups who think as a group can be very hazy about what they need. Besides, your greatest leverage is always in your own group.

➤ Diversify your portfolio. This is a competitive strategy (it makes you stronger) that requires pure collaboration—listening and talking to others, learning their skill sets and mind-sets, and most of all respecting the difference between what you do and what they do.

➤ Be willing to win, not for the sake of beating the other party, but just to come out on top for once. Everyone needs victories. A loser who wins just a few times quickly sheds the role.

To become more transcompetitive:

➤ Study your own past patterns of behavior. How have you competed in the past, and do people expect the same behavior from you now? Surprise them by showing a fresh vein of versatility.

➤ Place a higher priority on discovering what a win looks like for the other person. Pretend you are passing through a doorway. You know you will get through eventually, but what an improvement to the atmosphere when you defer until the other party has achieved its objective or is confident of doing so. In a world of Laurel and Hardys struggling to beat one another through the doorway, a little class goes a long way.

➤ Get interests and outcomes on the table. Until you know what all parties really want, you can't negotiate a successful solution for them.

➤ Be practical. What action on your part will satisfy both sides in a battle? What three things mean the difference between a done deal and a sunk one?

Now we'll spend a bit of time on each of the four archetypes. Each of them has three incarnations. The first, on the left side, is its competitive face, the one it shows in battle. The third is its collaborative face, that it reveals in time of peace. In between is the transcompetitive face, that it shows when it is thinking and deciding whether it will compete or collaborate.

We will explain the value each type brings to the table, how to recognize when you're dealing with that type, and how to deal with that type in such a way that they (or it, in the case of a whole organization) feel sufficiently comfortable to relax their competitive guard and do business.

Recognizing and Dealing with Brutes

COMPETITIVE ARCHETYPE The Brute	TRANSCOMPETITIVE POSSIBILITY The Orchestrator	COLLABORATIVE MANIFESTATION The Planner
Think of George Patton or Hercules. Brutes are people who must win and are not sensitive to the pain their winning inflicts on others. Brutes not only enjoy openly beating others, but believe it is a moral feat: Might makes right. Unabashed use of power is their solution to the problem of mistrust: If you can't join 'em, lick 'em. A straight line best describes their relationship to goals. Pulled into a transcompetitive orbit, the Brute becomes a mentor, a model, and a leader by example—someone who leads not by force but by blending the skills and attributes of others.	Nestled in the rational space between the Brute and the Planner, the Orchestrator has the ability to draw on the strengths of both to achieve outcomes in a forthright, planned, and coordinated manner. Not easily deterred from their mission, Orchestrators consider options and plan alternatives and "just in case" scenarios in order to minimize distractions on the march toward the goal. Don't get in their way. If you have to, provide value-added options so you're seen as helpful.	Like Brutes, Planners need to control their environment, but in a more indirect, much less offensive manner. Like declawed cats, they take to gentler activities that simulate control. They make lists. They are strategic in their thinking, bringing together disparate points of view to bear upon solutions to problems. They tolerate change well enough, so long as change doesn't interfere with the achievement of their ultimate goals (task completion and order). Jean Paul Marat, the fomenter of the French Revolution, was this kind of declawed cat, as are great athletes in retirement—potent, but passive.

Contribution

In any enterprise or industry, Brutes are the task experts. Their great value is in getting things done. They are simplifiers, results-oriented types whose motto is "Lead, follow, or get out of the way." The human race would long ago have been finished off by marauding bands of wild dogs had the Brute element of human nature not stood up and said, "Hey, no way."

Graft non-Brute attributes onto a Brute and you may end up with its transcompetitive alter ego, the Orchestrator. Orchestrators, like Brutes, are initiators. But they have developed new skills for connecting with people. Instead of bludgeoning, they are coaxing. Instead of ordering people around to fulfill their own vision, they are blending their voices and their input to create more intricate textures and harmonies.

Verbally, the Brute:

➤ Gets directly to the task at hand, with little or no small talk. Great habit, especially if the building is on fire.

➤ Does more talking than listening. Often, not such a great habit.

➤ Directs and controls pace of conversation. This is the dimension that, when amplified, is the key to the Brute's transcompetitive mutation to Orchestrator.

➤ Brings people continually back to the task—essential to leadership.

➤ Interrupts, finishes others' sentences. This drives more reflective types crazy.

➤ Speaks in a direct manner ("I want..." or "You need to..."). You never need to guess where a brute is coming from.

➤ Challenges others' thoughts and ideas. One of the most profound of the competitive attributes.

➤ Asks results-oriented "What" questions.

Nonverbally, you may recognize Brutes from their:

➤ Fast-paced gait. These people have places to get to.

➤ Forceful, commanding tone of voice. "Prepare to cross the Rubicon."

➤ Apparent confidence. Achilles may have sulked in his tent at the gates of Troy, but when he emerged, he was his old confident self.

➤ Show of impatience. They check their watches.

➤ Willingness to send cues. When a meeting is almost over, the Brute is already putting away materials.

➤ Words and deeds devoid of nuance. It's sometimes hard to read Brutes from the little things, like facial expressions. They will tell you what they think up front, but be less candid, or aware, of what they feel inside.

➤ Spartan decor. The walls of a Brute's office may feature nothing more than a clock and a few plaques and awards.

➤ Masculine demeanor. Both male and female Brutes have a no-nonsense, cut-to-the-chase way about them.

Luring a Brute to the transcompetitive side:

✓ Do "completed staff work" ahead of time. Be prepared. Dot *i*'s and cross *t*'s. Be prepared to back up what you say.

✓ Organize your thoughts and presentations for speed. Keep it moving. Brutes award no points for finesse, and deduct points for "on the other hand" thinking.

✓ Get to the task tout de suite and stick with it till it's done. Brutes probably don't care about your kids, nor do they wish to tell you about theirs.

✓ End early whenever possible and leave quickly. Brutes have places to be besides where you are, and people to be with besides you.

✓ Whenever possible, let them win; not beat you, necessarily, but win. Present options and let them decide.

✓ For God's sake, let them be in charge, to feel that they are, even when the org chart says they are not. Let them control how quickly or thoroughly you move through the material. If you are getting into a car, give a Brute the keys.

Recognizing and Dealing with Hermits

COMPETITIVE ARCHETYPE *The Hermit*	TRANSCOMPETITIVE POSSIBILITY *The Player*	COLLABORATIVE MANIFESTATION *The Analyzer*
These people have decided they are not going to compete in any way; withdrawal is their solution to the problem of mistrust. No line at all describes their relationship to goals—they have found peace by forsaking connectedness to people, and connecting instead to information. Hermits are the consummate detail people. You often find them in the introvert professions: computer science, finance, engineering. When their amygdalas are aroused, they abdicate. They feel safest away from the madding crowd, surrounded by things they know they can trust.	Brought out of their shell, made to feel valued for their analytical skills, you will find Players in the thick of things, willing to provide time and energy (such as it is) to help others achieve their outcomes. They want to be viewed as value-added, part of the action. When utilized correctly, they will volunteer for the most challenging and least desirable assignments. Get them turned on and it may be difficult to turn them off. Hermits may never become "people persons," but they can be real contributors, so that their valuable ideas and knowledge are not lost.	Competitive and collaborative Hermits are not all that different. Engaging Hermits in collaborative efforts is not as difficult as many would assume. They pride themselves on their ability to break a problem down into its component parts and view the world through totally logical eyes, Spock-like. They are thorough, dotting all the "i's" and crossing all the "t's." They provide value to any organization by making certain that information is complete (maybe too complete) and applying a critical review eye to all processes and procedures.

Contribution

At their best, Hermits are information experts. They deal in facts, data, and details. Their motto is, "The evidence speaks for itself." The trick is to bring them into the fold and make them feel valued—and not just for the data they amass.

Verbally, you can spot Hermits because they:

➤ Engage in very little small talk or socializing.

➤ Offer less in the way of disclosure of feelings or thoughts.

➤ Strongly prefer to focus discussion on the matter at hand.

➤ Make very few errors with facts or details, and are immensely proud of this.

➤ Use a large vocabulary.

➤ Ask a lot of questions, particularly of the "How" variety—the dreaded technical question.

➤ Share lots of data and information, often more than you want or are able to digest.

➤ May make decisions slowly and systematically.

➤ May be critical of others who are "less thorough."

Nonverbally, Hermits give off several clues to their nature:

➤ They speak slowly and deliberately. "I want to be certain you understand this."

➤ They share logic methodically.

➤ They show little animation or facial expression. Far be it from a hermit to wing it or to embellish.

➤ They exhibit very little movement or gesturing.

➤ They project a formal, conservative appearance. Think bow-tie.

➤ A Hermit's office will be functional, with plenty of storage space for information.

Luring a Hermit to the transcompetitive side:

✓ Send information package in advance to allow them processing time. Never mail-bomb a Hermit.

✓ Get right to the task. Create a meeting agenda and stick to it.

✓ Prepare thoroughly. Double check all your facts. Organize your material to flow linearly and logically. Plug all the holes with hard data. You will lose more points with amusing anecdotes and impromptu opinions than you will gain.

✓ Present a balanced case. Present the negatives as well as the positives. Offer concrete strategies for minimizing the negatives.

✓ If Hermits make a mistake, allow them to save face. Remember that they are tougher on themselves than you could possibly be. Hermits hate to be wrong or caught without information.

✓ Think through possible worst-case scenarios with them and develop contingency plans.

✓ Present realistic and detailed action plans and timelines.

Recognizing and Dealing with Pawns

COMPETITIVE ARCHETYPE The Pawn	TRANSCOMPETITIVE POSSIBILITY The Communicator	COLLABORATIVE MANIFESTATION The Comrade
Pawns are Everyperson, mensches, honest, eager to do right, but forever unsure of their position. Think of the pearl diver in Steinbeck's novel <u>The Pearl</u>, unable to capitalize, because of his position and ignorance, on the great find of his life. He is himself a pearl that the world does not appreciate, and he has grown hardened to his own inner beauty. Pawns yearn to win as much as the scariest supercompeter, but something in them always fails at the starting pistol. Their tragedy is a failure of confidence. Their typical solution to the problem of mistrust is unenthusiastic compliance. The motto they live by: Never volunteer. A dotted, uncertain line best describes their relationship to goals.	Pulled into a transcompetitive orbit, the Pawn becomes a contributor, an improver, a communicator, a coordinator. Positioned between the self-canceling stances of the Pawn and the Comrade, Communicators have the unique ability to help others better themselves. That's where they get their personal rewards. It's what charges their batteries. By helping others, they help themselves. They have a natural ability to link people with the resources they need to achieve outcomes or enhance their skill sets. They are the most patient of all the styles and, therefore, provide a much needed ear to those working through issues. They have their fingers on the pulse of the organization and therefore make great coaches when trained.	Empathy is the forte of this collaborative side of the Pawn. Comrades show great understanding for the needs of individuals and a concern for their well-being. They need to be liked by others and, as a result, go out of their way to make certain that people are informed and feel good about what is going on around them. They are continuously thinking about who needs to know what's happening and what is the best way to make the news palatable. The difference between a Comrade and a Communicator: Communicators enable change, while Comrades consolidate the status quo.

Contribution

Pawns are the team experts. They are good at recruiting people for causes and maintaining their franchise with others over time. Their motto is, "Make new friends and keep the old."

Verbally, you can spot Pawns because they:

➤ Ask a lot of questions to get others engaged.

➤ Particularly ask the "Who" kinds of questions, putting the team together and building constituency.

➤ Listen, paraphrase, and reflect feelings.

➤ May not be quick to disclose what they want; they often want to say things, but they are afraid to.

➤ Engage in small talk frequently.

Nonverbally, Pawns give off numerous clues to their nature:

➤ Their steady and even speech tempo.

➤ Their relaxed body language. "Hey, I'm nobody special, but I know who I am."

➤ Active listening: nodding and attentive posture. They are listening to you the way they wish people listened to them.

➤ Low volume; Pawns are not screamers.

➤ A casual but conforming appearance. A Pawn's office is likely to have family pictures, personal mementos, and plants.

Luring Pawns to the transcompetitive side:

✓ Engage in small talk. "How 'bout that game/the weather/the action movie?" Open up first to allow them to relax with you.

✓ Draw out their points of view. Listen for and reflect their feelings. Pawns are shown so little respect that yours will have impact.

✓ Clarify what is needed of them and offer your support.

✓ Work hard to maintain your franchise with them. Pawns want to like you and for you to like them.

✓ Take a sincere interest in their hopes and concerns. Show that you care.

Recognizing and Dealing with Tricksters

COMPETITIVE ARCHETYPE *The Trickster*	TRANSCOMPETITIVE POSSIBILITY *The Entrepreneur*	COLLABORATIVE MANIFESTATION *The Negotiator*
Tricksters are not automatic villains, but their talents are associated with treachery and craftiness, with the characters of Iago in <u>Othello</u>, Odysseus, and Jacob in the book of Genesis. Their great talent is their ability to control appearances—and sometimes to mask intentions. The type includes stand-up comedians, poets, artists, people who, lacking the power to bully their way to satisfaction, find it through circuitous means. Manipulation is their solution to the problem of mistrust. A twisty line best describes their relationship to goals.	In between the Trickster and the Negotiator is the Entrepreneur. Entrepreneurs draw on the talents of manipulation and multiple perceptions to notice and take advantage of opportunities that others might miss. They see the possibilities. Their value to any organization is to push the envelope of the acceptable, to challenge upward and open new vistas. They can also drive senior management nuts with their ceaseless energy. They stuff the suggestion boxes and respond well to the recognition they so desperately need to survive.	The collaborative side of the Trickster, the Negotiator uses a natural manipulative ability to view all sides of a problem. They are good at wearing others' shoes and therefore understanding differing perceptions of the same issue. This ability, when mastered via training, serves them well as negotiators and facilitators in times of crisis or stress. Negotiators are a valuable class unto themselves, even when they do not metamorphose into the more proactive Entrepreneurs: The world has too few people blessed with empathy, imagination, and evenhandedness.

Contribution

Tricksters are the communication experts, the silver-tongued devils who can make you see a thing 12 different ways and appreciate each one. They are enthusiastic influencers of others, and they play us with great skill. Nuance, style, slant, perspective, and fine shadings are everything. They believe that anything is possible if the imagination is put in service to it. Their motto is, "It's not just whether you win or lose, it's how you look when you play the game."

Verbally, you can spot Tricksters when they:

➤ Talk about their thoughts and feelings. Feelings are the reality of these soulful twisters.

➤ Tell stories and share anecdotes. If a consultant tells you that your story is your business, you have a Trickster for a consultant. But then, aren't they all?

➤ Describe things. They are so drawn to adjectives, descriptive phrases, and metaphors that they occasionally lose track of the point they are trying to get across. There is great charm in their language, but also great potential for distraction.

➤ Digress from the point at hand. They are less like arrows, shooting straight to a target, than like rivers, gently wending their way to the sea.

➤ Ask the "Why" questions: What is the rationale? What makes us want to do this? They are like actors forever pestering their director to understand their motivation.

➤ Persuade and sell. Half of the time they are persuading you in order to persuade themselves. But they are nature's sales force, eager to bridge communication gaps with insight, empathy, and words.

Nonverbally, Tricksters give off several clues to their nature:

➤ They speak quickly. Their words are surfing a wave of emotional propulsion, and if they slow down they will wipe out for sure.

➤ Animated, dramatic gestures and facial expressions. Think of Walt Disney enacting his vision of *Snow White* to animators. A shaman painting pictures in the fire is a Trickster through and through.

➤ Lots of vocal variety: inflection, volume, nuance; again, the Trickster as thespian.

➤ Smiling and head nodding. Agreement is built through sympathetic response and affirmation. ("Are you with me?")

➤ Stylish and fashionably current in appearance. Or sometimes a slob, but a slob for calculated effect.

➤ Kinetic, always in motion, lots of high energy.

➤ The Trickster's office will be stylish and maybe a bit flamboyant; or it may be somewhat cluttered and jumbled; look around and you're sure to find toys and cartoons.

Luring a trickster toward the transcompetitive side:

✓ Cut your material down to the high-level overview and present it in a lively way. Spend extra time to add zip to your presentation.

✓ Follow their lead. Engage in socializing when they do. Go to what interests them in your material. Go off on tangents with them, then bring them back to task gently if you must.

✓ Hit them where it matters. Think through what's in it for them and focus on that. What is the "why" for them?

✓ Involve them in a dialogue. Listen to them; *really* listen.

✓ Praise and support their ideas. This is not a bad strategy for all four types, but it hits home especially hard with Tricksters, who can feel underappreciated in the middle of a standing ovation.

✓ Provide an action plan, then seek their buy-in. These are people of adjectives, not verbs. *You* must supply the verb.

The Fruit of the Pineapple Tree

Grafting the transcompetitive habits

Before you go about blending the best of competition and the best of collaboration, you need to know which aspects of each are best. To that end, we've compiled a couple of short lists describing what the best times to compete are and the best ways to go about competing.

To Compete Successfully

➤ **Compete outward, not inward.** If you must ride into battle, do it against people who are not your colleagues, allies, and friends. There is no excuse for eviscerating your own people for the competitive joy of it. As General Electric's Jack Welch said, "Kill ABB. Kill Westinghouse. But don't kill the person at the next desk."[1]

Picture the universe of competition as a series of concentric circles, like a target. Proper competition occurs as far out on the circle as possible. Better to compete with another company than with a division of your company, with outsiders than insiders, with strangers than friends.

➤ **Pick your battles.** Compete where it makes sense, and when it makes sense. Listen to what McKinsey consultants Joel Bleeke and David Ernst say:

> Instead of competing blindly, companies should increasingly compete only in those precise areas where they have a durable advantage or where participation is necessary to preserve industry power to capture value.[2]

➤ **Shorten expectations.** Win/lose has an inherently short fuse. No sooner does one contest end than another begins, and the more you win, the better prepared your next opponent will be. The lament of the aging gunslinger applies here: "There is always a faster gun." The first question a World Series winner is asked is, "Can you repeat?" If victory is what you seek, be content with the short term—there's nothing wrong with it.

➤ **Have a tangible goal.** Competition turns sick when it becomes personal or the reason for it is unclear—when it's a compulsion, not a choice. Like compulsive gamblers, compulsive competers embarrass themselves when goals fuzz over and competing itself becomes the point of all interactions. You must have a point besides winning. Compete for something, not against someone: a trophy, a payout, recognition, a commission, a promotion, a respite from other competition.

➤ **Calibrate your firepower.** Don't take an elephant gun to a turkey shoot. Don't take candy from babies. But avoid Pyrrhic victories while you're at it. Choose goals that are achievable but still worthy of you. Amount of force should be proportional to need.

➤ **Know when to stop.** Alexander wept when he realized he had conquered the world. It's difficult to stop fighting once you have drawn blood, but pointless to continue after you have obtained the resources you set out to win.

Successful gamblers know when to fold. They put a limit on both ends of the scale: a limit to losses and a limit to winnings. Most of us can put a limit, say $200, on our losses. But when we are winning we think luck has taken over and we'll continue to win. Of course, the odds are always with the house, so stop at $200 or you will lose more in the longer term.

➤ **Don't cheat.** Fairness is important. If you're not being fair, it isn't competition, it's a rigged game. And if you're found out, as usually happens over time, the game will turn violently against you. Everyone may like a winner, but when cheaters are found out, as Ivan Boesky, Dennis Levine, and Martin Siegel are in the 1980s Wall Street insider trading scandal, they were disgraced, imprisoned, and eventually shunned—driven out of the tribe and left to fend for themselves. Tricksters forced to become Hermits, they will never compete again.

Swearing off dirty tricks isn't a moral issue, but a rational one connected to business success. Raising the price of umbrellas during a rainstorm will result in an easy short-term win. Angering future customers with your opportunism will make you a bigger loser in the long term.

➤ **Defend yourself.** When a competitor gives you no choice, don't hold back. But beware of the psychology of the preemptive attack—hitting them back before they hit you first.

➤ **Remember your humanity.** Competition is about obtaining resources (money, food, recognition), not bashing in the brains of your competitors. Healthy competition recognizes the connections between things, even as it seeks advantage for itself.

➤ **Chill.** Competition works when participants exercise restraint. Keep your eye on the ball, your objective. Do not go off on emotional tangents. Do not spike the ball, blow smoke from your finger, dance in the end zone, or taunt your opponent by insisting that you're number one. This is more than good manners, it is a matter of survival. You do not want to give whoever you just beat the motivation to come roaring back at you with everything they've got.

➤ **Collaborate.** Paradoxically, the best competitors in nature, business, and sports are those who recognize the value of teamwork in achieving objectives. In sports, the winningest teams are those that demonstrate teamwork. In business, the companies that prosper longest are those that adapt to the environment they compete in and find ways to allow all sides to do well.

To Collaborate Successfully

➤ **Choose wisely.** Collaboration is only valuable if the people collaborating are competent and are the right people for that task. What good is it to share crummy expertise?

➤ **Plan.** Collaboration can't overcome bad planning or a bad idea. Managers would like for teamwork to make all their decisions look good. But when that fails, guess who gets the blame.

➤ **Know why your team exists.** Teams lose perspective on their reason for being. They are not a team because they make a great team. They are a team because there is a job that needs doing and they are the best people to do that job. Collaboration is not the job; it is just the means for doing the job.

➤ **Choose wisely, Part II.** Teamwork requires character. Bad people—people who like to deceive, to cheat, to manipulate—make lousy collaborators. A team of supercompeters or go-to guys is not likely to be much of a team. Someone still needs to go to them—to pass the ball, to plan, to knit the task together. The trick here is to mix the fire of competition with the slick coordination of collaboration.

➤ **Beware of the star system.** You can't encourage collegiality if some colleagues matter and others don't. Leaders must make clear at the outset that the team rises and falls together, regardless of the heroics of individual members.

At the same time, individuals must be given their due. Teams that allot all rewards on a group basis teeter on the brink of communism—a brittle leveling that is a disincentive to individual excellence. Let your best people know their excellence is a treasure to the team, and encourage them to help make the rest of the team as good as they are.

➤ **Hide.** Collaboration occurs best when no one is looking. Teams operating under hot lights tend to melt. If you want to encourage collaboration, get people together, explain the job, and then leave them the hell alone.

➤ **Clarify.** Collaborative relationships are not managed, therefore the onus for role and goal clarity is on every member. Touch base for the purpose of clarification early and often.

➤ **Be prepared to wait.** Collaborative decisions take time. Group work is time-consuming. Sorry, that's just the way it is with the collaborative process. On the other hand, time is a transcompetitive treasure—continuous winning occurring over extended periods of time.

➤ **Draw dotted lines.** Successful collaborations rely on fill-in team members who contribute small but critical bits of technical or other information.

➤ **Be leery of technology.** Collaboration feeds on information. Teams kept in the dark waste quickly away. While networking can link a team across the globe, the linking is not as high-quality as the linking achieved by a team that lives in one another's face.

Computer and software systems, e-mail, Lotus Notes, and EDS constitute only a small part of this information, however. Use the best technology available and affordable to you, but do not let it become your information system. This system is best conducted not through wires and silicon but from one person to the next, and across such considerable barriers as rank, distance, mistrust, and interteam competitiveness.

➤ **Think small at first.** We are misled by our technology to think we can do business with one another across great gulfs of space and cultural disparity. *Global team* is an oxymoron. Teams can overcome great obstacles of physical distance, but first they must overcome obstacles of misunderstanding and group culture. Successful teams pretend they are close together even when they are not, and welcome everyday confusion and disagreements as a way to surface differences and deal with them.

➤ **At ease.** Teams need time off. The idea that teams are united at the antennae like ants, subject to the continuous electrical sparking of ideas and collaboration, is goofy. An extra hour of sleep is worth three additional hours of meetings.

➤ **Install an OFF switch.** When the task is completed, the team loses its reason to team. Disband them and form new teams to address the next job.

➤ **Compete.** When your customary mode is to collaborate, competitive action is a breath of fresh air, like a lifelong vegetarian biting into a burger—but be careful, as this makes some vegetarians throw up. It is a paradox, but collaboration thrives when individuals are acknowledged along with the group. Do not set people against one another, but remember that they all have egos and need victories.

Which Is Better?

Is it better to position oneself as a competer or a collaborator? Neither. The best position is rationality—to work one's way through difficulties on the basis of what you want and need, not the stance you wish to be remembered for.

The supercompeter at the party who bores everyone with tales of great deals bagged has been shut out of ten opportunities for every deal that was rammed mercilessly down a buyer's throat. The supercollaborator missed out on all eleven—hardly a prescription for success.

So be rational. Identify your baseline goal (the highest cost, in dollars, effort, and goodwill, that you can live with) and the other side's baseline goal (the lowest total price they will accept without bursting into tears).

Not every deal can be a win/win, but you can easily avoid deals whose long-term costs—loss of goodwill, damage to reputation, guilty feelings—outweigh the short-term advantage.

The rational way to do business is transcompetitive. How to graft the two themes into a powerful whole is the topic of the next section.

Mixing and Matching

One of the curious achievements of the human race has been genetic manipulation. Until Johann Gregor Mendelev discovered the principles of genetics in the 1840s, playing with pea plants in his monastery garden, and horticulturists like Luther Burbank later put these genetic insights into practical application, people left plants and animals alone; our role was to be their stewards and caretakers.

But once we learned it was possible to coax certain qualities out of species and to graft the best with the best, we became an acutely creative race of creatures, playing god with every other species. Broccoli was cheerfully crossed with cauliflower. Tomatoes were bred that could survive weeks in the back of a truck. Eventually we cloned sheep.

In our native Minnesota the sour *riparia* or riverbank grape, which can survive winters as cold as 80 degrees below zero, was crossed with tastier grapes from California and France. The resulting wines are no threat to the fine wines of the world, but they boast great shelf life. The way these wines taste, they need great shelf life.

Great shelf life is what you want your business to have.

Transcompetition is a graft. Imagine combining two very dissimilar trees—a pine and an apple. Get them to grow together as one and you have some interesting options:

PINE	APPLE
Grows wild.	Human-managed.
Pine cones survive fires to 800°F.	Apples good for pies, cider, applesauce.
Great at long-term survival.	Great at short-term production.
Process.	Results.

One tree bears edible fruit and the other produces nothing but pine cones. One is thorny and coniferous and evergreen, the other enjoys a beautiful cycle of leafing out, blossoming, bearing fruit, losing its leaves, and then (apparently) dying. A rational combining of the benefits of such a graft (a pineapple tree?) would obtain the best qualities of each: an incredibly hardy tree bearing edible fruit year-round. A bad combination of qualities, on the other hand, would result in less favorable characteristics: Imagine enjoying a slice of pine cone pie with cheese.

Think of transcompetition as the grafting of fruit from the two trees of competition and collaboration. Each tree has fruit that's good and fruit that's not so good. Your job is to combine the best of both trees, the best attributes of each approach, for the task currently facing you.

TRANSCOMPETITIVE VIRTUES
MIX and MATCH

COMPETITIVE ATTRIBUTES	COLLABORATIVE ATTRIBUTES
The will to greatness	The will to commonality
Focus (inwardness)	Empathy (outwardness)
Persistence	Insistence
Results	Process
An apptitude for play	An appetite for work
Opportunism	Consistency
Depersonalization	Personalization
Monopoly	Sameness
Loose	Tight
Killer instinct	Survival instinct

➤ **The will to greatness vs. the will to commonality.** The best competers are keyed to win for the best reason: to be the best at the task before them that they can be. It is a natural pull that is part of their personalities. People given naturally to sloppiness and apathy never experience this "will to greatness" unless they are the beneficiaries of an electric jolt to the seat of their pants. Many impressive leaders have been driven by the will to greatness. John Kennedy's style and rhetoric typified this kind of leader, exhortative, demanding, optimistic: "Be all you can be." Dick Gregory comes at it from another angle: "Just because you're common doesn't mean you have to be ordinary." The will to greatness seeks to put daylight between what is common and what is better. It is restless and quick to raise objections. The will to greatness, given free rein, becomes pure win/lose thinking.

The will to commonality, however, may be an even greater innate trait. It seeks to find win/win solutions, looking for common ground even when positions seem cast in stone. Like the will to greatness, the will to commonality is a talent some people are born with and most people must struggle to attain.

➤ **Focus** (inwardness) **vs. empathy** (outwardness). These are valuable but nearly opposite skills. The serious competer is capable of focusing on the task at hand to the exclusion of nearly everything else. It explains why an Olympic skater can be so good at the triple Lutz and so uninformed about etiquette and common decency. Almost all our business, technological, and athletic advances are made by people able to put everything out of their minds but the challenge they have set for themselves. If focus is *in-vision*, fixing on a single thing, empathy is *omnivision*, forever scanning the horizon for more to understand, from the outside in. Which is more important or transcompetitive? The one that is weakest in you.

➤ **The persistence of a serf vs. the insistence of a star.** They are as different as conquistador and native.

The star performer is constitutionally insensitive to difficulty. The type ignores setbacks and denies failure. Getting people like this to do what you want is like herding cats. The serf or compliant participant, by contrast, is easy to control. You tell them what to do and they are glad to do it. Their difference in outlook is total.

The star sees himself or herself as an adventurer in an alien landscape, on a mission to succeed at all costs. The star succeeds by an act of the will or heroism. The serf, who is much more sensitive to difficulty, finds virtues in defeat. The serf is a survivor at all costs, not seeing himself or herself as being on any mission, but as the property or prop of a familiar landscape, surviving by staying put.

Asked which is better, most companies will say star performers. But think again: Who is usually still around after the smoke of battle subsides—the company that knows it belongs? In business, star performers (Steve Jobs, Michael Milken, Henry Kaiser) come and go. The greater successes are the almost personality-less companies (Hewlett-Packard, Citicorp, United Parcel Service) who hunker down and vanish into the markets they serve.

Can an insistent leader manage a persistent organization? Maybe, but we can't think of one.

➤ **Results vs. process.** A results orientation is an attentiveness to the *what* of business: tangible prizes, quantifiable results usually involving quarterly return or percentage of market share. But a results orientation imposed from above is simple tyranny: "Give me my results and don't tell me how you do it."

The tyrant is seldom competent to describe meaningful results for every part of an organization. The tyrant in Rumpelstiltskin ordered the miller's daughter to spin straw into gold, little reckoning the havoc bales of gold would wreak on the precious metals markets, not to mention the disposition of the king's own heir-apparent.

Though process, an attentiveness to the way things are done, may seem less competitive, it is in fact much more competitive over the long term. While a results orientation leverages gimmicks (straw into gold, restructuring, outsourcing), a process orientation leverages meaning: What can we do to align our operations with our values? While the results organization chases dollars headlong until it stumbles, the process organization pursues purpose. And because it has purpose, it stumbles less often.

➤ **An aptitude for play vs. an appetite for work.** Play gets less respect in business circles than Rodney Dangerfield does anywhere.

Thomas Edison epitomizes the American work ethic with his famous dictum: "Success is 1 percent inspiration and 99 percent perspiration." You would deduce from this that Americans are compulsive toilers. But anyone who has wandered through a successful modern office knows 99 percent is a pretty high estimate.

Indian poet Rabindranath Tagore has a more luminous epigram: "The lord respects me when I work, but he loves me when I dance."[3]

Clearly, the aptitude for play, for "messing around," has always been the foundation for our inventions, improvements, strategies, and ideas, from Newton's apple to Alexander Fleming's bread mold to Art Fry's Post-it Notes discovery for 3M—a sticky substance that wasn't *too* sticky.

There is even reason to suspect play is the necessary precondition to successful work. Hirotaka Takeushi and Ikujiro Nonaka say that *tacit knowledge* (transferable knowledge) doesn't happen in a group until its members first develop intimate structures for sharing *implicit knowledge*. Thus do Japanese businesspeople strive to knock down social and competitive barriers through alcohol, bathing in hot springs, karaoke, and golf. Americans are less rigid to begin with, but they have always seen the value in bowling leagues, team parties, and company picnics.

There is a developmental twist to this. Humans are the slowest animals of all to mature from babyhood to adulthood, and for an interesting reason: Immaturity appears to be vital to our nature. Our need to play is probably hardwired into us, and while it fades with age, few of us overcome it completely.

Play and business have always been intertwined. We all think of the business bon vivants like Malcolm Forbes or Virgin Group's Sir Richard Branson going up, up, and away in their respective balloons. Work hard and play hard is the motto, and it occurs at lower levels as well. Companies like 3M have senior scientists whose sole responsibility is to play, working on projects that interest them apart from the applications the work might be put to. Honeywell hires project managers to comb through the trashcans of its play pens to examine the work underway and to identify applications for it. Southwest Airlines' motto looks for happiness at every level: "Have fun, but ensure the joy of those around you."

Imagine what human culture would be without this streak of childishness; imagine the effect on innovation, art, entertainment, and humor. Imagine a party at which everyone is "grown up."

For many of us, transcompetition means abandoning the pain principle of advancement for its diametric opposite, a pleasure principle of work for the fun of it.

➤ **Opportunism vs. consistency.** Capitalism is founded on the spirit of alertness: Whoever exploits value first is rewarded most. The entrepreneur is the visionary who sees future value while the crowd mills around items considered valuable yesterday. The leader is also a kind of entrepreneur, only instead of seeking material value he or she seeks human value, extracting the best effort that people can give. These are competitive virtues that no naturally collaborative soul can do without.

Consistency is also a virtue. The elimination of variation is a cornerstone of total quality management; it is the reason inspectors stood alongside production lines for years with calipers in their hands. But consistency for its own sake[4] quickly gives way to fetishism and obsessive-compulsiveness—dotting every *i*, sanding down every burr.

➤ **Depersonalization vs. personalization.** Personalization is the talent for communicating in such a way that the person you are talking to feels the message has been custom-tailored to his or her understanding. In an organizational culture that ignores individuality, personalization is a precious skill.

But depersonalization is also very powerful. It is the ability to see a thing without regard to its effect on you. It is wonderfully liberating to take oneself out of decision making. When detachment comes in, out go paranoia, disrespect, and the blindness that so often accompanies self-interest.

➤ **A knack for monopoly vs. an attraction to sameness.** Monopoly means doing something no one else is doing. We should say *mini-monopoly*, because the most successful monopolies are those willing to stay small. Yet another name is niche-making, the art of uniqueness.

The phenomenon occurs first in nature. On the eastern slopes of the Sierra Nevadas, four chipmunk species (the alpine, the lodgepole, the yellow pine, and the least chipmunk) all vie for the same nuts and berries. But they do not compete head to head, because they divide the terrain into four habitats, according to altitude.

Birds do it, too. In a single oak tree, three species of English tit have established niches. The blue tit resides way up in the upper crown. The marsh tit lives in the lower crown. Meanwhile, the great tit ekes out a living on the ground below the tree.[5]

People and organizations, as we shall see, are also practitioners of the art of niche-making, seeking pockets of opportunity where competition is reduced. It is the perfect alternative to destructive competition when resources are genuinely scarce.

Opposite niche-making is an attraction to sameness. Most organizations obey this urge to stay plain vanilla, to avoid detection by one's competitors by blending in with them. There is also the fetish of large organizations to impose conformity restrictions on workers and facilities. IBM in the 1960s and 1970s was the classic case of an organization in love with its own look and feel. The Big Blue logo appeared on every item, making it one of the fastest growing brands in the world. But look-and-feel came at a high cost: No division could release a product until it had been incorporated into other company technologies, or at least offered to other divisions. The cost was sluggishness and loss of technology leadership. Only in the 1990s was the company able to free itself of this value, spinning off formerly controlled business divisions like its Lexmark printers group.

➤ **Loose vs. tight.** Which structure is stronger, one that is elastic but encourages innovation and experimentation, or one that achieves coherence through the imposition of order? This is an issue not for individuals but for groups to resolve. Loose relationships like confederacies permit wider latitude for expression; but tighter relationships, unions and alliances, have the power to effectively guarantee compliance and uniformity. Let duration be your guide. If you are in imminent danger of destruction, tighten the bonds between yourself and others. If your survival issues are longer-term, loosen the line and encourage free minds to find solutions.

➤ **The killer instinct vs. the survival instinct.** Which brings us to the heart of the matter: how survival speaks to us from our characteristic location on the scale of connectedness. Some of us (Brutes) are equipped from birth with a natural rapacity, an ability to take what we need. Others are unable to assert ourselves as we might like, because it does not seem social or because we are afraid. The heart of transcompetition is to graft the conscience of the group onto the daring individual, or the tooth of a lion onto a timorous lamb.

The Transcompetitive Toolkit

Not every situation calls for you to exchange, encircle, and exact. Exchange, encircle, and exact is the process you use against worst-case offenders, supercompetitive predators, when all else has failed. Even in the info age, when it is possible to exchange more information than in previous times, the 3E's are not a lead-pipe cinch to work.

The more customary transcompetitive toolkit is stocked with less sexy, humble processes. They are all one form or another of negotiated settlement, deals you can cut with parties you are competing against in order to achieve greater success.

These approaches can be enlarged or reduced in scope to work at nearly every level, from the team level to negotiations between superpowers.

➤ **Censure and isolation.** If an entity refuses to play by civilized rules, have nothing to do with them. Whenever exchange, encircle, and exact fail to achieve the results you seek, you can fall back on its short-form cousin, censure and isolation. It is a form of shunning. You don't exact a change in behavior, but you signal in no uncertain terms that you are against it.

➤ **Arms talks.** When you are dealing with an obvious enemy, one with a supercompetitive orientation, the first thing you want to do is get the guns lowered. Nations conduct arms talks to achieve this end. Companies, teams, and individuals can also conduct arms talks. The guiding wisdom from the SALT talks with the Soviet Union in the 1980s holds true for us: "Negotiate, but verify." Individuals and companies can fashion arms agreements just as countries and alliances can.

➤ **Trade agreements.** Companies, industries, countries, and whole regions have negotiated agreements that encourage the sharing of information and the lowering of barriers. Spell out activities that will be condoned (benchmarking, talent raiding, non-compete clauses, litigation) and those that will not be (espionage, deception, cannibalism). Be specific.

➤ **Professional codes of conduct.** Every mature profession is aware that there are lines its practitioners must forbid one another from crossing. Pharmacists are not allowed to raid the controlled substances jar. Fisheries are not allowed to kill off whole oceans. Partners are not allowed to fix prices. Customers—yes, even they should be held to some kind of professional standard—should not be allowed to return merchandise after two years of use.

➤ **Free agency.** Sports learned long after other industries that it could open up a new era of fair treatment with the abolition of restrictive regulations. As Lincoln freed the slaves, you should free your people through the abolition of non-compete clauses, and your customers from entangling contracts. In the information age, no party will long endure confinement. Open the doors, before the people inside break out and come looking for you.

➤ **Bills of rights.** A bill of rights is a statement you create outlining general principles of power in a relationship. The U.S. Constitution added a bill of rights as a pot-sweetener to convince colonies that the new federal government was not going to snatch up powers left lying around. A good bill of rights is an empowering tool that tells customers, team members, shareholders, and other partners in broad outline what they can expect from you and what they can get away with.

➤ **Boundary management.** The problem with empowerment is that it is usually much too vague. Responsibilities must be spelled out with some specificity. If they are not, people will be doing things you don't want them to do, and not doing things you do want them to do. So spell them out in very specific terms. People will feel more secure and information will flow more freely.

➤ **Guarantees.** A guarantee is a bet you make with a customer, in which you essentially put a gun to your own head. "If I fail to come through for you, I will pay you." The customer can be anyone, from the end-customer to internal customers (other teams) to employees, suppliers, dealers, and even shareholders. The power of guarantees is that they promise good results, with a heavy penalty hanging overhead if the promise is not kept. The trick is to create a promise that is *specific* (that limits the failure to something nontrivial), *important* (you don't want to ensure something your customer doesn't care about), and *achievable* (no sense promising to blow your brains out if failure is inevitable).

➤ **Forgiveness.** When a partner lets you down, consider giving them a second chance. Often we betray one another without thinking of the cost. We do it because our internal needs take precedence over the external relationship. Don't be a doormat and invite multiple betrayals. But before you step onto the slippery slope of retribution and recrimination, consider explaining to the offending party how they hurt the relationship, and exact a promise not to do it again—laying out the consequences if they blow it again. You don't have to forgive everyone, especially the obvious predators and tricksters. But many times, groups that have the best intentions let one another down. Try again; it may save you from an expensive cycle of blame.

These tools are all intuitive. They are less about guerrilla action, in which the enemy is given one last chance before you open fire, than about sitting down and hammering out a solution that works for all sides.

The skills of transcompetition at this level are skills of negotiating. We don't have space here for a 90-day course on beefing up negotiating skills, but if you are interested, check out the bible on the subject, Roger Fisher and William Ury's *Getting to Yes* (Penguin Books); or Harvey Robbins' own *How to Communicate Effectively* (Amacom).

The New Versatility

There is no such thing as a guaranteed correct path to transcompetitive success, for several reasons.

The first is that there is no absolute right or wrong. A transcompetitive organization can look highly competitive or highly collaborative to the outsider. What makes it transcompetitive isn't the choices it makes, but the fact that it is making choices. Transcompeting means moving beyond the habitual to the rational, from reactive to proactive.

Put the transcompetitive virtues before you, pick and choose the ones that best complement your skills and predilections, and what you have conducted is an experiment in rational versatility.

Versatility is the ability to do many things. A versatile organization is one in which people know what other people are doing, and have mastered some of the basic skills of the people they work with. Instead of being squeezed into a narrow silo of functionality like accounting or engineering, throwing work over the wall to the next function when they are done with it, the walls are taken down and people begin peeking over one another's shoulders.

Think how much less time the engineer will waste on approaches that an accountant's mind-set would intuitively avoid. Think of the savings an accountant can achieve who understands the practical and well as financial implications of the numbers he or she is running.

Smaller companies have traditionally operated more flexibly than their larger counterparts because their people are ready to fill in as needed, across functional lines.

Versatility acknowledges that we cannot all be stars, but that we can all increase our value by being utility players, stepping from role to role as circumstances require. It is a collaborative skill providing a distinct competitive advantage.

Endnotes

[1] Remarks by Manfred Kets de Vries, The Masters Forum, Minneapolis, June 17, 1997.

[2] Joe Bleeke and David Ernst, *Collaborating to Compete*, John Wiley & Sons, 1993.

[3] Novelist Milan Kundera in *The Art of the Novel* completes the triptych with this addition, cautioning us against trying to reason everything to death: "God laughs when he sees me thinking."

[4] "The hobgoblin of small minds" was how Ralph Waldo Emerson put it.

[5] Robert Leo Smith, *Elements of Ecology and Field Biology*, Harper & Row, 1977.

Borrowing from Minneapolis to Pay St. Paul

Competition and teams

While you ponder a switch to transcompetitive habits and what that may demand, think local. If you focus on parts of your culture you can reach out and touch, you will be able to better comprehend your competitive culture and better able to give it a nudge.

In our case, we have a handy local example of how collaboration and competition can be mixed and matched—the Twin Cities where the two of us live.

They were never supposed to be "twin cities." They were settled seven miles apart in the 1840s for reasons logical to each: Minneapolis had a waterfall that could generate power, grind flour, and saw boards; and St. Paul, at the juncture of two great rivers, was a natural port. They gradually grew into one metropolis in this century, as people filled in the gaps between the cities. The closeness forced them to acknowledge issues of competition and collaboration more remote locales could ignore. The combination of the two helped create one of the more prosperous and progressive urban areas in North America. Though not the most exciting metropolis, the Twin Cities constitute an urban approximation of the principle of continuous winning.

Here are some of the ways the two cities bang their heads and put them together:

⟵ COMPETITIVE   COLLABORATIVE ⟶

⟵ **New Business.** The two cities compete against each other to bring in new businesses, jobs, and professional sports teams.

⇨ **Defense.** Old Fort Snelling, built between the two cities, made the area safe for settling and doing business.

↩ **Government Money.** The two cities have different congressional representatives, and the fight for spoils—bridges, highways, block grants—is often intense.

⇨ **Healthcare.** Minnesota helped invent HMOs in the 1920s. In the 1980s the state led in creating a health insurance plan for the poor.

↩ **Expansion.** Since the 1960s, Minneapolis sprinted ahead as a builder. Its downtown is an urban gem, while St. Paul's languishes.

⇨ **Education.** Minneapolis got the liberal arts and medical parts of the University of Minnesota; St. Paul won the farm campus.

↩ **Power.** St. Paul is the seat of government, but Minneapolis is clearly the source of more political clout these days.

⇨ **Community.** The Scandinavian tradition of sharing has always marked Minnesota politics, from barn raising to food shelves.

Generally speaking, Minnesota has been good enough at competing to keep its people employed without competing so well that it triggers a violent cycle of boom and bust, as occurs in other high-tech economic pockets—Silicon Valley, Boston, and Puget Sound, for example. While the region once competed solely on the basis of commodity plenty—lumber and grain—in our more shrunken world it maintains economic niche communities in agribusiness and the biomedical products industry. The new plenty, based on trading and inventing, is information-based: Because so many companies in these industries are clustered in the same area, there is a lot of expertise being shared from company to company.

Where We're Going

In a bit we shall see that there are limits on the region's collaborative goodwill, that its future vitality may depend on its ability to enlarge the circle of the known one more time. Meantime, it is as good an example of a transcompetitive "community of communities" as you'll find.

The Twin Cities never set out to be transcompetitive, of course. The rivalries of a hundred years ago continue, as the cities vie for bragging rights to scores of issues, from which city has the best ribs to which has the better lifestyle to which has the best parks and architecture, which newspaper arrives at the news scene first, whose high school basketball teams are best, whose citizens pay lower property taxes, and which city has the most cineplexes.

But these are all "competing on quality" issues, a noncannibalistic competition that challenges but does not destroy. It is a kind of competition that often brings out the best on all sides.

The next few sections will focus on transcompetitive challenges between different levels of entities. As we move from one to the next, they will telescope in dimension, from the very small and local to the very large and global:

➤ competition among and between teams;

➤ competition between unequal partners (your company and its suppliers and dealers);

➤ competition between equal partners (alliances and confederacies);

➤ competition among constituent groups (workers, customers, shareholders);

➤ competition among very large companies and entire regions.

At each level it is necessary to run a connectedness check to determine whether culture and practices are currently too competitive or not competitive enough, and to design systems that allow a more balanced and more rational way of doing things.

As we step from stone to stone, we will hearken occasionally to the example of the two cities in Minnesota whose fates are intertwined.

Comfortable Space

Take teams. A Portland, Oregon real estate developer we recently met, believing we were team freaks, asked if it wasn't true that people need to be on teams as a fundamental human hunger, and that teams need to be with one another, to colocate, to share physical space with one another, in order to function. He wanted us to say yes because that would justify his building a 200-office corporate office building (one office for each team), instead of the 125-office building that was probably more appropriate.

We said, well, yes, sort of. Among the ordinary human desires is the desire to socialize and to work together. It strikes most people as an empty experience to do something good and have no one to share it with or show it to. People not only crave company but they crave company that is like them. True team members are like family; when teams don't gel, it is often because they cannot approximate this near-family feeling.

We were reminded of this requirement in January 1997, when the space shuttle Atlantis ferried astronaut John Blaha home after 128 days on the Mir space station. Blaha, clearly drained by his four-month journey in space, startled reporters with his admission that he felt "alone and afraid" among his Russian counterparts, who had been together for many months already and whom he had not met prior to his mission. His complaint sounds unastronautish, and not quite politically correct, but his words come from the heart:

> "After I'd been there a month, I was a little bit getting psychologically depressed," the 54-year-old astronaut said.
>
> Blaha said he would have liked private quarters on the station and a fellow American on board to talk with.
>
> NASA has tried to be sensitive to the psychological needs of the astronauts who have stayed on Mir after the first astronaut on Mir, Norman Thagard, complained of "cultural isolation" during his 115-day stay in 1995.[1]

What happened was that the cultural differentness of the Mir cosmonauts and the stress of being in a very strange place shook Blaha to his foundations. In space you want a team you feel absolutely comfortable with, and he had strangers. At home in the psychological comfort of his own surroundings, Blaha would have been able to reach out to his unknown partners. In the lonely reaches of space, his amygdala decided for him, painting them as strangers and thus vaguely negative. The fact that Russia's and America's hopes for the experiment were sometimes competitive exacerbated Blaha's sense of team unease.

Team unease—when people are forced to be a team before they really are a team—is a primary reason teams don't work. Competition can be an enormous hindrance to the formation of team solidarity. Teams that are exposed to too high a dose of it, over too long a period, are on the brink of nonexistence even when every member is still showing up for work.

To help an uneasy team become a team at ease with itself, you do not need to impress upon members a vision of beatific brotherhood and universal cooperation. You don't need to convince them they have no enemies. You only need to inform them that the enemy isn't on their team, or between your team and another, and show them the advantages to everyone of continuous winning.

Some Party

You may be familiar with the phrase *matched team*. That sounds like the kind of team we would like to be on—a team on which all members share the same interests and behavioral patterns.

The phrase comes from animal husbandry, referring to oxen. Oxen are gelded bulls, and a matched team is a pair or quartet of oxen with the same strength, and who pull at the same rate and in the same direction. With oxen, this matching was very expensive: When one team member was unable to continue, the other was often slaughtered as well, because it was not possible to train it to work as effectively with another team member.

So much for our wanting to be on a matched team.

In certain places in the Twin Cities along the route of Interstate 94, which stretches from Chicago to Seattle, are the visible furrows of the Ox-Cart Trail, which was the superhighway pioneers used to get from the east to the west, and when things went sour, back east again.

The best story we know illustrating the perils of unmatched teams—the people being pulled by the oxen, not the oxen themselves—began in the spring of 1856, in similar furrows in lower Illinois. One of the human teams went by the name of Donner.

The Donner party was a caravan of several Illinois teams, families mostly, who attempted to cross the Truckee Route in the American west in the winter of 1846–47. Had they made it intact to

California, they would have been among the first dozen groups of Americans to settle there. Instead, their fate is commemorated in a park a few miles from the casinos of Lake Tahoe, Nevada.

In this park is a set of shacks, hastily erected to ward off nightly four-foot snowfalls. Here, trapped by snow and cold, their resources and strength depleted, families squabbled, people boiled cowhides to stay alive, and a few resorted to the far points on the connectedness scale: cannibalism.

There was not an experienced trailblazer in the entire group of 90. Instead there were several families of farmers, Donners and Reeds and others who saw the move west as a sound economic move but were unprepared for the difficulty of the crossing, the severity of the winter, and the quickness of its onset.

It could be argued that what defeated the Donner Party was not the snows but their own infighting. A frontier guesstimator named Lansford Hastings assured them the Truckee Route could shave 400 miles off their journey. As is the case with many change initiatives, Hastings did not mention that the shorter route would be straight uphill. Their party did not arrive at the Utah flats until late August, and nearly died in the six-day push across the salt and sand expanse there.

Instead of unifying them, the desert experience splintered the party into bitter factions. At one point a fight broke out, and before he knew it, team leader James Reed stabbed and killed a man. Reed was banished from the group and from that point on, desperately needing unity in the face of marauding Indians, bad weather, and treacherous terrain, the two main teams seldom spoke. They were as distant from one another in the wilderness as John Blaha was distant from his Russian colleagues orbiting the earth.

When they finally took camp in what is now known as Donner Pass, they were only three miles and a half-day's trek from safety. As they huddled in their separate shacks, wasting away, they could reflect on the cost of their infighting:

> It was not merely the cold, for there was plenty of firewood and, at first, men to cut it; nor was it the hunger and malnutrition, for at first there were a few beeves, oxen, then the remaining few horses, mules, and finally, dogs. Their inability to accept discipline or leadership, the inter-family hatreds that pursued them right down to their deaths, so that there was never any sharing of food or hope

or comfort ... these caused their slow destruction; these deprived them of their strongest psychological weapon for survival.

Any one day would have saved them: one of the four spent resting at Fort Bridger, one of the five spent waiting for Reed to return from his trip to overtake Hastings, one of the seven spent pursuing Hastings' trail south and then north again, one of the five in the Truckee meadows, the last day's refusal to push the final three miles behind Stanton; one day that the devastating snowstorms might have held off. Or any of the innumerable days spent in quarreling, refusing to help each other, to share food, water, oxen, friendship, leadership.[2]

Teaming Frenzy

Your organization may not be boiling cowhides yet, but chances are the analogy holds up on these counts:

➤ Factions competing within your company are preventing it from meeting its goals with its true competition.

➤ Destructive behaviors like malicious compliance and miscommunication are costing you precious days in bringing products and services to market.

➤ Envy, paranoia, and lose/lose thinking threaten to leave your outfit as cold and hungry as the Donners, until no sordid deed—sabotage? cannibalism?—is unthinkable.

Turf wars occur when teams are unable to work as teams. The opposite problem is just as dangerous: team frenzy, the insistence that every function be performed by teams, not individuals.

A sure sign that teams are going to be with us to the end of time was the conversion some years ago of big city newsrooms to teams.

Anyone who has ever worked in a newsroom knows that the spirit of this kind of place is pure individualism and pure competition. Newspapers have always striven, often desperately, to scoop one another. Within newsrooms, reporters have kept secrets from one another, in the style of Lois Lane and Clark Kent.

For the past 25 years, however, newspaper readership has been shrinking, two-edition papers have been consolidating to a single morning edition, and many cities have wound up with virtual monopolies. The Minneapolis *Star* and Minneapolis *Tribune* merged into one paper, the *Star Tribune*, in the 1970s. Across the river, the St. Paul *Pioneer Press* and St. Paul *Dispatch* did the same. In each case, the blending of newsrooms and the creation of one big staff at each paper caused great consternation and resistance.

But that was nothing compared to the 1990s and the arrival of teams. Teams have been the biggest of all management fads, adopted by more companies than the sum of companies adopting TQM, reengineering, and the learning organization. Teams, as opposed to the hierarchical boss–worker line of command, soon assumed an air of inevitability. Businesses that had no business turning to teams did, with bizarre results.

The St. Paul *Pioneer Press* (to which Mike contributes a weekly column) adopted teams in a pretty conventional way. People were introduced to the idea and taught the new rules of collaboration, and pretty soon everyone forgot about the idea, except that reporters rely on one another more in the editing stages and editors and writers have worked to achieve a less adversarial, more mentor–student relationship.

Upstream in Minneapolis, the story was very different. A passionate and visionary publisher, Joel Kramer, who believes papers must radically recreate their relationship with a changing readership, set the paper on an irreversible journey into what its own reporters call "The Strangeness."

> Beginning last fall, teams of formerly independent reporters and copyeditors and photographers and graphic artists started to work in unfamiliar collaborations. Stories ... no longer fall into predetermined spaces in the paper but rather float through the newsroom in search of a place in tomorrow's edition. A new newsroom leadership exists on paper, but in practice almost nobody tells anybody what to do anymore.
>
> The old understandings—all the terminologies and work patterns and lines of accountability that traditionally defined the way journalism has been practiced at a daily newspaper—have disappeared in a bewildering muddle of faddish business jargon and woozy New Age management stratagems. The objective is to make the staff less beholden to a daily routine that has as its focus the production of tomorrow's newspaper—to open them up to new prod-

ucts, new channels of communication, to the end of their world as they have always known it.

Only two constants have persisted through the tumult. One has been management's continuing inability to explain to the staff and to the outside world what they are trying to accomplish and why—to demonstrate, in short, a logic lurking in the flux they've created.[3]

The number one rule of teams, as we pointed out in *Why Teams Don't Work*, is that they must have a purpose. It was not clear to anyone what the purpose of teaming was at the *Star Tribune*—they did it because they felt they had to try something to forestall the tough economic times they saw coming, as newspapers seem less and less necessary to busy and increasingly less literate people. Now they are so committed to the change process, there is no turning back. Though their problem is too much teamwork instead of too little, their situation is not much better than that of the Donner Party, hunkered in amid the high Sierras, watching the snow fall around them.[4]

Individual Differences

It helps greatly to assess team members to understand their proclivities, to see who are the potential Brutes, who are the subtle Tricksters, who are content to suffer Pawn-bashing, and who has emotionally vacated the premises, Hermit-style.

Every team is different. You do not know, as you are introduced to the people you will be teaming with, what the individual styles of each member are or what the group style has been up until that point.

Beyond that, teams become more transcompetitive, more optimal in their behaviors, more conducive to continuous winning, as they choose how they will act on the basis of meeting actual, identifiable needs, and get away from reflexive actions that repeat a competitive behavior because it is the only one they know.

It is not true that a team must cleanse itself of extreme types to function, to drive away supercompeters and supercollaborators. It is true that these types may pose a danger to team success if they are unable to graduate from a habitual to a more conscious way of behaving.

Teams and Turf Wars

Turf wars are wars between teams for the purpose of surviving. These wars can have several causes:

➤ **Mission bloat**, whereby two teams believe they share a mission and each believes the mission belongs exclusively to that team. The manager of a Texas aerospace company believed two vice presidents had a personality conflict. As it turned out, each vice president and the divisions each represented were given the same job. Faced with this kind of systemic conflict, even Buddha's disciples would break into a fistfight.

➤ **Handoff anxiety**, in which one team feels its work (and its future) is compromised when it is passed on to the next team. A French machine tools company had a string of turf wars up and down its manufacturing division, until a consultant observed that face-to-face meetings between processes—design, production, distribution—were rare. Everyone was throwing work over the wall to the next team. The result was that no team was sure it was doing what the previous team wanted or what the next team needed.

➤ **Death struggle**, in which a team is convinced it is unappreciated and destined for the chopping block unless it can divert the blame, and the axe, to someone else. A Yokohama shipping company announced a spate of imminent layoffs. Teams who had enjoyed meals and recreation together for many years suddenly became blood enemies.

Managers tend to dismiss turf wars as childish, but there is nothing childish about these problems. Each one is a life-and-death struggle and so pushes team members' buttons to the fully locked positions. From that point on the biological and economic mission of personal and team survival becomes more important than the mission the team was established to address.

When this happens, both the team and the organization they are part of are sitting in deep snow that is only getting deeper.

Endnotes

[1]Jeff Foust, "Astronaut Admits to Loneliness in Space," *American Reporter*, January 23, 1997.

[2]Irving Stone, *Men to Match My Mountains*, Doubleday, 1956.

[3]William Souder, "Welcome to the Fun House: Strange Days at the *Star Tribune*," *Mpls-St. Paul* Magazine, June 1996.

[4]Alas, the effort to instill unconventional collaboration and thus save the newspaper failed. In November, 1997, the *Star Tribune* was sold to the McClatchey chain of "Bee" papers—a notoriously conventional group.

Dead Men
and Headmen

Leading a team of competers

We've talked about problems within teams and problems between teams. We need to talk a bit about the problems of leading teams beyond competition.

Leading a team of strong competers often calls for a collaborative style of leadership. Collaborative leadership means being a coach, a cheerleader, a counselor, a taskmaster, a constant reminder of the goal, and a nag about best practices and good habits. More than anything it means constant attention and hard work. It is seldom glamorous and never glorious.

Anthropologist Marvin Harris describes the workday of a tribal taskmaster, or headman, of a group living along the upper Amazon:

> Headmanship can be a frustrating and irksome job. Among Brazilian Indian groups such as the Mehinacu of Brazil's Xingu National Park, headmen remind one of zealous scoutmasters on overnight cookouts.
>
> The first one up in the morning, the headman tries to rouse his companions by standing in the middle of the village plaza and shouting at them. If something needs to be done, it is the headman who starts doing it, and it is the headman who works harder at it than anyone else. He sets an example not only for hard work but for generosity. After a fishing or hunting expedition, he gives away more of the catch than anyone else; and in trading with other groups, he is careful not to keep the best items for himself.

In the evening he stands in the center of the plaza and exhorts his people to be good. He calls upon them to control their sexual appetites, work hard in their gardens, and take frequent baths in the river. He tells them not to sleep during the day or bear grudges against each other. All the while he carefully avoids making accusations of wrongdoing against a specific individual.[1]

Only team members imagine that team leadership is an honor. Team leaders—effective ones, anyway—know differently.

The Story of Digit

Leaders of native groups are lucky in one way: Their culture defines the role they must play. In our more freewheeling society where anything goes, leaders are left to their own devices.

When Dian Fossey worked with the highland gorillas of Rwanda in the 1970s, she discovered each individual had a distinct personality but each was committed to the happiness of the group. One young silverback, Digit, was so sociable he appeared on tourism posters, until he came to a grisly end at the hands of poachers.

It was Ian who found Digit's mutilated corpse in the corner of a blood-soaked area of flattened vegetation. Digit's head and hands had been hacked off; his body bore multiple spear wounds.

There are times when one cannot accept facts for fear of shattering one's being. As I listened to Ian's news all of Digit's life, since my first meeting with him as a playful little ball of fluff ten years earlier, passed through my mind.

Digit, long vital to his group as a sentry, was killed in this service by poachers on December 31, 1977. That day Digit took five mortal spear wounds into his body, held off six poachers and their dogs in order to allow his family members, including his mate Simba and their unborn infant, to flee to safety. Digit's last battle had been a lonely and courageous one. During his valiant struggle he managed to kill one of the poacher's dogs before dying. I have tried not to allow myself to think of Digit's anguish, pain, and the total comprehension he must have suffered in knowing what humans were doing to him.[2]

The lesson of Digit's leadership is that one does not always lead from the front. Digit was the derriere garde of an extremely peaceable, collaborative group, whose existence was threatened by the encroachment of highly competitive poachers. Collaborative by nature, Digit gave the last full measure of devotion to buy time for his team.

Silverbacks and Graybeards

But Digit's devotion was not enough. Ron Heifetz, author of *Leadership without Easy Answers*, describes[3] the shortcomings of leadership that operates, like Digit's, in a closed system.

Heifetz described the communal lifestyle of the same highland gorillas Fossey lived with. The gorillas live in bands of 15 or 20 individuals, always with a dominant male called a silverback because of the color of his hair. The silverback is silver because he's older, and he's more experienced than the others in the band. The silverback is a living example of traditional leadership—in charge because he's been around and knows the score.

He knows, for openers, where the berries are, and berries are big business for highland gorillas. In the morning when the gorillas wake up, they all turn to the silverback for direction. Eventually he too wakes up, thumps his chest, and they all follow him to the desired berry-picking site.

The silverback performs five basic tasks of leadership:

➤ **He provides direction** by helping the band find berries.

➤ **He protects the group** he leads. If a leopard is in the vicinity, the leader either gathers the band around him so that no stray gorilla can be picked off, or he leads them in bellowing and waving at the leopard until it slinks away.

➤ **He orients the group.** There is an order to the way gorillas move, with the silverback first, followed by nursing mothers, then older kids and males and females. Bringing up the rear is another adult male. When it is time to rest, the band waits till the silverback makes his nest, then they locate themselves in relation to him.

➤ **He mediates conflict.** Disagreements break out even among these peaceable creatures. The silverback reminds them that group integrity is more important than individual issues.

➤ **He models and maintains norms of behavior.** Gorillas aren't born knowing how to be gorillas. The silverback is the shaper of group behavior.

So the question is, are the skills of the silverback enough to keep the team he leads on track and alive? Yes, if the system is one that is finite and knowable. No, if new variables are introduced at random intervals. To the gorillas, the arrival of poachers with semi-automatic weapons was unforeseeable, and no existing defense mechanism—not clustering, or chest beating, or bush swinging, or face making—had any effect against the long bullets.

The moment a new situation presents itself—new market conditions, new technologies, changes in customer tastes, nuclear winter—the team must adapt. A silverback response will seldom be adequate. Think how much more of a hero Digit would be, and less of a tragic figure, had he been able to galvanize a new and effective response to the poachers, like hiding. But gorillas don't hide.

Presidential Vomit

Heifetz compares President Bush to the murdered gorilla when Bush, a lifelong free marketer and believer in competition, was manipulated by the Big Three automakers to perform the ultimate collaborative service to them.

In 1969 the balance of trade deficit was accelerating out of control, and U.S. carmakers were frustrated that Japanese consumers were not snapping up Chevys and Fords. Big Republican donors that they were, they manipulated Bush into traveling with them to Japan, not to lay down the competitive gauntlet ("Open your markets to our cars and we'll drop our barriers to yours") but to beg their number one trade rival to please, please sell more U.S. cars in Japan.[4]

It was a complete disconnect for Bush, advocating something he had opposed for his entire career. The Japanese were puzzled by the new face Bush was showing them. The men from Detroit were puzzled that Bush was not a better salesman for them. Perhaps it was this ideological contradiction that led to a fevered Bush vomiting in the arms of Japan's prime minister at a state function. In the struggle to lead people who would not be led to a mission he did not believe in, something had to give.

Broken Lance

Excessive competition is poison to teams because it erodes their sense of pride. When it is taken to its extreme, team members become not eaters of meat but the meat itself, too demoralized to function as they are trained and rewarded to do. When that happens, teams and the company they comprise go into a freefall together, the teams desperately needing a victory to sustain their sense of self, and the company blaming the teams for not being competitive enough. Recriminations, dismissals, and exhortations to extinguish the fires that are popping up everywhere only make matters worse.

Here is an example involving a friend of ours, whom we will call Lance. Lance is a divisional head for a Minnesota communications company. We know from our dealings of many years with Lance that he is a super-motivated, highly competent, very intelligent manager, with considerable personal charm.

But he is also an all-out workaholic Brute, desiring victory over his market competition so fervently that very often it is the most important thing to him. In the past 20 years he has headed half a dozen teams. Each time he has begun with a bright vision and tremendous personal commitment. Seventy-hour work weeks are nothing to him, and he naturally expects, as we all tend to, that the people he surrounds himself with will share his rabid appetite to win.

Lance has worn out and depressed every talented group he has assembled. Everyone starts out as teammates and friends, high-fiving and pledging up-against-the-wall competitiveness. But no one can match Lance's foaming-mouth intensity for long, and the products he competes against are not much different from his own—he has created no secure niche in which to do business. So there is really no opportunity for victory. Instead, blaming sets in and it quickly becomes personal. Soon an important teammate loses his or her status as go-to guy or gal and from then on is seen as an impediment or, worse, someone consorting with the enemy. Something that began healthily becomes quite sick.

Our own friendship with Lance has been downgraded over the years because he has seen us, ultimately, as cut from a less sturdy bolt of cloth than himself. In a pointless war of self-destructive competitiveness, we were not go-to guys.

The future for Lance, for all his competence and industry, is uncertain. He lives in a wonderful big home, but he can't relax in it. He is on his umpty-umpth team now. They keep getting younger and easier to inspire, program, or dominate in the early going. But his reputation as an eventual cannibal precedes him into relationships even with these neophytes. None plan to be with him long, just long enough to pick up the credential and search for greener pastures—among Lance's sworn enemies.

Lance's personal charm does not make him any more lovable to the teams he tyrannizes. Nor does it bolster the muscle tissues of a heart that has been diagnosed as overworked from the stress and tension Lance visits upon it.

Our hope for Lance is that he will find his path to a more transcompetitive, less compulsive way of working. We suspect he will always be a supercompeter; it is in his blood. But he must know that a longer-term success and life are possible if he can master his need to be master.

Vertical Competition

People on teams engage in destructive competition. Whole teams do battle with one another, to no positive outcome. Worst of all may be the competition between lord and laborer that has deepened in the winner-take-all economy.

We call the competition for profits between managers and workers *vertical competition*. Executives negotiating huge salaries and bonuses argue that their leadership is the key to company profitability, and thus, job creation. Workers who have seen their salaries and job descriptions frozen, or worse, scaled back, wonder whose side of the game the CEOs are on.

In 1996 the average pay raise for top executives was 54 percent, compared to a typical 3 percent boost for factory workers, according to a *Business Week* survey. That means the average CEO paycheck, with stock options, incentives, and bonuses included, was 209 times that of the average worker. The average CEO's salary at 365 companies was $5.8 million.

> At the top of the pack is a relative unknown, Lawrence Coss, chairman and chief executive officer of Green Tree Financial Corp. of St.

Paul, Minn., who brought home $102.4 million last year based on 2.5 percent of Green Tree's pretax income.

Andrew Grove of Intel was second with nearly $97.6 million, followed by Sanford Weill of the Travelers Group, nearly $94.2 million; Theodore Waitt of Gateway 2000, $81.3 million; and Anthony O'Reilly of H.J. Heinz, $64.2 million.

The switch to more stock options was supposed to make CEOs seem tethered to their companies, assuaging stockholders about where the chief executives' priorities lay.

"It's a soothing lullaby, but shareholders are starting to wake up to some sour notes," the magazine wrote. "The CEO's gains often exceed the company's own strong year proportionally ... options have hidden costs and are diluting those gains to the tune of tens of millions of dollars."[5]

CEO pay is a structural problem. In current business fashion, companies build themselves around superstar managers and so feel compelled to pay superstar salaries. In a world in which basketball players and rock stars make even more, it is not hard to justify.

But think of the morale problems such salaries inevitably cause. Even Disney, putatively the "happiest place on earth," is groaning under the weight of Michael Eisner's $200 million compensation package. Even *The Wall Street Journal*, no enemy to executive aspirations, wondered aloud about where the salary component of the Brute Cycle would end:

With even weak CEOs pocketing gigantic gains last year from the long bull market, boards—and some chiefs—have begun to ask the once unthinkable question: How rich is too rich?[6]

Endnotes

[1]Marvin Harris, *Our Kind*, Harper & Row, 1989.

[2]Dian Fossey, *Gorillas in the Mist*.

[3]Remarks by Ron Heifetz, The Masters Forum, Minneapolis, March 4, 1997.

[4]Ibid, Heifetz.

[5]Associated Press, April 10, 1997, reporting on an April 21 *Business Week* story.

[6]David Sarasohn, "How rich is too rich?" Newhouse News, appeared in the *Star Tribune* April 29, 1997.

Pain and Partnering

Why intercompany teaming seldom works

We are seeing a proliferation of new relationships between companies: partnering, strategic alliances, virtual organizations, and other arrangements. Some of these are bursting with potential; others (like virtuality) are flawed from the human engineering standpoint, because the wiring connecting the far-flung parts is too fine to convey the full of range of knowledge—the intuitive and cultural along with the factual—required for success.

Some companies don't set out to be partners, but they are stuck with the fact: The nature of their businesses lashes them together inextricably for life.

➤ One company is an inevitable supplier to another (US Steel's metal for Isuzu's cars, Canon's disposable drums for Hewlett-Packard laser printers, ConAgra's grain for General Mills' cereals).

➤ Two organizations team up to provide one another's services and thus broaden their service base (a printer partnering with a graphic design firm, a bank partnering with a mutual fund family, an airline and a ground transportation provider).

➤ Some companies are the delivery or marketing or licensing or manufacturing mechanism for another (local bottlers for Coca Cola, auto showrooms for Volkswagen and Audi, local affiliates for television networks, the New York Stock Exchange for member companies).

➤ An anchor company sells partnerships to franchisees (Subway, Jenny Craig, Firestone, Starbuck's, the National Football League).

➤ Companies form alliances with one another to solve problems neither can solve by itself (Apple and IBM working on a new chip).

➤ Organizations from different spheres team up to do things impossible in one sphere alone (NASA and Martin Marietta, Japan's Ministry of Trade and Information and Japanese manufacturers, Mexico's nationally owned energy company, Pemex and consultants from the world of commercial oil and gas).

In each case, partnership assumes an open boundary between once-sealed organizations. Partnerships fail when the boundary is too open or when it is more open for movement in one direction than in the other. When the urge to compete occludes the advantages of working together, partnerships fail.

Howdy, Pardner

The word partnership sounds easygoing. It conjures up images of cowpokes poking along the high chaparral together, providing one another with defense, complementary skills (cookwagon, branding, roping, blacksmithery), and companionship.

But it necessarily involves tension.

The idea of intercompany collaboration is not new. Most businesses have always enjoyed close relationships with a few suppliers or dealers. What is new is the extent to which partnering has increased both the number of these relationships and the closeness between them. Many companies, like Chrysler and Eaton Corp., or Airborne Express and its corporate partners, or just about any company and its provider of temporary employees, are so inextricably partnered that there is only a dotted-line difference between them. They share information systems. They share office space. They share leadership. They behave like a single company.

It is a stretch to call Chrysler Corp., an ocean liner's ocean liner, a model of flexibility. Yet it has seized on a substantial value differentiation from the other two American car companies by outsourcing, of all things, the design of its cars.

Chrysler has turned over substantial responsibility for auto design to Eaton Corp., and in true partnership fashion shares both credit and the profits with its suppliers. This stands in sharp contrast to the devious practices the industry is accustomed to, in which suppliers submit ideas and GM or Ford reverse-engineer them, paying nothing. GM's putative savior, J. Ignacio Lopez de Arriortua, is said to have set back supplier relationships ten years in six months with his brutal treatment.

Now, for the first time, Chrysler has the design advantage. Suppliers happily part with their best ideas, knowing they will not be ripped off. Chrysler saves hundreds of millions in infrastructure costs—and the designs for its Neon, Ram pickup, and Viper are winning awards by the armful and new customers by the carload.[1]

But partnerships do not always result in a happy or consistent company.

Partnering Pratfalls

True partners must learn to behave as if they were one company, and that means getting beyond the old win/lose mentality and adopting a win/win mentality. Partnering cannot succeed if one party is preying on the other.

➤ **Some equals are more equal than others.** When a bigger hub partner promises to let you maintain your identity, check your wallet. When Canadian newspaper giant International Thomson wooed New Jersey trade publisher Peterson's (our publisher at one time), Thomson promised virtual partnership and a strict hands-off policy regarding operations. Within six months, every person we knew at Peterson's was gone—quit, canned, or missing in action. Equal doesn't mean much when one equal buys the other one all of its food. Inevitably, the larger (and usually more predatory) culture will dominate the smaller.

➤ **Add their problem to yours.** You may be three years into an ISO 9000 registration plan, but your new hub partner wants you to do the Baldrige assessment as well. To get on the same page with your partner, you will either have to force employees through two mind-wrenching regimens, or dump one that people were committed to.

➤ **Sell the farm.** Many companies have partnered themselves into the intellectual graveyard, spinning off competencies that lay too close to the core. Kodak lets IBM do its data processing, which is fine. But Chrysler and Toyota both farm their auto designs to design partners. If they can continue to do that and still be seen as car companies, they will have redefined their industry.

➤ **Strings attached.** When Control Data restructured in the 1980s it created a partner to perform human relations tasks and charged it to market its skills to the outside world. Before letting it go, though, it crippled the new creature by saddling it with units that could not pay their way, putting a major drain on the new entity's prospects.

➤ **The carnivorous collaborator.** Most outsourcing is done to cut costs. By retaining high-value competencies while farming out lower-value competencies, an organization signals that the partner is little more than a sweatshop, working its people to the bone while the hub partner buys another ten years of the good life.

➤ **No one said partners can't be mutually brutal.** Some of the more frightening alignments occur when two giants team up to kick everyone else in the ass. In the summer of 1997, *The New York Times Book Review,* publishing's most influential journal, joined with Barnes & Noble, publishing's most powerful retail outlet, to form an online link. Reading the review, one is invited to buy the book—from a single vendor, Barnes & Noble. The combination of highbrow influence and discounting moxie sent a wave of fear through the nation's independent booksellers.[2]

➤ **How convenient.** Many partnerships move accountability outside the hub organization's control. You say your offshore partner uses prison slave labor, or makes Bangladeshi kids work 12-hour days? News to us. File this tactic under "plausible deniability."

They Can See You Now

The most celebrated recent case of wobbly partnering involves talk show host Kathie Lee Gifford and revelations that her line of women's wear clothing for Wal-Mart was outsourcing production to a Dickensian Honduran subcontractor—a sweatshop. In May 1996, Gifford went on national TV to issue a tearful denial that she was making money at the expense of Honduran children. (She was not alone. In June of that year, reports surfaced that Michael Jordan's line of Nike sneakers were made by children in Indonesia working for 19 cents an hour.)

> At a news conference held Wednesday (5-28) on Capitol Hill, a fifteen-year-old girl told of abuses in a sweatshop in her native Honduras that made clothing for retail giant Wal-Mart's Kathy Lee Gifford line of clothing. Wendy Diaz said about 100 minors as young as 12 years old worked 13 hours a day for a wage of 31 cents an hour in the factory. She spoke of verbal and physical abuse by employers toward the children, as well as sexual harassment and intimidation to keep them working until 6:30 a.m. at times.
>
> Diaz said the Global Fashions company tried to force pregnant women to quit in order to avoid paying maternity leave, forcing the women to stand for 12 hours in the heat of the pressing room. Workers were only allowed two trips to the bathroom all day, and were fired if they tried to organize a union.[3]

Because of the ties to big names like Kathie Lee Gifford and supercompeter Michael Jordan, the child labor issue lurched back into the public eye. But the problem of child labor is nothing new. It is as old as the idea that winning is worth anything, even the health and happiness of those least able to compete.

The contrast between the breezy glamour of Gifford's lifestyle (recall her singing "If you could see me now" for Friendship Cruises) and the squalid exploitation of her production partner could not have been greater. Newspapers and Gifford's own talk-show colleagues pulled the Brute Cycle response on her—they exchanged information, encircled her with the broiling power of media heat, and exacted the most humiliating retribution.

To the credit of her public relations advisors, Gifford turned the scandal around by becoming a champion for fair wages and decent working conditions at third world partners, on camera at least. But the lesson was plain. Partnering in the years ahead isn't going to be the same old, same old, with the anchor partner calling every shot and the junior partner bowing and stooping and claiming to like it.

Musketeers, Watch Your Backs

In the big game, opportunities for betrayal are everywhere. Consider the knots in the relationship Compaq shares with Intel.

Compaq has struggled to maintain its position as the number one maker of PCs, and throughout this period it has sought to portray itself as the third corner of an essential technology triangle: Intel providing indispensable microprocessors, Microsoft providing indispensable software, and Compaq providing what they hope is indispensable hardware. They were like the Three Musketeers, all for one and one for all.

Never mind that Compaq has always yearned for a cheaper supplier of chips, and that Compaq provides no essential value that other clone makers do not also provide. Or that Intel and Microsoft are both past masters of the brutal art of isolating companies who threaten them, as Intel showed in the spring of 1997 when it cut off shipments of chips to Digital Equipment because Digital allegedly incorporated into its Alpha chips proprietary features of Intel chips.

But see what happens when Compaq messes with a fellow musketeer. In 1996 Compaq struck a deal to buy cheaper chips from Cyrix Corp., a maker of knockoff Intel-type chips. Within hours, Compaq CEO Erhard Pfeiffer was getting reamed out on the phone by Intel's Andy Grove.

> Andy Grove was not pleased. Intel and Compaq had supposedly turned the page since a bitter public feud two years earlier soured their relationship. But now it was back to the future.
>
> "If you help my enemy, you are my enemy," Grove supposedly told Pfeiffer.
>
> Whether the story was apocryphal or not—it's since made the rounds at Compaq—the episode underscored the brittle relationship that still exists between the two industry giants.
>
> The last rift between the two companies occurred in September 1994 when Pfeiffer played the role of Don Corleone. Standing up at an industry conference in Spain, Pfeiffer declared that Compaq was fed up with Intel, reciting a litany of complaints in front of an astonished audience.

The relationship improved for a while, but hit the rocks again when Compaq started buying from Cyrix. Intel turned the tables by offering (Compaq alleges) Pentium chips to *its* archnemesis, Packard Bell, at below-market cost.

> "They knew we were coming out with the Cyrix stuff so they cut a deal with Packard Bell," said a Compaq source. "Those guys can be pains in the butt."

Over the years, a variety of industry executives have grumbled, sotto voce, about Intel's aggressive tactics. In the back of their minds, executives say, they know Intel can exercise a carrot-and-stick discipline.

"You might not get shipment allocations on time, or they could cut you down a tier on pricing," said a Compaq source. "They can make your life impossible."[4]

Compaq, a supercompetitive company in a supercompetitive industry, is not known for playing footsie with its other suppliers. But its relationship with Intel is so critical to its future it has been forced to swallow its pride and go along.

Franchise Frustrations

A franchise is a way for very small players to enjoy some of the clout of their bigger partners. For a few thousand dollars, individuals can buy into a large marketing organization's identity. In a happy franchising partnership, the anchor partner supplies the franchise partners, both sides play by the rules, and everyone is happy.

Sometimes the anchor partner breaks the rules. Carvel Ice Cream Bakery of Connecticut lured many hundreds of franchise owners in, promising them exclusive territories, only to turn around and sell their products to competing retail stores. Carvel franchisees revolted, hiring an expensive lawyer to fight their anchor partner in court. So much for that one big happy family.

In North Carolina, a judge ordered Meineke Muffler to pay its franchisees $601 million to repay money the company had collected for advertising but had pocketed for itself. Other franchisees, including Dairy Queen, 7-Eleven, and Little Caesar's Pizza Shops, have taken arms against their parent partners, for offenses ranging from one-sided contracts to problems with location to overly restrictive rules and regulations.[5]

Franchisees are grappling to understand the rules of engagement in the transcompetitive age. Can an anchor company and its franchisees work together toward a common goal? Or are franchisees constrained by the need of the anchor company to win in the relationship?

It Isn't Such a Wonderful Life

Partnering also occurs between corporate entities, and cultural differences between business units cause many stresses and conflicts. Sometimes partners collide not because of competitive practices but because of their opposite, collaborative policies.

Comedy Central announced plans to make a spoof of the holiday movie classic, *It's a Wonderful Life*. The parody would show George Bailey, the character played by Jimmy Stewart, as gay and wanting to star in action movies. Perhaps they could have lured George Clooney to play Bailey, with Robin Williams subbing for Clarence, the angel trainee. Doesn't that sound like a sure hit?

But in November 1996, Comedy Central said it was dropping the plan. The reason? The original movie is still owned by Republic Pictures. Comedy Central did not even realize that it and Republic were both owned by the same media conglomerate, Viacom, Inc. Republic, for some strange reason, was not eager to sell the rights to its greatest treasure for an inane spoof.

Rather than step on the toes of a partner it did not even know it had, Comedy Central canceled a sure moneymaker.[6] This was a gesture of collaborative solidarity: one partner forsaking sure advantage rather than step on the toes of another.

The remake of *It's a Wonderful Life* would doubtless have been a crappy movie, but a moneymaking one. But the story points out the handcuffing potential of partnering. Independent companies do not feel constrained by the rights and traditions of other companies; they compete unaware of these limits. If you were a shareholder of Viacom, would you be happy to know one division lost money because of the druthers of another?

Endnotes

[1] Remarks by Michael Treacy, The Masters Forum, Minneapolis, April 11, 1995.

[2] George Beran, "One for the Books," St. Paul *Pioneer Press*, August 18, 1997.

[3] "Honduran Girl Exposes Sweatshop Abuses," *Feminist News*, http://www.feminist.org/news/newsbyte/may96/0530.html.

[4] By Charles Cooper, "Intel and Compaq: Punch and Judy till the end," *PC Week Online*, April 10, 1997.

[5] "Franchise Flare-Up," by David Segal, *Washington Post*, April 24, 1977.

[6] Associated Press, November 11, 1996.

Red Rover, Red Rover

Linking arms with one's enemies

When we were in Brazil in September of 1997, an executive of a plastics company asked us a poignant question:

"How do you collaborate with someone you have always considered an enemy?"

The question is especially tough when the enemy is someone you have been doing battle with for years: a company you have held rallies to taunt and denounce, that hired away some of your best people over the years, and that obtained inside information about your company and its plans.

There is no love lost when elephants do battle, but much grass is trampled. Patching together a peace afterward is no sure thing.

The problem is especially acute in a society like the United States, where supercompetitiveness is given free rein, where there are no collegial keiretsus or chaebols (Korea's equivalent of the Japanese network) setting ground rules for combatants, and where corporate cultures vary widely.

Apple and IBM

Head-to-head warriors Apple and IBM were given very little hope of success when they entered into a joint venture with Hewlett-Packard in 1992 to create a common operating system, nicknamed *Pink*, and sure enough, the project was a bust, even after spinning off the new technology to jointly-owned Taligent Corp. The venture cost the three companies $100 million, and ended in squabbling over who would get what.[1] But despite the predictions of many industry observers, the reason for the failure ultimately had little to do with the clash of corporate cultures.

Apple had always defined itself as the opposite of whatever IBM was. If IBM was East Coast, suit and tie, middle-aged, and business-savvy, Apple took pains to be West Coast, jeans and T-shirt, twentysomething, and more interested in technology than business.

Taligent went belly up, and no one ever made a nickel off Pink. But the collaboration proved a powerful point to the two former competitors and was the genesis of a new kind of relationship between the two companies.

First, the two companies found out they are *both* global and *both* middle-aged. The cultural differences were not so important as people thought they would be. Second, the two staunch competitors had a reason to come together: to join forces to hold off an even more fearsome competitor, Microsoft, that had stolen IBM's dinner right off its plate and treated the Macintosh standard with condescension and contempt.

The operating system joint venture went nowhere, but it laid the groundwork for a more profound alliance involving microprocessors. Eventually, Motorola, IBM, and Apple would join together to create the PowerPC chip, which came the closest of any chip in the mid-1990s to competing against Intel's Pentium chip. And IBM and Apple would find common cause with a large number of other companies that were alarmed at the Microsoft/Intel relationship: Novell, Netscape, Adobe, Sun Microsystems, Symantec, and ADM. In effect, they became an American keiretsu, joined arm-in-arm to defend themselves against a common enemy.

Collaborative Rationalization

The answer to the question, "Why should competitors collaborate?" is that they do it out of self-interest. Nemesis wars are wars of assured mutual destruction. Unless the competition is fixed (you hit us, then we hit you, but we take pains not to actually do one another any damage), head-to-head competitors exact a terrible toll on one another in resources, resilience, and rationality. It becomes a habit, and not a happy one; from that point on it is simply a game in which two dummies slug one another.

When enmity is high, rationality is low. You must rein in these extremes or you risk going over the deep end.

It seems heretical to say this, but even in the din of battle, nemesis competitors need one another. Apple and IBM, even as they struggled to outdo one another, profited greatly from one another's existence. Apple inspired IBM to participate in the small systems market, and IBM legitimized Apple's participation in it.

If there is no battle, consumers may never know about your product. The Apple/IBM war was a spectator sport, and millions of people around the world looked up to see how it was going—more than would have tuned in to an informational commercial about the Apple II.

Head-to-head competitors have found that they can compete while at the same time cooperating on marketing initiatives. In Mike's sleepy urban neighborhood of Merriam Park in St. Paul, there is a street called Selby Avenue. For years, a handful of antique dealers and furniture restorers were scattered along the length of three blocks. Antiquing is a low-margin business, but the people who go into it want to succeed as much as anyone. The shopkeepers will tell you that when a customer went into one shop instead of theirs, they bit their knuckles out of jealousy.

It was not until 1996 that they decided their competition was a blessing. They formed a merchant's alliance with one another and renamed their stretch of the neighborhood Antique Row. They painted murals between the shops, promoted joint events, and reached out to any nearby business that had a tangential interest to join them—coffee shops, bike shops, used clothing shops, a bank. Now when a customer goes into one shop instead of another, the proprietor may still bite a knuckle. But at least the customer came to Antique Row. Chances of each merchant getting a visit from that customer are much greater than if the customer had never come by.

Come On, Baby, Do the Colocation

Colocation is a phrase that arose from collaborative practices of the last few years. Teams function better when they are in physical proximity to one another (within reason). So whenever possible, if the personalities and schedules of the principals mesh, they are put together to work.

Colocation works best when it is done with respect for team differences. Putting a bunch of avid supercompeters together in a room may make for interesting viewing from behind a two-way mirror, but quickly turns into a frenzy of high-fiving.

"Putting them together in a room" is poor colocation, anyway. Most people need some degree of privacy. Visioning teams as a barracks experience in which everyone inhales everyone else's exhalations is an invitation to team ennui, not to mention the need for room freshener.

More interestingly, however, colocation works just as well among fierce external competitors as among internal team members.

Consultant and author Michael Porter is regarded as a god among competitive strategic thinkers. All his books have *competitive* in the title.[2] One of his latest uncovered the peculiar insight that competitors do better, and reach a new plateau of intraindustry collaboration, when they colocate in the same zip code or locale.

It works within countries as well. Thus New York is the center for advertising, publishing, and finance; Amsterdam for diamonds; Seattle for aircraft equipment and design; Milan for shoes; Cleveland for paint; Britain for high-performance cars; Carlsbad, California for golf equipment; and Minnesota for biomedical instruments.

Companies need to be aware of and influence this geographical determinism. If you want your region to be competitive, invite in other competitors. Take an active role in improving local infrastructure and schools. Work with associations to strengthen intercorporate bridges and to speak to government in a single voice. For its part, government can provide stability, predictability, an economic vision, and assistance in building industrial clusters.

The first paradox is that in a global world, locale still means something. Not only do companies do better in some places than others, but they do better by marketing locally to the different needs and tastes of those markets.

The second is that companies compete better when they are surrounded by competitors. "Trust networks" can spring up laterally when professionals from different industries work in the same area.

Identifying Gaps

The main reason enemy businesses are reaching out to one another is that there are gaps in the competition—markets where the two organizations are not engaged in struggle with one another. Where these gaps exist, or where a compelling other reason exists, such as joining together to fight an even more despised enemy, opportunity also exists.

It happens often at the large corporation level: Apple and IBM and Motorola deciding to make a new chip; the Defense Department and McDonnell Douglas and a thousand other large weapons subcontractors collaborating; Hitachi of Japan and Olivetti of Italy, agreeing to open up markets to one another in their respective continents; NEC of Japan and Bull of France joining together to get NEC in the mainframe business; Peugeot and Renault's decision to make electrical cars together.

It occurs at the smaller company level as well. Paragon Decision Resources is a 60-employee service company based in Irvine, California that specializes in relocating people. It also publishes a newsletter about employers for employees, and another newsletter about employees for employers. Many of Paragon's employees work at client sites, working out details for people who must move from one locale to another, buying and selling homes, solving problems relating to schools and eldercare.

But Paragon, which often competes harshly against other relocation firms to win jobs, often turns around and gives referral business to the same competitors it beat out or that beat it out. Why? Because they often have areas of strength that Paragon can't match, such as local real estate know-how.

It doesn't matter to Paragon if they hand off occasional small jobs to competitors, provided the end-customer is still happy it contacted Paragon first. The long-term customer relationship, not the sideshow competition with other firms, is where Paragon's best interests lie.[3]

"And why not?" asks *Wall Street Journal* columnist Thomas Petzinger, Jr. "Competition and collaboration are merely two aspects of the same wealth-creation process." While the mantra of business used to be "location, location, location," Petzinger said, "those days are gone. Now it's 'connection, connection, connection.'"

Transcompetitive Tips

There are five strategies for hammering swords into transcompetitive plowshares.

➤ **Trustbuilding.** Lifelong rivals have ample reason to be distrustful. Each side knows things the other side desperately needs to know. So long as the atmosphere is contaminated by this distrust, there is little chance of working together effectively. Sharing information communicates the idea that mutual gain is a possibility—that I don't have to succeed by making you fail.

Does this mean that the transcompetitive company promptly hands over all sensitive information to prospective partners? No.

It does mean that negotiators must prioritize their concerns. They are not at the table to keep secrets or to gain personal credit for being tough, but to make good deals. If sharing information moves the process forward, it is a sensible strategy.

Likewise, if the objective of partnering is to create opportunities that would not otherwise exist, both sides will need information to work from the biggest picture possible. Without information, there can be no collaboration.

The whole idea of partnering is to agree to be open—to imagine that the walls now dividing you are gone. That's why you must meet in the transcompetitive zone, where you fight for common ground but verify everything.

➤ **Inquisition.** The ideal partnership is one in which you already have all the information you need—then you don't have to worm it out of your partners. The problem is that your data about them are never as good as their own data about themselves. Their data are more accurate, more reliable, and more balanced. Why not just ask them, pointblank, for the information?

You may say, "Why should my competitor answer my questions?" The answer is that your chances of getting information are greater if you ask than if you don't ask.

True, your prospective partner may not want to divulge information on sensitive issues, such as the cost of capital, what their alternative plans are, etc. But by giving them a chance to divulge, you learn what points are sensitive to them, and that is valuable information too.

When dealing with a lifelong adversary, it is very difficult to keep an open mind. It is easy to get distracted by hostile challenges or thinking of what you will say in reply. At such times it is critical to favor listening over replying.

➤ **Uniting.** Alliances require some sort of structure, whether it is tight or loose. Most collaborations between equals are loose, with every measure subject to the approval of every member of the alliance, or the measure doesn't carry.

This form is called a *confederacy*, and it is the preferred American way of uniting, going back to the strong feeling Americans have for local control. When American Indian tribes united as in the Adirondack area in the eighteenth century, they formed loose coalitions. The United States' first government was based not on the Constitution but on the Articles of Confederation—which some scholars suggest was based to some degree on the Algonquin Indian confederacy. When the Civil War began, Southerners reverted to this loose format. (It is noteworthy that government by the Articles had to be replaced by the tighter federal constitution, and that the South, which lacked the ability to tax itself as part of its confederate structure, lost the war.)

Authorities disagree on the issue of loose vs. tight coalitions. Economist Lester Thurow believes that the European Union will have a big advantage over NAFTA because unions are tighter and better able to police themselves. The natural fractiousness of Americans will be their undoing. Others say the opposite: that a quarrelsome, individualistic union will be more flexible and more open to new ideas. Confederacies like St. Paul's Antique Row are probably the best way for small players to compete against their corporate cousins. The form has extended the lives of independent grocers in the IGA chain, the coop members of Farmland USA, the family of franchisers in the Hardware Hank family, and the various statewide associations of independent bankers.

➤ **Disclosure.** Give something valuable away, some tidbit of information that shows you mean business. Strange things happen when you divulge information. You can see it in the expressions on the other side's faces: astonishment, relief, something close to joy. Not the lawyers' faces, though—never look a lawyer in the face.

We're not saying Coke should blurt out its sales strategy to Pepsi, or that McDonald's should confess to Burger King the ingredients of its secret sauce. But there are things they are dying to know that will cost you nothing. Why not tell them, to get the ball rolling? You will likely find that the gift is reciprocated. If it isn't, slow down. Their hesitation is a sign they are not as ready do work together as you are.

➤ **Exploring.** The biggest mistake rivals make in partnering is building a firewall around the partnering project. Instead of protecting the enterprise against further partnering, you should be looking for other areas to collaborate on. The catastrophic alliances that make news are those that limit their interactions to such a narrowly defined pilot that they are swamped by the bad blood that dominates the companies' historic relationship. The cure for bad blood is new blood—new ideas, multiple projects, the support of a broad base of leaders on both sides.

Endnotes

[1]Linda Picarille, "Investors may pull Taligent plug," *Computerworld*, October 2, 1995.

[2]*Competitive Advantage*, Free Press, 1990; *Competitive Strategy*, Free Press, 1993; *The Competitive Advantage between Nations*, Free Press, 1995.

[3]Thomas Petzinger, Jr., "Joe Morabito Beats the Competition with Collaboration," *The Wall Street Journal*, February 7, 1997.

Competing
with Employees

More tales of corporate cannibalism

There are many companies today that have bent over backward to make the people who work for them feel like part of the business. Empowerment, participative management, profit- and gainsharing, quality circles, and open book management all send the message to employees that they matter, that they are a valued part of the overall team, and that success for the enterprise and their own personal successes are intertwined.

United Airlines was perhaps the biggest organization to send this message, when its employees bought 55 percent of the company's stock in July 1994. The acquisition was a tradeoff, because workers had to give up $4.8 billion in wages and benefits. Symbolic of the new arrangement was the removal of the heavy glass doors separating the executive office area at the company's Chicago headquarters.

The United buyout became the largest employee buyout ever, and it has proved a success as United stanched the flow of red ink ($800 million in the previous three years) and expanded service on two continents. The buyout was a terrific example of a business and its people joining hands for long-term success.[1]

Business Week described United's takeoff as the fruit of an unthinkable collaboration between workers and managers:

> For example, after the buyout a group of pilots, ramp workers, and managers devised a simple way to use electricity instead of jet fuel when planes are idling at the gate, thus saving the airline about $20 million a year. The only capital investment required was longer ladders so the ramp workers could plug in the electric

cables. "In the past, we would have sent out an edict and nothing would have changed," the executive in charge of fuel explained.[2]

But many companies compete against their own people. They lose sight, whether at the businesswide or departmental level, of the goals of the business, and focus instead on the emotional goal of not letting hired hands get the better of them. From that moment on, the relationship is hopelessly adversarial, with employees seeing the employer as a brutal ogre and the company seeing employees as untrustable upstarts who must not be allowed to win.

Sometimes companies are so competitive that they reach out across death itself to score the last goal. Here's a story of benchplay worthy of Robert Grisham:

> An elderly widow was allegedly handed a bill for more than £12,000 [$19,645] by the firm of solicitors her son worked for, after they went to his house and found him dead. Irene Brierley, 80, of Henley-in-Arden, Warwickshire, was said to have been charged £150 for being told her son, a solicitor, was dead and an extra £300 for his firm to identify his body at the mortuary.

> Searching his office to sort out affairs cost another £750, and £5,799 was charged for writing 172 letters and receiving 64. The total bill from the legal firm James Beauchamp of Edgbaston, Birmingham, came to £12,278.16, it was claimed.

> Mr. Bryant's sister, Melanie Weerdmeester, said: "He was a very well respected lawyer. He was unscrupulously honest, he was just a very, very fine professional." Mrs. Weerdmeester, 45, of Snitterfield, Warwickshire, added: "He was just totally honest and loved the law, that was his life."

> Mr. Bryant, who graduated with first class honours from an Oxford masters degree, was a former chairman of Moseley Rugby Club.[3]

Competition against employees varies a lot from culture to culture. Few cultures draw the line as firmly as China. Nobody, but nobody, makes the system there look ridiculous. Ethicist Thomas Donaldson tells the story of an American manager operating in China who caught an employee stealing. Thinking she was doing the right thing, and that it would be wrong to interfere in a local matter, she reported him to the local authorities. Later, she was aghast to discover that the employee had been taken out and shot for his crime.[4]

Relationships decay in Canada, too, though with less fatal results. In February 1997, Wal-Mart, which enjoys an extraordinary price partnership with its customers worldwide, demonstrated a less than perfect partnership with its workers in Ontario. The provincial Labor Relations Board overrode a vote by one store's workers and ordered United Steelworkers certification for all Wal-Mart employees at a Windsor store. What made this reversal noteworthy is that it was the first time Wal-Mart, with a global chain of almost 3,000 stores, had ever lost a labor dispute. Since it was founded in Arkansas by Sam Walton in 1962, Wal-Mart has defeated every attempt to unionize. Wal-Mart's initial response: Close the store rather than deal with workers.

At the heart of the dispute is a paradox. On the one hand, Wal-Mart is a big believer in financial incentives. Though it pays its associates bottom dollar, it rewards them with stock ownership and talk of empowerment. But heaven help the employee who takes empowerment to the logical stage of negotiating working contracts. In 1994 the company had paid $15,000 to settle a complaint by a New Hampshire store clerk who was fired for trying to organize coworkers.

> "I can't believe we won," said Mary MacArthur, a worker at the Windsor store who helped lead the organizing drive. The union argued that the May vote was not a free expression of opinion. Marie Kelly, a lawyer for the union, said Wal-Mart managers had left the impression that the store might close by refusing to answer questions about what would happen if the workers voted for certification.[5]

The best evidence that companies compete actively against their own workers is the practice of downsizing. Between 1985 and 1995 some 22 million jobs were cut from Wilshire 5000 companies, all in the name of becoming more competitive.

Many of these companies used restructuring to reinvigorate themselves, and ultimately hired back as many as they let go or more. A more common experience, however, was that the company expected the people remaining after the downsizing to pick up the slack and be more productive; but they weren't.

People don't compete well when their supply of confidence and self-esteem has been reduced to zero. But Brute companies, seeking to extract victories wherever they can—even at the expense of their own team—keep flicking the restructuring switch. One definition of insanity is to keep doing the same thing, hoping it will work when it has never worked before. Bludgeoning employees in order to free up their competitive spirits must surely qualify.

Competing through Non-Competes

One of the more demoralizing trends in recent years has been the rush to hang non-compete clauses onto employment contracts. The trend is a sick side-effect of our metamorphosis into a knowledge economy. Companies are finally recognizing that their employees are valuable because of their skills and knowledge base. But instead of treasuring employees for this reason, companies are imposing career limitations on them.

Consider the case of a lowly reporter for *MplsStPaul* magazine, a regional magazine about personalities, lifestyles, and the arts. Hayes and other writers were informed that the new publisher, former owner of a law book publishing company, expected people to sign non-compete statements if they wanted to keep their jobs. The clauses forbade them from taking their inside information to other publishers within two years of leaving the magazine.

Hayes balked. Minnesota is a small media outlet, and the non-compete clause effectively made him an indentured servant—he couldn't leave, and thus he lost all negotiating leverage. The clause was a career-killer. Hayes, 42, saw the move for what it was, a chance for the magazine to bottle up all available talent and keep a lid on the price.

> For his part, Hayes thought the MSP non-compete contract was preposterous. Though Hayes was among *MplsStPaul*'s most competent writers, he did not consider himself a "marquee name"—like the news anchor and radio personalities frequently bound by such contracts—and denied his absence would cost the magazine substantial readers.
>
> But Hayes said he knew little of consequence about his employer, *MplsStPaul* magazine—certainly nothing of value to a competitor. "They wouldn't even tell me where the copy paper was," he said.
>
> Hayes, 42, was making slightly more than $28,000. What Hayes and his colleagues did have, according to his former employer, was a new kind of workplace currency: Knowledge.

"There is nothing more proprietary than intellectual property," said Gary Johnson, chief operating officer for MSP publications. "Our assets are the brains of the people who sit in our offices. We do not make widgets, we produce information."[6]

And so it was that the new publisher, surrounded by attorneys, cast a noose around the necks of the people they purported to value.

Non-compete clauses have been around for a long time, but they have typically been confined to holders of mission-critical knowledge, for example, people in product development or sales management, who could deliver a devastating blow if they went to work for a head-to-head competitor.

But the new trend is to throw the rope around the necks of less critical employees, like Hayes. Employees who decline to pledge allegiance to the company can legally be denied yearly raises, promotions, and other benefits.

The irony is appalling: First the company says these people are corporate treasure; then it herds them into a doghouse. Later, the company will wonder why the creative types inside don't seem happy and aren't putting out like they used to. Perhaps they lack competitive fire.

The employer's view lacks no such fire: Whether employee fears about non-competes are legitimate or not, said *MplsStPaul*'s Gary Johnson, competition forces companies to implement them. "We'd be crazy if we just sat there and let rivals cherry-pick off our staff," he said.

A transcompetitive company would direct this fire at the external competition, not at its own people. In the words of Hayes: "They are trying to manage by contract, which is the easy thing to do. The harder thing to do is to win people's trust so they don't want to take another job."

Networks of Trust

Francis Fukuyama, author of *The Last Man and the End of History*, calls transcompetitive relationships *trust networks*—any relationship between individuals or groups of individuals whose continued success requires that they minimize mutual suspicions and security measures.

A trust community can be any group of people bound together by an ethic more compelling than profit or self-interest: one's ethnicity, one's religious heritage, one's professional code of behavior, one's political ideology, or one's commitment to the broader community.

That's why architects, because of their professional code, conform to building standards more stringent than bottom-line requirements.

That's why in certain industries, collaboration across corporate lines is common: in Silicon Valley, 80 percent of bosses once worked for Fairchild Semiconductor. That commonality of origin creates a network of trust within the industry.

That's why, in Little Tokyo as a boy, Fukuyama heard his father explain why he bought a hammer from a Japanese-American owned hardware store, instead of getting a cheaper one from, say, Sears: "I trust the Japanese merchant."

That's why friends within an organization, from different functions or divisions, share information in advance of official notice by the company. *Something more powerful than the hierarchy takes precedence over it.*

In flat organizations where workers supervise themselves, such trust networks are critical. When Saturn or Toyota empowers individual workers on the manufacturing line to shut down the line, it is saying that it trusts the workers to use good judgment. A work environment riddled with distrust, by contrast, is one ripe for employee sabotage.

Likewise, in virtual corporations, it is essential to trust the outlying members of the partnership, even though they are out of sight. Without this trust, the spontaneous organization will sputter to a stop.

A trust network is not a substitute for a hierarchy, but a supplement to one. All organizations properly partake of both the formal mechanical model for organization and the informal biological one.[7]

Because they are informal, trust networks reduce transaction costs, such as negotiating, contracting, litigating, enforcing, etc. The New York diamond market is an example of this. "People move diamonds around as if they were pinto beans," in Fukuyama's phrase, with relatively minor worries about security.

Where does the trust come from? Nearly all the market's participants are Orthodox Jews of the same sect, so the odds of one cheating the other are low. Consider the arrangement in Silicon Valley: Companies subcontract freely to people who work for competitors. In that kind of knowledge-based market, the ethic of technological advancement outweighs the skirmishing of individual companies—transcompetition in action.

Hierarchies order the vertical flow of information through an organization. Networks of trust do the opposite, freeing information to flow laterally across organizational boundaries to the trust community.

Trust networks are not for everyone. Don't expect the new Barings Bank, burned in the $14 billion Nick Leeson Singapore fiasco, to move too rapidly toward a trust network and away from command and control. Neither will governmental bodies resort any time soon to trust as a referee—the public demands accountability from the public sector, even at the cost of inefficiency. When people are sure the government has ceased buying $600 hammers at their expense, trust in government may begin to blossom.

Trust networks must also walk a tightrope between extending natural favor to members of the network—Orthodox Jews in the diamond exchange, for example—and systematically excluding others. The "good old boy" system is a trust network, but that doesn't mean it's good. Favoritism and nepotism foster trust in the narrow community, but annihilate it in the larger one.

Likewise, the new form cannot take shape if principals cling to the old ways. Trust networks cannot coexist with excessive compartmentalizing, keeping members in the dark about other projects and functions. Status barriers must all be torn down. Fretting nonstop about what the competitors will find out prevents the development of trust across corporate membranes. And there is the ever-present danger of supercollaboration: Imagine simple tasks complicated needlessly by chaotic processes.

The Grammar of Transcompetition

A friend of ours, writer and consultant Jerry de Jaager, had the good fortune to work as a consultant during the early days of NUMMI (New United Motor Manufacturing, Inc.). NUMMI is a joint venture between Toyota and General Motors that has been hailed as one of the greatest transformations ever, and Jerry describes his NUMMI experience as one of the most remarkable he has had. The determination to blend the best aspects of fiery competition and teamwork into a single powerful instrument reached all the way down to everyday grammar:

> The degree to which teamwork mattered at NUMMI was driven home to me one day when I was leading a project-management training session.
>
> At NUMMI, all employees are referred to as "team members," and there are no distinctions in dress or deference among managers, team leaders, and other team members. I had taken on an actual project—the creation of a manual of travel guidelines—as the basis for my class, and I ran into trouble right at the beginning, when I was describing the objectives for that project.
>
> Knowing how intensely participative everything was there, I proudly wrote as an objective, "The manual must be approved by all team members." I could see severe looks of disapproval among the Japanese participants, so I asked what the problem was.
>
> "Here at NUMMI," I was told, "team members are the subject of all sentences, not the tail end of prepositional phrases. Your objective should read, 'All team members must approve the manual.'" A lesson I've never forgotten in the difference between "being" and just "doing."

What NUMMI achieved was the creation of a transcompetitive culture out of the ashes of a plant that was the most abysmal in the GM system, a new kind of bureaucracy that, instead of stamping out innovation and commitment, actually encouraged it.

GM-Fremont had been a disaster. One manager called it "the worst plant in the world." Productivity was among the lowest of any General Motors site. Quality lagged terribly. Morale was so bad and drug and alcohol abuse were so rampant that the plant employed 20 percent more workers than it needed just to ensure an adequate labor force on any given day. The local United Auto Workers unit was angry and activist in character, and not afraid to walk out when their demands were not met. The place was a mess.

When the Toyota-GM management team came in to rebuild, they hired from scratch—new people, untainted by the years of bitterness. That, plus the new training in quality and teamwork, resulted in a completely different story.

How would they effect this sea change of mind-set? First, they unapologetically broke American cultural norms and installed a bottom-line guarantee of no layoffs in return for solid teamwork.

Second, the company worked overtime to eliminate the customary we–they divisions between American workers and management. It tossed out traditional perks and privileges like special parking and separate dining rooms for managers.

Third, they did the unthinkable in America: They instituted a uniform dress code, and everyone had to abide by it.

Fourth, Toyota planted the idea in workers' heads that the company was not the property of management; it belonged, rather, to everyone that was there, from the lowest person in the hierarchy on up. Management only existed in order to support the production teams with its problem-solving expertise.

Finally, managers spent time on every individual hired and inculcated each one with the vision of a plant they could be proud of, a plant that would build "the finest vehicles in America."

A NUMMI report lays out the significance of the turn-around:

> What the NUMMI experiment shows is that hierarchy and standardization, with all their known advantages for efficiency, need not build on the logic of coercion. They can build instead on the logic of learning, a logic that motivates workers and taps their potential contribution to continuous improvement.
>
> NUMMI seeks to build an atmosphere of trust and common purpose. NUMMI maintains exceptional consistency in its strategies and principles, it carefully builds consensus around important decisions, and it has programs ensuring adequate communication of results and other essential information.[8]

From these collaborative measures, Toyota fashioned a powerful competitive weapon. Within two years NUMMI's productivity was higher than that of any other GM plant. In fact, it nearly matched the performance of the legendary Toyota Takaoka plant. The problems of absenteeism and substance abuse dwindled to insignificance.

A Brand New Bag

Is your organization ready to trust its own people?

First, be sure you understand the requirements. You have to relax your sense of organizational boundaries. You have to develop a consuming commitment to keeping people educated. And you have to be doing business in a society that also shows a certain level of trust: Transcompetitive organizations can't happen in paranoid or totalitarian environments.

Most importantly, you have to continually deserve trust. Reciprocity is the fuel of trust: Give in order to get. Germany and Japan enjoy world-class trust networks because management does not screw with workers' heads. Their commitment to workers is lifelong and reliable. Companies in the U.S. have not been so deft, talking trust one moment and downsizing the next.

If you can view workers not as short-term costs but as long-term assets, you may be ready for a brand new bag.

Endnotes

[1]Roger E. Alcaly, "Reinventing the Corporation," *The New York Review of Books*, April 10, 1977.

[2]"United We Own," *Business Week*, March 18, 1996; cited in Alcaly.

[3]"Law firm hit mother, 80, with £12,000 death bill," London *Independent*, March 14, 1997.

[4]Patricia Digh, "Shades of Gray in the Global Marketplace," *HR Magazine*, April 1997.

[5]Associated Press clip, February 12, 1994.

[6]Jon Tevlin, "Non-compete pacts are growing trend," *Star Tribune*, May 23, 1997.

[7]From remarks by Fukuyama at The Masters Forum's Tomorrowday II conference, 1996.

[8]Jerry de Jaager, "Loyalty and Involvement: Two Things Not to Be Confused with Commitment," Masters Forum Application Kit, April 1996.

Swallowing the Hand That Feeds You

Competing with your customers

One of the funnier bits on the TV show *Seinfeld* involved a restaurateur whose style was to badger customers to keep moving down the buffet line, to use their napkins, and to eat what's put in front of them. The bit, which came to be known as the "Soup Nazi" episode, was based on real-life New York soupseller Al Yeganeh. The charm of the episode lay in the notion that one can berate and abuse one's own customers and stay in business.

In the summer of 1997, Yeganeh signed a nonaggression pact with longtime rival, Soup Man International. ABC News says that means that his soups will be sold in airports, in gourmet shops, and at international chains.

If the Soup Nazi and the Soup Man International can work together, who are we to hold out?

Despite this success at partnering, Yegeneh is unhappy. Even though the *Seinfeld* episode thrust him into the pop culture limelight, Yeganeh issued a statement saying he still wants to be rid of the Soup Nazi label. And he wants an apology from the person who put him in the global spotlight, Jerry Seinfeld himself.

Is that any way to treat a customer?

The Barbie Betrayal

We like to say we are living in the age of customer satisfaction, but there are gaping holes in this contract between businesses and the people who do business with them. Many organizations see their customers not as the reason for being in business but as a force to be tricked, lied to, bullied, and ignored. This improbable super-competitive attitude toward customers is more common than we like to think.

The relationship between businesses and their customers has often been parasitic. On the connectedness scale, parasitism is just one notch away from cannibalism. It's a relationship, but not much of one.

Take Barbie dolls, the world's best-selling toy. There are 250,000 people around the world who collect the dolls as an invest-ment hobby. In recent years these collectors have begun to grumble that Mattel, the maker of the dolls, has been skimping on materials, issuing inappropriate versions of Barbie and outfits that didn't fit.

> The dispute stems, in part, from a series of manufacturing goofs and marketing blunders that hurt collectors.
>
> Poodle Parade Barbie, a replica of a 1965 doll, was released with hair seemingly trimmed with a chain saw. Then came Barbie's friend, Francie, another vintage doll reissue, whose undersized shoes split when placed on her feet.
>
> Mattel also misjudged the market, underproducing some collector dolls and overproducing others, causing prices to soar, then fall. Early buyers of Star Trek Barbie who paid nearly $80 each got burned, for example, when store prices later dropped to about $30 per doll.[1]

But the final straw was when Mattel sued a fanzine for trade-mark infringement after the magazine satirically portrayed a Barbie with alcohol and pills. Facing the storm from faithful customers, many of whom buy 50 Barbies a year, Mattel CEO Jill Barad vowed not to give an inch. "What I do in my job, first and foremost," Barad said, "is protect Barbie."

Trademark infringement is a great way for companies to exer-cise the bully within, and there is never a shortage of corporate lawyers to suggest this course of action. The anecdotes of overzealous litigation are as ridiculous as they are legion. Here are some recent cases of big companies stomping on isolated individuals:

➤ Time Warner, owner of the rights to Batman memorabilia, sued a Denton, Texas rock band that was using the name Riddle Me This.

Time Warner contended people would mistakenly assume the band is associated with *Batman and Robin*, the fourth installment in the Batman series. "I think the absurdity of it speaks for itself," says Eric Keyes, the lead singer and founder of the 6-year-old band.[2]

➤ If you worked at Kmart over the summer and found it wanting as a career experience, and decide to post your own personal "Kmart Sucks" profile online, describing the personal habits of your immediate supervisor and the existential tawdriness of life under the blue lights, that long shadow over your lawn will be the giant red K come to discuss trademark infringement with your parents.

➤ If you're a lover of M.C. Escher's weird drawings, and you posted some on your website imagining that any copyright on this 60-year-old art had expired, think again. Escher's estate has sold the rights to a CD-ROM publisher and is bullying every site that has put up Escher images to take them down, or to severely limit their use.

➤ If you're a lifelong admirer of J. D. Salinger's *Catcher in the Rye* (the favorite book of four out of five unbalanced loners) and post excerpts from the book on your website, the agent of the author will come rapping on your virtual door. By all accounts, the reclusive and seemingly indifferent J. D. Salinger has the most ruthless agent of any living writer.

➤ Most absurd of all, in our view, Toys R Us came down hard in September 1996 on a website with the easily confused name of Roadkills R Us.[3]

Note that none of these people are selling goods under the aggrieved company's name. Few are even in the same business. Most are fans of the suing company's products. But the lawyers say that unless the trademark is defended it becomes void, as happened to Frigidaire and Xerox and Polaroid and Scotch Tape. Wait, aren't those trademarks still valid?

In the 1960s, Walt Disney sued penniless underground publisher Paul Krassner over a poster Krassner created showing Snow White and the Seven Dwarfs engaged in an elaborate animated orgy. The intent was clearly to shield Disney characters from satirical intent. Disney won and put a unique publication out of business. But by crushing Krassner, Disney put itself on course to become the company it is today, making as much money merchandising its name and characters as it does by making movies. Where does an 800-pound mouse sit down? Anywhere it wants to.

The moral: Intellectual property should be defended, but when the mighty squash the puny, beware the Brute Cycle.

Lost in Cyberspace

Another good example of customer bashing is occurring in cyberspace. A major debate of the last couple of years has been the right of commercial mailers to bombard customers with junk e-mail. You know the type of mailing: offers to sell business kits, credit cards, hard porn, investment opportunities, miracle drugs, magazine subscriptions. If this mail were faxed it would be illegal, because it ties up the recipient's equipment without permission. But no such law protects customers from junk e-mailers.

It is sinfully easily to compile e-mail address lists. Programs called spiders can cull 75,000 names per hour from a host of Internet sources, then turn around and mail to 1,000,000 people in a single day, without the sender spending a cent on postage or printing. The typical customer gets five or six pieces of this stuff every day, and unless the activity is criminalized, that number will leap exponentially in the months ahead. It is time-consuming and annoying to have to shovel one's virtual sidewalk clear of cyber-debris every few hours.

The point is that the relationship between seller (the bulk e-mailer) and customers is way on the left side of the scale of connectedness. Forget the customer as partner—these customers are no more meaningful to the sellers than plankton to a whale. Indeed, they don't consider end-customers "customers" at all; they are simply data their paying customers (the businesses that buy lists or buy list-making software) gobble up.

As ever in such relationships, the Brute Cycle is automatically invoked. Already suits have been filed against websites and conduits like Cyberpromo for behaving bestially in cyberspace. At the speed the Internet is growing, Cyperpromo may be driven out of business by enraged customers by the time you read this. Like many a predator, their deal may not seem so bad—short-term riches, followed by a bloody uprising.

The final obvious great example in our time is Major League Baseball and the Players Association. In a sport that is ostensibly about competition, most players compete more for salaries and bonuses than to win games. Teams care more for getting free new stadiums from their communities or better offers from other communities.

As prices skyrocket, the thing that made baseball great—the bond between players on the field and spectators in the stands—has vanished. In the free agency era, teams mean nothing. In a global system, locale itself means nothing. Who wants to spend $100 on an event that means nothing, and where the popcorn was popped three days earlier? What is there to root for but empty professionalism?

Compare the empty spectacle of American baseball with the collaborative brand of social soccer played in Africa:

> I was in the city of Douala in Cameroon, and the Cameroonian team had somehow gotten to the quarterfinals of the World Cup, playing England, and so the whole city, the whole nation, was involved in this one game. The people thronged together in the streets to watch on public TV sets, or massed in bars, with dirt floors, if they had the wherewithal to buy one beer and the emotional forbearance to nurse it. Nowhere, ever, have I seen people care so about their one thing, this game of their country. This was not overemphasizing sport. It was overemphasizing belonging.[4]

When the customer is brought back into the equation, baseball may begin to rebuild its status as a national pastime, but not before. The game is bullying its own fans, and those fans will apply the Brute Cycle with a hot dog and relish.

It Works Both Ways

Of course, Brutes don't have to be managers or organizations. Workers can behave abominably, as the history of labor shows. Customers can be the worst of all. Think of drunken louts at the ball park or high school students who attack their teachers. Even Nordstrom, the department store that set new records for bending over backward to please customers, won't take abuse at the hands of customers with obvious larceny in their hearts.

In each case, the solution is to turn the Brute Cycle to your favor. Encircle and expose. Eighty-six (ostracize) the hell-raising fans for life. Brand the attack on the teacher as the act of cowardice that it is, and communicate to other kids the uncoolness of it. Spread information about devious customers to every branch of your company and across company lines so that your competitors will also forego the pleasure of those customers' business.

Endnotes

[1]Associated Press, May 10, 1997.

[2]Associated Press, June 20, 1997.

[3]"Trademark Wars on the Web," http://www.muchmusic.com/muchmusic/cyberfax/trademark.html.

[4]Frank DeFord, "How We Lost Our Pastime," *Newsweek*, December 30, 1996–January 6, 1997.

The Sign of the Scorpion

Competing with shareholders

There is a fable about a scorpion who talked a frog into helping him cross a stream. The frog demurred, certain the scorpion would sting him. The scorpion assured him that it would be irrational to sting the frog, because then he too would drown. You know the rest. The frog gets halfway across the stream and the scorpion stings him. Both animals are going down fast. The convulsing frog is just able to ask why and the scorpion can only answer that he did what he did because it was in his nature.

Now, you would think it would go against a company's nature to compete against its shareholders. After all, what is the number one thing companies get grief for? It is their determination to reward first-line investors more than other constituent groups—workers, customers, the community they do business in. That is the purpose of businesses: to enrich the owners.

Every business has sacred constituents whose interests the people in that business are supposed to put above their own interests. The Hippocratic oath circumscribes medicine's reach. In real estate the prime constituent is the seller. In corporate life, it is the stockholder. Corporate management is no more likely to betray the interests of investors than government, say, can ignore the interests of the everyday citizen.

In theory.

Choking the Chicken

But it happens, and it happens because management's super-competitive traits lead it to forget about corporate profit being a team sport. When managers withhold information about losses from stock-holders, for instance, they are stealing from them. The Boston Chicken restaurant chain was one of the fastest growing in recent years, and its stock was for many months one of Wall Street's favorites.

But the company's rapid expansion came at the expense of numerous franchises that were financially unequipped, or simply incompetent, to handle the responsibilities of running a restaurant. The chain showed very little diligence in identifying weak franchisers, and even less diligence in informing investors that the value of their rapid growth was suspect. While the company's stock inflated like a rubber chicken, the chain squeezed out reliable information to investors. Over the course of two quarters, the company's stock fell from $41.50 a share to a low of $15.67.

According to a lawsuit filed by one shareholder in June 1997, at no time did the company lay it on the line for investors that its franchise base was thin. By the time the fat hit the fryer, the company had reduced its workforce by a third. Investors? Caveat emptor seemed to be the company's policy—a policy that ran afoul of SEC regulations.[1]

Insider Trading

When managers take advantage of insider information in their own investing, they are stealing from their own shareholders. That insider trading is wrong is implicit in the exchange-encircle-exact dynamic, because information is not circulating as it must. Too often, the sacred constituency gets burned at the altar.

Take a case from the Twin Cities that went all the way to the Supreme Court. A respected attorney at the firm of Dorsey & Whitney, James O'Hagan had an interesting meeting with a client, Grand Metropolitan PLC of London, in which he learned that Grand Met was planning to make a tender offer for all shares of the Pillsbury Co. Grand Met soon left Dorsey & Whitney, but the inside info stayed in O'Hagan's head.

O'Hagan, despite his grandfatherly appearance, was the sort of reckless individual who liked to play games with other people's money and imagined that since he was clever, he would never get caught, a trickster's Trickster. He decided to become a player himself, and over the next year parlayed $4.3 million in gains, using client moneys to buy at a low price shares he knew would soon skyrocket in price. They did.

O'Hagan was eventually tried in local courts, found guilty of swindling his law clients, and ordered to serve 30 months in jail. Then a federal court indicted him and found him guilty of 57 counts of mail fraud, securities fraud, and money laundering. Sentence: 41 months. O'Hagan, lawyerly to the end, appealed his conviction at every level until it was turned down by the Supreme Court, which found his defense, that he couldn't be guilty of insider trading because he didn't actually work *inside* Grand Met, to be a little light on the merit side. It was a breathtaking legal precedent, which held for the first time that a swindle is a swindle, even when the swindler is a member of the bar.[2]

Takeover Mutinies

During corporate takeovers, management often mutinies against shareholders, because their interests (keeping the company under their control or seeking acquisition terms favorable to them) and the interests of shareholders (windfall returns) have bifurcated. The Brute Cycle kicks into high gear very quickly, since shareholders swivel rapidly to a new management in order to get rid of the old management. But even then it comes at a horrific high cost.

Managers like Ross Johnson of RJR Nabisco show what happens when they put their own interests ahead of the interests of shareholders. Johnson sought in 1987 to buy the company away from investors at a bargain price, primarily to enrich himself and other top management. But Johnson, RJR Nabisco's CEO, learned a painful lesson, that one does not initiate a stealth operation with a hog call. As soon as its leveraged buyout plans became public, a bigger hog, Kohlberg Kravis Roberts (KKR) moved in, outmaneuvered Johnson, and took the company away from him, installing American Express's Louis Gerstner in his place.

This particular tale of damn-the-stockholders took several more years to play out, however. KKR, which took such delight in stealing Johnson's company from him, wound up enriching RJR

Nabisco's investors and punishing its own. The massive debt the buy-out incurred, plus the fading appeal of the companies' many brands, resulted in a final KKR stockholder profit of only 11 cents a share.

It Cuts Both Ways

Shareholders, for their part, can exert a collaborative drag upon a company. When all 99 percent of investors want from a company is to keep the cream coming, a great fear of action sets in, and management feels that fear like a cold hand around its throat. Many companies have met untimely deaths because stockholders were unwilling to see the companies plunge into the bath of change. No managers have ever been let go while the company kept delivering regular dividends, even while those payments masked structural and strategic problems that spelled long-term doom.

Can a Stock Exchange Cry?

It may seem that we have wandered far from the customary pastures of industrial psychology. But the higher you go into our institutions, the greater the role played by the supercompetitiveness ethos. Eventually you come to the holy of holies, the free market system itself, in which dogs eat dogs and the devil take the hindmost.

Look down upon the frantic goings-on in the pit of the New York Stock Exchange and you perceive a competitive arena that puts the Olympics to shame. For a sixteenth of a point over an hour's time, mature adults trained in the philosophy of a rational marketplace will push their grandmothers down the stairs and sell their children into slavery.

At first glance, cannibalism is the law of the free market: For every winner (buy low, sell high) there must be a loser (buy high, sell low). Buying a share of stock always represents a gamble that the stock will do better for you than it did for the person selling that same share. A definite star system is at work: *The Wall Street Journal* holds ongoing contests with top brokers, headlining the stockpicker who finishes the quarter with the highest gains. There are short speculators whose mission in life is to achieve short-term gains by betting against the market. Their role appears unsavory at first, but they play a vital ecological role in clearing the street of carrion.

To overlook this pressurized supercompetition betrays the spirit of transcompetition.

But times are changing. The colorful world of the trading pit is a relic of an earlier time. Before another ten years pass, we expect to see it replaced by a system of almost pure information. Instead of buzzers, markers, tickers, and exhausted people in damp shirtsleeves, the system will be run by computers, following the NASDAQ model, but worldwide and round-the-clock. All the stock markets and bourses will feed into one large system, a kind of financial Internet.

Our sense is that this streamlining of the world of investment will have a powerful transcompetitive effect. When it is in place we will have moved in less than a century from a series of national economies in which a handful of diamond-stickpin Brutes with inside information feasted on the wealth of others to a transglobal economy in which information and opportunities are available to all.

Already, our thinking about money and wealth has undergone a major transcompetitive shift. The very concept of a bull market meets that description: A market that is good for everyone, a rising tide that lifts all boats. The diversification and low entry costs of investing via mutual funds and large group investment pools like pension and 401(k) funds allow us to enjoy an above-average profit while running below-average risk. Pool investors are like armed warriors, protecting one another with their very numbers. There are even ideological pools, the so-called ethical funds that seek to invest in companies that do not pollute, that treat workers well, and that aren't involved in the sale of tobacco, liquor, or guns.

We have evolved from a market on the lookout for a fool to buy at the highest price to a community that invests at staged intervals, stays in the market for decades at a time, and roots for everyone's success.

Many of the competitive practices of Wall Street are less competitive than they appear at first glance. One of the habits of fundamental analysis is to view companies only through the lens of how they are faring against other companies in their category. Thus everyone in the aerospace industry is considered to be competing against one another, even though only a select few vie for the same contracts. From the art of niche-making, we know that listed competitors are not always actual competitors. Yes, Arco and Chevron compete against one another, especially in some regions. But does Encyclopedia Britannica really compete against Simon & Schuster? Does Cray Research (now part of Silicon Graphics) compete against NCR? Does Glaxo Wellcome compete against Johnson & Johnson? No, no, and no. The competition is mostly in our minds.

A surprisingly collaborative force, the Federal Reserve Bank, is trying to protect all Americans from the go-go enthusiasm of a few. Senator Daniel Patrick Moynihan made the observation in a television interview[3] that Americans live in "earthshaking economic times" because the longest period of continuing negative economic growth in the 35 years from 1960 to 1995 was only 14 months. Under the tutelage of Alan Greenspan, the Fed has buffered a nation undergoing rapid change with an economy that knows when to cut the throttle and glide. There are no guarantees that we will not see a crash or panic at any time. But there is a clear intention to guide the market so that the largest possible number of people benefit from it for the longest possible period.

In Albert Brooks' 1983 comedy, *Lost in America*, he quits his job and invests his savings in an RV to travel around the country experiencing life. The very next day he and his otherwise sensible wife, played by Julie Hagerty, squander their life savings at the craps tables in Las Vegas. Desperate to undo the damage, Brooks beseeches the casino managers to return his money and to start a new era, as the "casino that cares."

It was asking too much of Las Vegas, but it may not be too much to ask of Wall Street. Indeed, with the decline of the billionaire class and the rise of pooled investments, a market that looks out for its participants may be the only one people will participate in.

Endnotes

[1] Associated Press, June 25, 1997.

[2] Tom Hamburger and David Phelps, "High court says O'Hagan conviction on firm ground," (Minneapolis) *Star Tribune*, June 26, 1997.

[3] *Charlie Rose*, PBS, broadcast in Minnesota on January 13, 1997.

Global Economic Warfare

Competitiveness between economic regions

In the last few chapters we have been looking at transcompetitive dynamics, starting very close up, looking at the factors of personality that determine a person's competitive nature, then slowly pulling away to look at more complex entities:

➤ competition within work teams and competition between work teams;

➤ issues affecting entire companies as they partner with suppliers and distributors;

➤ companies that can't keep themselves from competing against their own constituencies;

➤ the difficulty of cooperation between large competing entities.

Now we open the lens full wide and look at the entire world as a transcompetitive organism, with one region locked in competition against another, with the remote possibility of easing that competition sometime in the future.

Lester Thurow describes the transcompetitive world in terms of shifting tectonic plates. Each plate is always doing something, and as information moves more rapidly from one plate to the next, the actions of one region affect the other. The great economic regions each constitute a plate—the Pacific Rim, Southern Asia, the Middle East, Europe, the Americas.

Plate tectonics is important because it explains why the earth gets the shimmies every now and then. Earthquakes occur because something happened underneath our feet. A card was pulled out of a house of cards, and the rest of the cards bore the brunt of the change.

> But plate tectonics also causes the slower, almost imperceptible changes that fundamentally alter the earth's surface within what are for geology short periods of time. What seems static, the surface of the earth, is in reality in constant flux. The Indian plate pushes under the European plate, and what is by weight the world's largest mountain massif, Nanga Parbat, in the Himalayas, rises more than two feet every hundred years. Relatively quickly something significant happens—Nanga Parbat becomes the world's tallest, as well as the world's heaviest, mountain.[1]

Could there be a more coherent image for the scale of connectedness? Everything we do affects everything everyone else does. Though we seem separate, we are in fact in continuous contact with one another, in a continuous dance of stimulus and response.

More importantly, we must deal with the fact that the economic plates, unlike the geological ones, are within our control. They are conscious. Though what our neighbors do affects us and may trigger a unrecallable reaction, we don't have to initiate any kind of shift unless we want to.

The In-Between Age

What are the plates doing right now? They are seeking to achieve and maintain peaceful alignment: They, and we, are enjoying a transcompetitive phase. NAFTA is linking the countries of North America to one another and will soon add more, starting with Chile. The short-term results of NAFTA have been mostly bad, but the countries involved swear their best bet is regional cooperation.

The European Union is stronger than NAFTA because it is a union with teeth, not just a loose confederation. Countries like the U.K. and Denmark continue to drag their feet on the issues of sovereignty and identity, but the Union goes forward nonetheless.

Though developed Asian nations belong to APEC, Asia is less united than either Europe or the Americas. But it does not need unity. It has something more precious: momentum. China's economy is growing at a faster rate than any large nation in history, and with no obvious ill effects. The U.S. keeps extending China most favored

nation status, in hopes China will encircle its outlaw industries—
everything from shoemaking to software piracy—and exact change.
(This, despite the fact that the worst pirates in China appear to be its
own army, freelancing in the music and software counterfeiting business to pay its bills.) Japan, in the fourth year of negative growth, is
like the snake that ate a great meal and is now pausing to digest it.
The second-tier countries of the Pacific Rim and Southeast Asia, from
Korea to Singapore and Thailand, seem unstoppable in their determination to compete on a global basis. Not even the financial free fall
of late 1997 seems able to slow their rapid growth. Even India is flex-
ing its strength as an arm's-length provider of high-tech services,
including software programming, to the world.

But it is a tenuous phase. The new world order still has one
foot in a dreadful past of pogroms and invasions, and one in the
hopeful future of people prospering by getting along. The new age
described in books never seems to arrive. We are always in an in-
between age, like a boat on a river, forever approaching the next bend.

William Greider, author of *One World, Ready or Not*, worries
that, behind the curtain of international cooperation, supercompetition is hard at work, an engine revving the world up to global cata-
clysm. "Global capitalism," he said, "is running out of control to
some kind of abyss."

> Greider surveyed the world, and found much that is ominous,
> including the way "global finance turns manic ... as an army of
> Luddites assembles across the world."
>
> Does free trade benefit the world? He cited a visit to a Chinese fac-
> tory where machinists make $50 a month to assemble parts for
> Boeing, all under the eyes of Communist cadres. The process seems
> brutal. But, as a Boeing engineer there said, it was once worse.
> "They used to shoot them."
>
> Moreover, how long can Boeing's $4,000 a month machinists com-
> pete with the Chinese machinists? Greider cited Boeing engineers
> who told him, "The things you talk about are the things we talk
> about every day of the week at the Boeing Company."
>
> In textbooks free trade benefits everyone, Greider said. But in the
> real world, it doesn't work that way. China forces Boeing to farm
> out work to China. Someday China may be able to build its own
> aircraft and compete with Boeing. Trade agreements are no help,

Greider said. "Boeing is not going to complain about its customers in China."[2]

While the big players play footsie with one another, the little players get hurt. Greider visited the site of a factory in Bangkok where 185 workers died in a fire in 1996. It was the worst accident in the history of capitalism, worse than the infamous Triangle Shirtwaist Factory Fire in 1911. But the world was less desensitized to industrial deaths then. The Triangle fire provoked shame and outrage. But had you even heard of the 1996 fire, the worst in the history of capitalism? In the calculation to provide low-cost goods to Western buyers, 185 lives were never factored.

When we first began writing this book, one publisher we approached was overjoyed at the topic. But we found out his reason was less happiness than horror.

"Thank God someone is doing this," he said.

> You know, we put out all these books on the new age, and how everything is getting to be so rosy, with empowerment and customer focus and workplace democracy. But it just isn't like that out there. The stories we are hearing about competition at the international level are bloodcurdling. Companies are buying and selling the countries they do business in. Workforces are being cashed in on a whim, and work is being sourced for a third of the cost 5,000 miles away.
>
> I really feel that we are drawing close to a blowup of the kind we haven't seen since the beginning of World War II. And the cause won't be borders or ethnic cleansing or political ambition. It will be because a few companies were helpless to control their own will to win.

Endnotes

[1] Lester Thurow, *The Future of Capitalism*, William Morrow, 1996.

[2] Jim Tynen, "Look at a New World," *American Reporter*, February 5, 1997.

The Flight of the Billionaires

An unlikely source of transcompetitive thinking

Competition and capitalism are like an old married couple that eat together, walk together, and snore together in bed. But lately, just when it seemed they had smooth sailing till death did them part, a few cracks have been showing up in the relationship. Some of the world's foremost supercompeters have been indicating that enough is enough.

> Things fall apart; the center cannot hold;
> Mere anarchy is loosed upon the world;
> the blood-dimmed tide is loosed, and everywhere
> The ceremony of innocence is drowned;
> The best lack all conviction, while the worst
> Are full of passionate intensity.
>
> **William Butler Yeats**

Lord knows the world needs more billionaires. In 1996, best estimates put the world's population of this species at 358. But they are not without resources. The combined wealth of these 358 people is neatly counterbalanced by the combined wealth of the world's 2.3 billion poorest people.[1] So there is hope.

Consider the case of George Soros. A fabulously successful investor and one of the world's richest men, Soros has lived a dual life of commercial brutality and social philanthropy. In 1992 he made a currency play on the British pound that plunged the United Kingdom into monetary crisis. In business he has not cared if people get hurt, so long as he has fun. On the other hand, in one of those classic paradoxes of capitalism, he has given away many millions to support emerging Eastern European nations. Perhaps his generosity is how he atones for his brutality.

227

Another way has been his reconsideration, in recent years, of the competitive instinct itself. He has become a kind of armchair philosopher for an "open society," a balanced economic lifestyle in which people are free to do things, short of nailing one another to trees. It was odd to read of this international predator saying in the *Atlantic Monthly* that unfettered competition posed a mortal challenge to continued civilization:

> Insofar as there is a dominant belief in our society today, it is a belief in the magic of the marketplace. The doctrine of laissez-faire capitalism holds that the common good is best served by the uninhibited pursuit of self-interest. Unless it is tempered by the recognition of a common interest that ought to take precedence over particular interests, our present system—which, however imperfect, qualifies as an "open society"—is liable to break down.

> I want to emphasize, however, that I am not putting laissez-faire capitalism in the same category as Naziism or communism. Totalitarian ideologies deliberately seek to destroy the open society; laissez-faire policies may endanger it, but only inadvertently.... Nevertheless, because communism and even socialism have been thoroughly discredited, I consider the threat from the laissez-faire side more potent today than the threat from totalitarian ideologies. We are enjoying a truly global market economy in which goods, services, capital, and even people move around quite freely, but we fail to recognize the need to sustain the values and institutions of an open society.[2]

After Soros made his plea for an open society, the orthodox press nearly hooted him off the planet. *Newsweek* economist Robert J. Samuelson dismissed him as a "crackpot" writing "rambling," "incoherent" "rubbish,"[3] who had dared look sideways at the same free market that had made him rich. *The New York Times* followed with a sarcastic feature titled "Look Who's Carping Most about Capitalism," lumping Soros together with other breast-beating oligarchs, who met at the World Economic Forum in Switzerland[4] to ponder ways of ameliorating the worst consequences of economic competitiveness—why, for instance, it is so hard for a world loaded with food and other resources to feed its own hungry people.

Oddly, it is the billionaires who worry the most about the free market. The oil sheiks of the Middle East were the first to see that wealth creates disequilibrium, and disequilibrium invites turmoil—

the Brute Cycle. American billionaire Ross Perot and British billionaires James Goldsmith and Paul McCartney have both sounded the trumpet against unrestricted free trade, Perot against NAFTA and Goldsmith and McCartney against the European Union.[5]

Warren Buffett, the wizard of Berkshire Hathaway, was advising his own investors in mid-1997 to invest not in his stock but in index funds—perhaps the most collaborative investment there is.[6] Even Bill Gates, the monopolist of the age, is conscious of his image of being a predator in the information marketplace, and stages public relations events to display his collaborative side:

> Even Microsoft, notoriously aloof from the communities it serves, has gotten in on the act. At the end of May, chairman and CEO Bill Gates visited Boston's Computer Museum and announced the company's donation of $100,000 in cash, software and hardware to expand the Museum's Computer Clubhouse—an after-school learning environment designed to help young people become more comfortable with technology by exploring their own interests— into under-served communities such as Roxbury and Boston's South End.

> "Microsoft is working with a variety of partners across the country to help create a connected learning community, one in which parents, teachers, librarians, community advocates and museum directors can collaborate via the Internet on a child or an adult's life-long learning," says Gates. "The Computer Museum is at the forefront of providing access to these technologies in disadvantaged communities."[7]

But when the bullies are global, the consequences of their tumbling are too. The competing mega-interests of the world fit together, like Lester Thurow's tectonic plates.[8] When one plate shifts, even slightly, as the Japanese economy has from 1994 to 1997, the whole world trembles. The U.S. economy itself is no longer safe. When the Euro dollar finally comes on board in 1999, currency speculators like Soros will have a foil to turn to for bringing the dollar down. Imagine the mighty American economy, felled in the millennium year to put a few hundred billion in cash into a few opportunistic pockets.

If the billionaires are all wet, it will be a first. You don't become billionaires by being wrong. What their critics are really jumping on are some of the solutions Soros and others have put forth, requiring greater governmental restrictions on competition.

Walling countries off against one another strikes supercompetitive free marketers as a ticket not to an open society but to local tyranny. Brute government is no cure for brute multinational business, they are saying; keep looking for another solution.

The paradigm of exchange, encircle, and exact is the other solution. It's really no more than the mice putting a bell around the cat's neck. A cat that tinkles every time it takes a step is a lot less dangerous.

Does belling the cat constitute Karl Popper's open society? Probably not; the open society advocates always envisioned governmental discipline of business excess, a kind of economic United Nations.

But exchange, encircle, and exact is the best counterweight currently at our disposal—awareness and joint action versus marketplace brutality. Brute cannot quash Brute any more than Rock can overcome Rock; only the combined force and knowledge of all assembled can paper over the misbehaviors of the neighborhood bully.

It isn't perfect by a long shot. There will always be bullies, corporate and individual, because it is in our nature as human beings to be diverse. Some vigorous figure will always be out there on the left side of the connectedness scale, cheerfully cheating, pillaging, and bulldozing neighbors, and scoring each destructive act as a win.

Wouldn't it be nice if we could have the older, sober billionaires sit down and have a talk with the rising young billionaires, and explain to them the eventual emptiness of all that winning?

Endnotes

[1] James Gustave Spaeth, "Global Inequality," *NPQ*, Fall 1996.

[2] "The Capitalist Threat," *Atlantic Monthly*, February 1997.

[3] Robert J. Samuelson, "Crackpot Prophet," *Newsweek*, March 10, 1977.

[4] David E. Sanger, "Look Who's Carping Most about Capitalism," *The New York Times*, April 6, 1977.

[5] "I view this partnership as a bummer," McCartney told *The New York Times* (May 25, 1997). "'We'll then have a common flag, so the Union Jack means nothing,' he says, 'and one common anthem.' He slumps against his seat cushion. 'Actually, that was what got me—the anthem.'"

[6] Dylan Ratigan, "Berkshire investors head to Omaha," *Bloomburg News*, May 3, 1997.

[7] PR Central, Reputation Management, "Technology: Creating a Generation of Haves and Have-Nots?" http://www.prcentral.com/rmja96haves.htm.

[8] Thurow, *The Future of Capitalism*.

The New
Art of Unknowing

Why exchange, encircle, and exact works

Let us end where we began, by considering the traits of the human mind. We have looked at companies and countries, teams and tectonic plates, but in the end all that matters is what we do when confronted with new knowledge.

Transcompetition is a call to rationality, but it does not presume that people are rational. We know that what makes us go is still a lopsided contest between the part of our brain that compiles and processes information, and the other part, that just wants to beat someone to death.

Tacit and Explicit Knowledge

We compared people to other creatures that live in communities—ants, fish, lions, and apes. Language, opposing thumbs, and wearing clothes are important differences. But the big difference between animals and people is that we are the only beings who traffic in explicit knowledge: thinking that can be permanentized on paper and ported to one another over distance and time.

Chimpanzees can't do that. They may learn how to capture ants with a stick dipped in honey, and they may exult in that new knowledge and communicate to their relatives how happy they are with it. The exulting and boasting are tacit knowledge, knowledge that you know or feel, but that is hard to put into words.

What chimpanzees cannot do is package their insights, arrange them on a slide carousel, take them on the road, and instruct others in their discovery at major jungle chimposiums. Because their information cannot be ported, chimpanzees operate under severe constraints. They have little chance of becoming wiser over time.

We do, because we know how to manage explicit knowledge. We know how to port it whole from one mind to another, from one life to another. Just as importantly, we know how to convert tacit knowledge (knowledge of experience) into explicit knowledge (a written record).

It is not a perfect process. We often disagree about what meaning or interpretation to assign to explicit knowledge. But it is durable beyond the moment it took us to acquire the knowledge, because we have written it down or recorded it as audio or video or as electronic bits. When we succeed in converting something that is tacit and elusive into something that can be shared universally, as in a painting or a poem, it is the glory of our kind.[1]

Knowledge and Collaboration

Knowledge diffusion is not a static thing. During some periods it occurs freely, and at other times it is dammed up. Its movement fluctuates according to whether an environment is competitive or collaborative.

Explicit knowledge occurs only on the right side of the scale of connectedness. Creatures who cannibalize one another generally do not seek to enhance one another's knowledge base. Only creatures who care about one another as a tribe and can write, will write down information and store it for posterity. There is no higher sign of humanness than a library.

Being the only creature that stores knowledge is very good for the unique half of our brain, the neocortex, the curious, inquisitive part of us that continually needs new information. But it causes problems for the old brain in us, the amygdala, the part whose job it is to sound the alarm when it encounters something unknown.

Perhaps this is why for every library patron happily hunkered in among stacks of books there are dozens of people who never set foot in a library. Eager users encounter the unknown in a more positive, peaceful way than do the taxpayers who drive by the library as anxious as if it were a cemetery. For them the library is a fearful place, whose every book reminds them of their ignorance. For people who have never opened a book, a shelf full of books is a hostile tribe shaking spears.

One reason people resort to supercompetitive strategies is that they can't find a way to know each other; they can't port information about one another's inner reality.

While our reasonable neocortex urges us to learn about strangers, we resist that message because our amygdala is screaming at us to get away from the frightening new person as quickly as possible. The amygdala is only comfortable with what it already knows, and new people represent a universe of alien information.

You can map how the brain works and how people learn using a JoHari window:

	WHAT I KNOW	WHAT I DON'T KNOW
WHAT YOU KNOW	The Known	
WHAT YOU DON'T KNOW		The Unknown

The box shows that, whenever two people are together, there is information that both have in common (language, orientation, basic knowledge), knowledge that is exclusive to each of the people, and an area neither knows anything about, the Unknown. The old brain or amygdala is never comfortable with anything but the first box, What I Know. If you know it, too, that's good: The amygdala likes it when people agree with us.

In reality, the boxes are never the same size, of course. In a time of little explicit knowledge movement, like the Middle Ages, the JoHari window looks like this:

	WHAT I KNOW	WHAT I DON'T KNOW
WHAT YOU KNOW	The Known	
WHAT YOU DON'T KNOW		The Unknown

The Middle Ages
Avoidance of the Unknown

In the medieval scriptorium, where monks copied books from antiquity by candlelight, it was possible for one person to know everything that was explicitly knowable. The great library of Lindisfarne totaled only a few hundred books—impressive at the time, but quite manageable for a curator of breadth and intellect. Whoever did master such knowledge, or who had resident scholars to do it, was at a tremendous predatory advantage over everyone else.

The Unknown was huge, information was at a standstill, and fear was king. The world had frozen in supercollaborative mode: the big vague.

The supercompetitive age we live in is the exact opposite. Explicit knowledge is shooting at us in a constant, powerful stream, whether we want to accept it (our neocortexes are eager to learn) or not (our amygdalas start spinning around like police flashers).

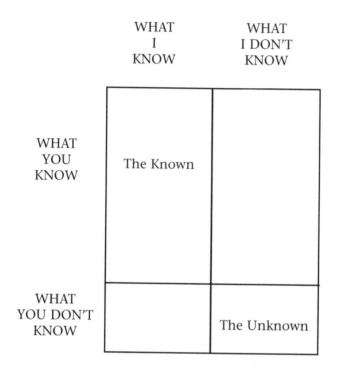

The Current Age
Management of the Unknown

One person can't do it anymore. A single person is not even capable of knowing everything in one field—medicine, investments, law, agriculture. There is too much to know and to keep up with, thus the need for collaborative information-sharing. While the task of the medieval organization was to hoard The Known and avoid The Unknown, the task of the modern organization is to disseminate The Known and to confront and absorb as much of The Unknown as possible.

If the medieval model of knowledge was a fortified castle, allowing new knowledge in by permission only, the current model is a microchip, along whose pathways knowledge flows at continuous high speeds, billions of instructions per second.

From the amygdala's point of view, the Middle Ages made more sense than the current age. In confronting and absorbing The Unknown at megahertz speed, we are going directly against our own brains.

The "something, someone" we are afraid of are the very people we must learn to deal with in order to make the most of our knowledge—our teammates, customers, partners, and even our competitors.

While our neocortexes are anxious to receive the incoming flood of knowledge, our old brains rebel at the vast and hateful ocean of Unknown that comes with it. The people we must work with in the university, hospital, and army are strangers to us. They come to us from other functions, other organizations, and other locales. They may speak other languages and be from other cultures. They have otherness written all over them, and to the old brain, that's bad.

If we are ever able to take The Unknown that hangs in the air between strangers, and learn to stop fearing it and to transmute it to a Known that we can port from place to place, we'll have licked one of the most frustrating aspects of human nature—our need to win at one another's expense. Our approach is to do it one step at a time: inching toward a greater comfort level with collaboration, and easing away from our competitive excesses.

Endnotes

[1]The vocabulary of explicit and tacit knowledge comes to us from Ikujiro Nonaka and Hirotaka Takeuchi, authors of *The Knowledge-Creating Company*, Oxford University Press, 1995.

The Synedelphia Story

The future of competition

So, we've been told to bank our competitive fires and alter the wiring of our brains. We have identified our competitive archetypes and made plans to coax them toward the transcompetitive center. We have mixed and matched our competitive and collaborative options to create a rational new way of doing business. We have exchanged, encircled, and exacted till we're exhausted.

Have we achieved anything? Can we even hope to?

Several people told us, one very emphatically, that writing this book was useless. "People are put on earth to duke it out," a very beefy man at a Rotary lunch said. "Duking it out is the only chance we have."

Others let us know that, if they had the choice, they would gladly opt for a more genteel way of doing business. Competitiveness arises from market forces, they insisted, not from their personalities. Maybe other companies in our industry are predators, but *we're* not. We're just responding to their aggressive actions. Sometimes those responses are preemptive—striking them before they strike us.

This is the reasoning of people like Wayne Sanders of Kimberly-Clark, whose quote, "Every morning I look in the mirror and ask how I can beat the hell out of Procter & Gamble," appeared on the cover of *Forbes*.[1] (Inside, he added, in a whisper: "And I want every one of my employees to do the same.")

Kimberly-Clark was the obvious underdog in the disposable diaper wars against mighty Procter & Gamble. P&G responded to K-C's challenge with everything in its arsenal, from legal challenges to marketing blitzes to price wars, all designed to bury the Wisconsin paper products company. Surely P&G was the supercompetitive Brute of the piece, and K-C was merely displaying admirable competitive pluck?

Maybe. But we spy a clue in the quote. When you wake up every morning plotting to beat the hell out of someone, you are no longer merely reacting. You inhabit an irrational zone by habit. You're into it.

Competition steps over the line when it becomes compulsion, and compulsion is bad because it sidesteps a company's carefully planned and stated mission—in this case, opportunities for workers, return for shareholders, and growth for the company—all for the thrill of the engagement.

Companies that forsake niche-making in favor of head-to-head, win/lose confrontations must recognize that they are operating not from a deck of 52 orderly playing cards but from a mysterious tarot deck whose every card is the face of an unconscious impulse; and the deck is not being dealt from the top.

If leaders lose this high-stakes game and all that goes with it—jobs, invested dollars, and a future—will they be able to shrug it off to the company's stakeholders as a good game?

Meanwhile, things change. Every thousand years our neocortexes get a little curlier, and the amygdala occupies a smaller portion of the cranium. The explicit knowledge we've been sharing, the sum of all our books and phone calls and conversations and dictabelts, evolves slowly into something like wisdom.

This is the wisdom that we see at work in the Microsoft–Apple collaboration, two sworn enemies finding a common cause. We see it in South Africa, where whites and blacks are working together to fight racism, street crime, and a legacy of cruelty. We see it at United Airlines, where workers are owners and entrepreneurial spirits are flying high. We see it at the NUMMI plant in Fresno, California, where management and workers are setting aside ancient misgivings to make the best cars in North America. We see it in the city of Hong Kong, where an extraordinary amalgam of competitive capitalism and collaborative socialism is fashioning a world city for a new millennium. And, God bless them, we even see it at the nexus of American competitive fervor, Nike, Inc., which is moving forward on, of all things, collaborative sports sponsorship ventures with Japan and Brazil. People are overcoming human nature by putting human nature more fully into play.

Our utopia would be one in which our skills of societal restraint become so great that we curb our worst excesses, and our communities become places where people can do interesting things without doing them at one another's mortal expense.

In our research, we came across a wonderful obscure word describing this version of the open society: *Synedelphia*, literally, "the city of connectedness," a place where continuous winning is the order of the day, and violators of the order are kept on a taut psychological leash.

If there is a weakness to this scheme, it is that it is fundamentally rational. In a world of many little Hitlers we are calling for balance and reason, and failing those, eternal vigilance. Perhaps one or two Hitlers can be reasoned with, but certainly not all of them.

If you assume competition and collaboration are hardwired into you, that they are in your brain and your genes like sexual preference or eye color, you and your organization will not be able to make much headway against them. But if you believe that you are rational and have free will and can alter or shape, if not root out completely, those habits you identify as destructive or counterproductive, then there is hope.

Though we have pushed examples of nature upon you all through this book, we ultimately urge that you go against nature, and work less from your amygdala and more from your neocortex. People, by being conscious, are unlike other creatures; we have the unique capacity to step beyond instinct and intuition to create conscious new paths for ourselves, to change our natures.

Brutes are not Brutes because they make rational choices to be that way, anymore than Hermits or Pawns decide consciously every day to spend their time hiding under rocks or wincing under the lash. The moment we become rational, we move inward from the extremes of the scale. Transcompetition is the art of tinkering with our natural inclinations and devising strategies for ourselves that are based on long-term, not short-term, advantage.

In Synedelphia we have choices, transcompetitive choices to elect the best tactics from both ends of the scale. We can choose the best approach for the situation at hand, or we can continue to operate out of our blind habits of choice—cruelty, deception, submission, and withdrawal.

We can do better.

Endnotes

[1]Robert Lenzner and Carrie Shook, "The Battle of the Bottoms," *Forbes*, March 24, 1977.

Pop Quiz

Sometimes people think they've read a book, but they haven't paused to knit it all together, so its lessons are quickly lost. Here, in a nutshell, are the key points of this book:

1. Did you figure out what your dominant personal style of competing is? What the style of your organization is?
2. Did you ask yourself where that style came from, who you got it from, or what experiences led you to adopt it?
3. Have you analyzed how well and under what circumstances it works, and when it doesn't?
4. Have you stopped in the middle of a competitive act and pondered an alternative response, borrowing from the other side of the competitive scale?
5. Have you been a part of an exchange, encircle, and exact movement? Have you experienced one directed against you?
6. Have you learned how to deal with other competitive types and bring out the best in each of them?
7. Have you tried the other transcompetitive tools—arms agreements, boundary management, guarantees, creating a bill of rights for your constituents?
8. Have you mixed and matched the transcompetitive virtues? Have you tried on an attribute that was never your strong suit and worked to make it stronger?
9. Have you ever forgiven a company that violated its spirit of connectedness to you and given them one more chance?
10. Have you forgiven yourself for the times you have come up short—and let the lesson sink in, and moved on?

To Contact the Authors

Harvey Robbins
Robbins & Robbins
2475 Ridgewater Drive
Minnetonka, MN 55305
612-544-9260
robbi004@maroon.tc.umn.edu

Michael Finley
1841 Dayton Avenue
St. Paul, MN 55104
612-644-4540
mfinley@skypoint.com
http://www.skypoint.com/~mfinley

Index

About the Authors

Harvey Robbins is a practicing psychologist, business consultant, trainer, and author specializing in teams and organizational behavior, with clients such as 3M and Honeywell. He lives in Minnetonka, MN, with his family.

Michael Finley is a syndicated business and technology columnist. He and coauthor Harvey Robbins received the Financial Times/Booz Allen & Hamilton Global Book Award for their previous book, *Why Teams Don't Work*. The two also collaborated on *Why Change Doesn't Work*. Mr. Finley lives in St. Paul, MN, with his family.